THE GOOD MAN'S DILEMMA

AMS Studies in Modern Literature, No. 5

ISSN 0270-2983

Other titles in this series:

No. 1. Richard E. Amacher and Margaret F. Rule, compilers. *Edward Albee at Home and Abroad: A Bibliography, 1958 to June 1968.* 1973.

No. 2. Richard G. Morgan, editor. *Kenneth Patchen: A Collection of Essays.* 1977.

No. 3. Philip Grover, editor. *Ezra Pound, the London Years, 1908-1920.* 1978.

No. 4. Daniel J. Casey and Robert E. Rhodes, editors. *Irish-American Fiction: Essays in Criticism.* 1979.

No. 6. Charles L. Green, compiler. *Edward Albee: An Annotated Bibliography, 1968-1977.* 1980.

The Good Man's Dilemma

SOCIAL CRITICISM
IN THE FICTION OF BERNARD MALAMUD

Iska Alter

AMS PRESS, INC.
NEW YORK, N.Y.

Library of Congress Cataloging in Publication Data

Alter, Iska.
  The good man's dilemma.

  (AMS studies in modern literature; no. 5)
  Bibliography: p.
  Includes index.
  1. Malamud, Bernard—Criticism and interpretation—
Addresses, essays, lectures. I. Title. II. Series.
PS3563.A4Z5   813'.54   79-8836
ISBN 0-404-18038-8

MANUFACTURED IN THE UNITED STATES
OF AMERICA

To my Father,
Saul Alter

Acknowledgments

Because this project has been so long aborning, there are many people whose kindness, help, and support must be acknowledged. Without the initial encouragement of Professor Arthur Zeiger of The City College of New York, I would not have had the confidence to begin. I am especially grateful to Professor James W. Tuttleton, Chairman, New York University English Department, whose patience with eccentricity was admirable to the last. Many thanks are due also to the good will of Bob and Dot Bone whose house on Hummock Pond Road, Nantucket, provided the perfect place to work. To Irene Alterbaum, Beryl York Malawsky, and Laurie Orseck whose friendship remains valuable, I record my appreciation. To my parents, Sylvia and Benjamin Protter, my debt is deep and real: their support and generosity have been unstinting and unqualified, even when they could not possibly be sure that I had made the right choices. And there is Bill, most of all, who read my handwriting (no mean feat), sustained me through depressions (which were frequent), and insisted that the project must be done (in spite of resistence, doubt, and hostility).

Annandale-on-Hudson, N.Y., 1979

Contents

THE GOOD MAN'S DILEMMA

The Natural, The Assistant, and American Materialism

In the explosion of Jewish-American fiction that has characterized this country's literary history since the Second World War,
Bernard Malamud's work retains a certain singularity in both
subject matter and form. Without the exuberant self-promotion of
Norman Mailer, the black and bitter humor of Joseph Heller, the
increasing self-absorption of Philip Roth, or, more significantly,
the moral comedy of Saul Bellow, Malamud has continued to be a
humanistic spokesman, albeit a frequently disappointed one in
recent years, for responsibility, compassion, and goodness in a
world spinning out of control with frightening speed. To embody
his concerns as a Jew, an artist, and a moral man, Malamud has
evolved a style that is uniquely his. Its fusion of the fabulous and
the factual, called "lyrical realism" by the Yiddish critic Mayer
Shticker,[1] is the fictive analogue to the Chasidic belief that the
mystical connection to God is to be found not in ascetic isolation,
but through man's participation in the ordinary activities and
mundane events of daily existence.[2]

Given Malamud's not-quite-fashionable content[3] and his
paradoxical technique, it should not be surprising that the critical
response to his fiction has been varied, and sometimes contradictory.
On the one hand, he is condemned by Philip Roth[4] for his distance

from an actual, firmly presented social environment; on the other, he is praised by Tony Tanner[5] for this very same quality. Within this range of opposites, several distinct orientations are apparent. For example, Alfred Kazin denigrates *The Natural* because it is rooted in fantasy, preferring those novels and short stories that seem to be a more naturalistic portrayal of the Jew's experiential reality,[6] while Marcus Klein notes Malamud's variations on the accommodationist spirit that Klein perceives as the major force in post-World War II literature. Like Kazin, Klein is not entirely comfortable with what he believes to be Malamud's intense, parochial exoticism. But he recognizes that the characters in Malamud's fiction are driven "to be out of this world and in a more certainly felt reality.... And their adventure is precisely their frustration; the end of straining and the beginning of heroism, if achieved, is the beginning of acceptance.... His hero's heroism is his hero's loss."[7]

There are critics such as Leslie Fiedler,[8] Stanley Edgar Hyman,[9] and Earl Wasserman,[10] who view Malamud only in his mythic context, counting as most worthy those works with an explicitly archetypal content, esteeming *The Natural*, in particular, for its lively sense of mythic play. Others belonging to this school are more interested in tracing the continuity of archetypal patterns from novel to novel.[11] Of course, and with good reason, there are those who consider Malamud primarily as a Jewish-American writer mindful only of his use of Jewish motifs. Mayer Shticker has noted that with *The Assistant* Bernard Malamud "has brought into American literature . . . the emotional sensibility of the heart [*herzlekhayt*] that reminds us so strongly of the great masters of Jewish writing, Sholem Aleichem, Peretz, and David Bergelson."[12] Robert Alter, however, believes that all but *The Fixer* are a vulgarization of that illustrious Yiddish tradition.[13] For Josephine Zadovsky Knopp, the concept of *mentshlekhayt* is at the core of Malamud's work and is the source of its strength.[14]

It would be foolish to deny or minimize the validity of much that the critics have observed and written about Bernard Malamud; yet there is one whole area of the author's fiction, his social criticism, that has been neglected, ignored, or even declared non-existent.[15] Indeed, the later novels, whose judgments about society are more pronounced, have usually been accorded less value than *The Assistant* or *The Magic Barrel*. But Malamud has, in fact, shown a constant awareness of the societies in which his fictions take place. He is not only interested in describing actual social structures, or the human interactions that sustain them; he is also concerned with defining and dramatizing the underlying forces which form the bases upon which a given community is built. This study will attempt to show that from the myth of *The Natural* to the apocalyptic design of *The Tenants*, Malamud has fictively presented the decline of the American dream into the nightmare of an entire civilization in decay, a surprising theme, perhaps, from an author supposedly unconcerned with the difficult realities of society and the problems of a disintegrating culture.

It is with *The Natural* (1952), his first novel, that Malamud begins to suggest and depict the frauds perpetrated on men by an established order, particularly the bogus values and the fakery that seem to be as much a part of the American dream as its hopes and promises. The American dream: a paradox to be sure, one that embodies both the idealism of the nation and the corrosive materialism that appears to be its tangible outgrowth. This democratic dream speaks of a society that welcomes another's exiles; where the barriers against individual fulfillment are absent and the self can flourish, releasing the vitality of future possibilities; where the *I* can expand to encompass the universe.

However, those very elements that constitute the culture's visionary potential are also the source of its terror: alienation, loneliness, transience, the psychological and geographical movement from roots and tradition. It is also a civilization that defines achievement externally and success acquisitively, making failure a punishment, poverty a sin, and love a purchasable commodity. And it is an increasingly firm axiom of Malamud's fiction that to succeed in such an environment is to lose one's soul; to fail is to preserve one's moral integrity.

Utilizing this series of assumptions to shape his version of the democratic dilemma, Malamud in *The Natural* offers a variant of the Horatio Alger archetype wherein the hero must choose between two opposing concepts of success. Roy Hobbs can be a true democratic hero, self-created, faithful to his natural talent and individual possibility, believing in and accepting the power of the middle class version of the good life: "a house they had bought, with a redheaded baby on her lap, and himself going fishing in a way that made it satisfying to fish, knowing that everything was all right behind him, and the home-cooked meal would be hot and plentiful, and the kid would carry the name of Roy Hobbs into generations his old man would never know. With this in mind he fished the stream in peace...."[16]

Or Roy Hobbs, succumbing to his status as celebrated cultural product, can betray his true capacities as one of Nature's noblemen in order to obtain the outward signs of socially approved success: money, power, things, which are represented not by the fruitful Iris Lemon, but by the barren Memo Paris, the boss's niece, failed movie starlet of Miss America perfection. Her siren's song is that of a typically American Lorelei, whose chant is the dream turned rapacious:

> I am afraid to be poor. . . . Maybe I am weak or spoiled, but I am the type who has to have somebody who can support her in a decent way. I'm sick of living like a slave. I got to have a house of my own, a maid to help me with the hard work, a decent car to shop with and a fur coat for winter time when it's cold. I don't want to have to worry every time a can of beans jumps a nickel. I suppose it's wrong to want all of that but I can't help it. I've been around too long and seen too much. I saw how my mother lived and I know it killed her. I made up my mind to have certain things. . . . You're thirty-five now and that don't give you much time left as a ball player. . . . I'm sorry to say this, Roy, but I have to be practical. Suppose the next one is your last season, or that you will have one more after that? Sure, you'll probably get a good contract till then but it costs money to live, and then what'll we do for the rest of our lives?" [199-200].

The source of decay in the mythic American landscape of *The Natural* is money, poisoning even the pure idealism of the country's symbolic national pastime (hence the verbal echoes of the 1919 Black Sox scandal that close the book).[17] Wealth is obviously important in any social system, but in a democratic one such as America, predicated on the premise of human equality, the possession of money as a major external token denoting difference, separation, and inequity becomes a more ambiguous force, perhaps threatening to the fabric of the national community. On the one hand, the acquisition of money is proof that an open society still operates, that money is the just reward for living the letter of the American dream. On the other hand, the possession of money bears witness to the destruction of traditional values, beliefs, and commitments, an indication not of continued vitality but of the nation's flaws, the disintegration of its promise. For Malamud, the need for money, and therefore power, becomes the concrete emblem of popular, superficial notions of success and accomplishment, ultimately corrupting all facets of the national experience—moral, economic, and sensual.

Goodwill Banner (a suitably ironic name for a notoriously bad-tempered individual) is the embodiment of a morally corrupt, exploitative America. He instinctively recognizes that this society not only prefers things to people, but also that its materialistic ethic rationalizes the transformation of people into things, objects to be manipulated. His wealth, obtained illegally, through the exercise of established capitalistic virtues based on the management of human weakness and greed, is put at the service of this awareness, thereby justifying his appetite for control. The crowds who come to his stadium are merely coins, Pop Fisher is an obstruction to be bought out by any means, and Roy Hobbs is a life-sized toy to be used in order to acquire *more*. Fittingly, the trophy in his tower office is a stuffed shark.

As a judge, Banner also dispenses dark wisdom, parables and aphorisms which punctuate his conversation, making him seem a cynical Poor Richard: "The dog is turned to his vomit again" [96]. "The love of money is the root of all evil" [99]. "He that maketh haste to be rich shall not be innocent" [101]. "Put a knife to thy throat if thou be a man given to appetite" [101]. "Resist all evil" [102]. He is, in fact, enamoured of darkness, planning to write a disquisition on the subject entitled "On the Harmony of Darkness; Can Evil Exist in Harmony?" (echoing, no doubt, Melville's "On the Whiteness of the Whale"): "There is in the darkness a unity, if you will, that cannot be achieved in any other environment, a blending of the self with what the self perceives ..." [100]. And like a perverse and pessimistic Ben Franklin or Jay Gatsby, the Judge is, in a very American way, self-invented: "As a youngster I was frightened of the dark—used to wake up sobbing in it, as if it were water and I were drowning—but you will observe that I have so disciplined myself thoroughly against that fear, that I much prefer a dark to a lit room, and water is my favorite beverage" [100].

Goodwill Banner has decided against the vision of a sunny, jovial America; and in his treatment of fellow human beings, he has passed judgment on American innocence and found it suitable for purchase. Working in collusion with Judge Banner is Gus Sands, the one-eyed Supreme Bookie, a representation of economic corruption and the decline of American capitalism.

To be sure, the original impetus of the American economic system had been to insure growth, progress, and the pursuit of happiness. Capitalism is, indeed, the financial analogue to the psychic and political freedoms on which the country was founded. It reinforced the idea of individual ability as the way to true achievement; it exalted the willingness to risk, the capacity to take a chance, and the readiness to seize the moment; it made real the national rags-to-riches mythology; it allowed more people to have a share in society's affluence. But for Malamud these factors no longer work as theorized. The economic system that was once the hope of the shopkeeper, the small farmer, the businessman with little capital and much ability, has become the servant of the rich who use it to drain and profit from those who have less.

Gus Sands, partially blind, seeing the individual only as an expendable commodity, is one such exploiter. Like the Judge, Sands has amassed a fortune by trading in human frailty, in this case the impulse bred into the American to get rich quick, to reach for the fast buck, no matter how. For if money is that necessary icon, the indispensable sign of acceptance, approval, goodness, wisdom, and power, then the means by which it is to be procured is irrelevant. Gus, secure in his knowledge of the secret heart of his countrymen, is, like the serpent in Eden (Roy Hobbs even calls him "wormy"), a masterful tempter.

He is also more than simply the Supreme Bookie. As a gambler, he is the epitome of the risk-taker, the speculative capitalist whose product, in this instance, just happens to be money:

> "Didn't know you bet on any special player."
> "On anybody or anything. We bet on strikes, balls, hits, runs, innings, and full games. If a good team plays a lousy team we will bet on the spread of runs. We cover anything anyone wants to bet on. Once in a Series games I bet a hundred grand on three pitched balls."
> "How'd you make out on that?"
> "Guess."
> "I guess you didn't.
> "Right, I didn't. . . . But it don't matter. The next week I ruined the guy in a different deal. Sometimes we win, sometimes we don't but the percentage is for us. Today we lost on you, some other time we will clean up double" [108].

And though dependent on luck and accident, like a good entrepreneur he controls luck and minimizes accident through bribery ("Say the word, slugger, and you can make yourself a nice pile of dough quick" [174]), seduction, dishonesty, and the chicanery that has become an established part of American business practice.

Memo Paris (whose name—a memory of Paris—may suggest the treacherous Helen of Troy or that sensual, erotic, tempting City of Lights), seductive agent of Judge Banner and Gus Sands, is clearly an exponent of the business of commercial sensuality. That she may be a national symbol of sorts is indicated by Roy's seeing her "as a truly beautiful doll with a form like Miss America" [166]. She is, indeed, a doll, an object, all surface prettiness with little emotional depth or internal integrity. And as a beauty contest winner, value has necessarily been placed on those superficial qualities that guarantee victory. Just as Roy Hobbs attempts to succeed in a particular area of mass entertainment, so too does Memo Paris. But she chooses the Hollywood dream factory, where success is contingent upon appearance far more than it is dependent upon talent. She fails, however, not because she lacks outward beauty, but because she lacks talent. She has no inner resources to draw on; she possesses a limited, closed self that has been determined by her external attractiveness:

> "I won a beauty contest where they picked a winner from each state and she was sent to Hollywood to be a starlet. For a few weeks I felt like the Queen of the May, then they took a screen test and though I had the looks and figure my test did not come out so good in acting and they practically told me to go home.... I stayed there for three more years, doing night club work and going to an acting school besides, hoping that I would some day be a good enough actress, but it didn't take. I knew what *I was supposed to do but I couldn't make myself, in my thoughts, into somebody else.* You're supposed to forget who you are" [119-120].[18]

As we have already seen, Memo's wants are not only conditioned by her fear of poverty, but also by what society has legitimized as essential for happiness: maids, fur coats, houses, cars. And she has been taught by that society that it is perfectly appropriate to sell herself in order to secure those things. Marketing her sensuality, however, corrupts the buyer as well. Memo Paris is, in fact, negotiable merchandise to be bought at the right price—a man's soul.

Into this knotty web of societal decay comes Roy Hobbs, a natural man, whose notable American innocence has prevented his education through experience; this difficult process has never been a popular American ideal, much to Malamud's disappointment. Roy is to be the authentic American hero whose adventures take place on the field of mass ritual—baseball—not in the realm of elite diversion to please the few. There is no question that he has great talent, the kind of native ability meant to be nurtured in a democracy. But his ambition is narrow and unchanging. It is expressed in the same language at the outset of his career at the age of nineteen—"Sometimes when I walk down the street I bet people

will say there goes Roy Hobbs, the best there ever was in the game"
[33]—and then at its resumption, age thirty-five: "Maybe I might
break my back while I am at it, . . . but I will do my best—the best I
am able—to be the greatest there ever was in the game" [114].

And his desires are at the mercy of social and cultural
influences that stress money, possessions, acquisitiveness:

> It had to be something big or it wouldn't pay back enough. And if it
> was a big company he could take it a little easy. . . . He pondered
> where to get another twenty-five thousand, and it had to be before
> the start of the next baseball season because as soon as everybody saw
> he wasn't playing, it wouldn't be easy to cash in on his name. . . . He
> thought of other means to earn money fast—selling the story of his
> life to the papers, barnstorming a bit this fall and winter. . . . But
> neither of these things added up to much—not twenty-five grand
> [201].

Because he does not grasp the meaning of the heroic beyond its
simplest definition; because his society has deceived him about
what is to be truly valued in life; because he accepts the tokens of
success rather than actual accomplishment, he chooses fidelity to
his genius too late, after he has already betrayed it for cash. Roy is
therefore doomed to repeat his suffering without understanding its
significance: "I never did learn anything out of my past life, now I
have to suffer again" [236].

If *The Natural* presents a simplified definition of the
American experience where villainy is easily identifiable and the
pattern of right action obvious, *The Assistant* offers complex,
perhaps perplexing, ambiguities. The world of *The Assistant* seems
closed, rigid, without opportunity or economic progress, where the
traditional values of honesty, thrift, and hard work go unrewarded,
and may, in fact, even be meaningless. It is an America inhabited by
the marginal, the frustrated, the luckless, whom a hungry, active,
pushing civilization has discarded as useless: immigrant Jews left
behind in the rush toward assimilation and the good life; would-be
criminals successful only in their failure; the trapped, who are
caught forever in a net of unfulfilled expectations.[19]

In this society of the powerless, so unlike that of *The Natural*,
evil is neither predatory, nor sinister, nor particularly threatening.
It is, rather, clumsy, slightly comical, and "Karping." Yet in such a
defeatist environment, characters seem nevertheless capable of
moral choice; positive human change can occur. Ultimately,
however, though choices are undoubtedly made and changes
certainly do occur, they are equivocal and claustrophobic,

imprisoning rather than liberating. Perhaps this paradox is an indication that such virtues as honor, duty, responsibility, and goodness are a hindrance in an aggressive society addicted to the pursuit of externally determined success, not its internal reality; that morality and ethical behavior are signs marking only the failed, the lost.

Walter Shear has rightly perceived *The Assistant* to be a dramatization of the never-quite-resolved conflict between two cultures—the Jewish tradition of the Bobers, Pearls, and Karps and the American heritage, the wisdom of the old world versus the utilitarianism of the new.[20] This analysis is true as far as it goes. But the encounter as presented in the novel is more subtly ironic. The Jewish tradition, as Malamud depicts it, may be morally admirable; but it is essentially heterodox and secular, divorced from its sources in orthodox Judaism and the European situation that conditioned it, and no longer appropriate in an open, liberal social system.[21] Morris Bober may have brought with him his own entombment but without sufficient spiritual consolation to sustain him. And the American heritage, vital and promising as it may be, stands not only as a mockery of hopes betrayed, or as a series of poisoned expectations, but as a sardonic tribute to the hypocrisy that is also a part of the American dream. Karp succeeds in the financially approved way, but it is without joy and without love.

We begin with the only Jewish families who inhabit, resentfully, uncomfortably, an impoverished, decaying, non-Jewish neighborhood in New York—the Karps, the Pearls, the Bobers: "She [Ida Bober] had waked that morning resenting the grocer for having dragged her, so many years ago, out of a Jewish neighborhood into this. She missed to this day their old friends and landsleit—lost for parnusseh unrealized."[22] Each represents, in some way, a facet of the Jewish experience in this *goldene medinah*, this golden land. While these families do have those aspirations common to American imagination, they are Jews who have, for the most part, been unable to enter the mainstream of middle-class life and acceptability. They are reminders of the immigrant past for whom the promise of *better* has not been kept. Fulfillment is for their children—Louis, Nat, and Helen. They are the generation who will belong. Although the patriarchs are entrepreneurs, self-employed businessmen—ironic exemplars of the classic American prescription for success—the isolated condition of these three Jewish families makes them vulnerable, susceptible to paralyzing memories of their ghetto history. Although these families are still

anxious to participate in the flawed American dream, they are
viewed by many of the Gentiles in the community as seeming
embodiments of the anti-semite's stereotypical Jew, and therefore as
legitimate targets for robbery and violence.

Julius Karp is the wealthy exception among the three families.
At the end of Prohibition, good businessman that he was, Karp
astutely (by society's valuation of such things) acquired the
necessary license to transform cheap shoes into expensive bottles.
The liquor store, not surprisingly, did well in so poor a
neighborhood, and Karp flourished. But for Malamud, Karp's
success had been bought at dehumanizing cost. After all, his
wealth, like Judge Banner's or Gus Sands's, is based on the
exploitation of human frailty. "A business for drunken bums" [9],
says Morris Bober, the novel's moral voice, judging with
disapproval and contempt. Karp, in an act that signifies the
breaking of the human connections that have tied him to his fellow
Jews, has also moved out of the neighborhood into "a big house on
the Parkway ... complete with two-car garage and Mercury" [16],
the middle-class American's vision of accomplishment. It is worth
noting here how often success, in this country, is measured by the
geographical distance one has moved from his origins and roots—
the further one goes, the more one has achieved. This fact has
allowed Karp to become an absentee exploiter, using the neighborhood for his own, as property, then leaving it to die from his
poison, a singular example of the abdication of moral responsibility
in favor of personal financial satisfaction.

But Julius Karp's deficiencies as a human being are more
extensive. Having become the kind of success society values, he is
now free to exercise the power conferred by money: the ability to
transform human beings into commodities to be manipulated for
gain. Because he has attained position, Julius Karp assumes also
that he has been given wisdom. In this culture, the ability to
acquire money attests to sagacity; therefore Karp is free to "run
down the store and spout unwanted advice" [22]. After all, since
Morris Bober is a poor man, a failure by anyone's estimation, what
can he possibly know that is worth anything? And Karp, assuming
that the world, as he knows, dances only to the tune of cash, even
converts love into a business proposition with Helen Bober an
object to be traded for financial security:

> Karp felt he could ease his son's way to Helen by making Morris a
> proposition he had had in the back of his head for almost a year. He
> would describe Louis' prospects after marriage in terms of cold cash

and other advantages, and suggest that Morris speak to Helen on the subject of going with him seriously. If they went together a couple of months—Louis would give her an extravagant good time—and the combination worked out, it would benefit not only the daughter, but the grocer as well, for then Karp would take over Morris's sad gesheft and renovate and enlarge it into a self-service market with the latest fixtures and goods.... With himself as the silent partner giving practical advice, it would take a marvelous catastrophe to keep the grocer from earning a decent living . . . [151].

Finally, and perhaps most significantly, Karp betrays friendship, loyalty, and his own humanity for a mercenary reward by allowing into the neighborhood another grocery store to compete with the unfortunate Morris for business, since competition is the essence of the American way. Karp does this first at the beginning of the novel when, rejecting Morris's pleas, he sells the empty tailor shop to Schmitz: "Morris ran to Karp. 'What did you do to me?' The liquor dealer said with a one-shouldered shrug, 'You saw how long stayed empty the store. Who will pay my taxes? But don't worry,' he added, 'he'll sell more delicatessen but you'll sell more groceries. Wait, you'll see he'll bring you in customers'" [11]. And he resells to Taast and Pederson, knowing full well that such competition will be destructive:

> "What happened to Schmitz?"
> "He has a bad blood disease and lays now in the hospital."
> "Poor man," the grocer sighed.... "Will he give the store in auction?"
> Karp was devastating, "What do you mean give in auction? It's a good store. He sold it Wednesday to two up-to-date Norwegian partners and they will open next week a modern fancy grocery and delicatessen. You will see where your business will go.... What could I do? I couldn't tell him to go in auction if he had a chance to sell" [155].

That Karp chooses, in both instances, to sell to *goyim* is a further betrayal of Morris, who is portrayed as the essence of Jewishness.

Yet in Karp there exists a vague, ineffable, dissatisfaction, an unconscious recognition that perhaps his kind of achievement is incomplete, a suspicion that something is indeed more vital than dollars. For, like the crooked Charlie Sobeloff, Morris's former partner made rich at the expense of Bober's trusting innocence, Karp finds it necessary to have Morris's approval and acceptance: "For some reason that was not clear to him Karp liked Morris to like him . . ." [149]. True wisdom makes itself known even to the most hardened.

As for the next generation, Louis Karp is the son of such a father. And it is hardly surprising that his ambitions are narrow, limited to those obtainable by purchase:

> "Louis," she [Helen Bober] said, watching a far-off light on the water, "what do you want out of your life?"
> He kept his arm around her. "The same thing I got—plus."
> "Plus what?"
> "Plus more, so my wife and family can have also" [43].

However, in this version of America, unlike the landscape of *The Natural*, there is retribution for those who have made their pact with the American serpent, who have been seduced by the force and potency of economic materialism. Karp's liquor store, feeding on itself, is burnt to the ground by Ward Minogue, an ironic avenging angel. Karp himself has a heart attack, and he can no longer continue those activities that have given justification to his existence. And Louis, interested in immediate gain, goes to work as a salesman for a liquor concern, rather than rebuild his father's business. Perhaps punishment is possible because in *The Assistant* Malamud has chosen to portray a society of the helpless where there is only minimal power to be exercised, rather than the omnipotence of Judge Banner and Gus Sands.

The Pearls are also foils for the values represented by Morris. Sam, in spite of his poor candy store, is an entrepreneurial success after a fashion, although not within the *legitimate* economic structure employed by Karp. While he "neglected the store . . . Sam's luck with the nags was exceptional and he had nicely supported Nat in college until the scholarships started rolling in" [15]. Like any good risk-taking capitalist, he spends his days brooding over the dope sheets in much the same way a broker studies stock quotations and Dow Jones averages—and to much the same end. And such an occupation requires a fierce dedication to the study of the main chance in order that every possible money-making opportunity be exploited. However, this commitment, according to Malamud, narrows one's encounters with the world and with humanity, a weakness that once again only Morris recognizes for what it is: "Morris took the *Forward* from the newsstand and dropped a nickel into the cigar box. Sam Pearl, working over a green racing sheet, gave him a wave of his hammy hand. They never bothered to talk. What did he know about race horses? And what did the other know of the tragic quality of life? Wisdom flew over his hard head" [17-18].

More relevant for the novel's antipathy to America's driving materialism is the character of Nat Pearl, "magna cum laude, Columbia, now in his second year at law school" [14], and, as Helen observes, a soon-to-be professional "with first-rate prospects, also rich friends he had never bothered to introduce her to" [14]. By virtue of his education, his job choice, and those values inherited from his father and the culture at large, Nat ultimately will become part of society's controlling machinery. That Nat has chosen the law is obviously significant, for, as a profession, it provides easy access to real wealth and power, temptation enough for anyone, let alone the son of immigrants: "Nat Pearl wanted to be 'somebody,' but to him this meant making money to lead the life of some of his well-to-do friends at law school" [133]. How unlike Morris, for whom the Law (always capitalized in Morris's usage) is seen as a mode of ethical behavior and right conduct.

It is important to understand how Nat's acceptance (and perhaps America's as well) of the law as a tool, simply a pragmatic device whose function is to wheedle, to manipulate, to justify, and to excuse wrong action, shapes his dealings with Helen Bober. First, however, it is necessary to acknowledge how much that relationship has been conditioned by the very fact of Nat's promise rather than his beliefs. This recognition is particularly fitting considering that America has always been the civilization symbolized by a commitment to a better future for all its inhabitants. Helen is acutely aware that the society's respect for Nat's possibilities has allowed her to act against her own personally developed moral sense: "Nat Pearl, handsome, cleft-chinned, gifted, ambitious, had wanted without too much trouble a lay and she, half in love, had obliged and regretted. Not the loving, but that it had taken her so long to realize how little he wanted" [14]. Nat, like Louis Karp, regards Helen as an object to be acquired and used. Louis offers money and fails. Nat, more sophisticated, knowing that he stands, in some way, for entry into that culture that has labelled the Bobers outsiders, offers possibilities and succeeds. But when Helen, recognizing the nature of her seduction, develops scruples, Nat does not hesitate to use a kind of legal chop-logic to defend his behavior and to demean her conscience—that is what being a lawyer means:

> "Helen, I honestly want to know how somebody's supposed to defend himself when he hasn't any idea what's in the indictment against him? What kind of crime have I committed? . . ."
> "I'm not a lawyer—I don't make indictments. . . ."

"You're a funny kid," Nat was saying. "You've got some old-
fashioned values about some things. I always told you you punish
yourself too much. Why should anybody have such a hot and heavy
conscience in these times? People are freer in the twentieth
century.... What," Nat argued, "would peoples' lives be like if
everybody regretted every beautiful minute of all that happened?
Where's the poetry of living?" [109].

When Helen finally rejects Nat and what he represents, she
becomes for him only "You bitch." And Nat, because of an
allegiance to a philosophy which turns people into things—a kind
of transformational materialism endemic in American society—
must suffer the loss of wisdom; hardly much of a loss, he would
suspect, if it is to be defined by Morris Bober.

The Bobers are clearly failures, at least as society would judge
them. They have neither money, nor power, nor the intense drive to
belong that is characteristic of so many immigrants. And they lack
that seemingly national trait, crucial if one is to succeed in
America, the ability to create their own destiny. They do not
control fate; it controls them. The Bobers are, in fact, frightened
and disappointed in the country they have escaped to. They take no
risks; they do not gamble (except on the grocery store—a losing
proposition if there ever was one); they cannot hear opportunity's
knock. And they are immobile, stationary, afraid to venture beyond
the block. To a large degree, they are responsible for their
entombment in that grave of a business, for their attitudes are
unsuitable to achievement and accomplishment in American
terms. Finally, Ida and Morris have, in the worst betrayal of the
American dream, deprived their child of a future in this new golden
land. Yet the Bobers, as a family, seem to represent a source of
strength, goodness, wisdom, and morality unavailable to the rest of
society, and perhaps unattainable if the price be social and
economic failure.

Ida Bober, however, is considerably less willing to accept
moral virtue if it is unaccompanied by sufficient financial rewards.
In fact, Ida is obsessed by her need for monetary security to a degree
that often dehumanizes her. She is suspicious of anyone who may
attack what little position and self-respect she has acquired. She is
therefore hostile to the newcomer Frank Alpine on two counts: as a
stranger, he may steal money; and, as a non-Jew, he might steal a
more valuable piece of property, a key to the future, her daughter.
And because Ida is wise in the ways of the American world, her
Cassandra-like prophecies of doom have much accuracy. Unlike

Morris, she believes "a business is a business" [9] even if the money is made at the expense of another's weakness. She clearly resents her husband's claims to superior moral sensitivity, "everybody is a stupe but not Morris Bober" [10], especially if it means a loss in dollars. She nags if Morris trusts enough to give credit. Her measurement of human worth is material possessions. And significantly it is only Ida who respects and even admires Julius Karp for his foresight and his success, though it be to her husband's cost:

> "Why does he bring me buyers? Why didn't he keep out the German around the corner?"
> She sighed. "He tries to help you now because he feels sorry for you."
> "Who needs his sorrow?" Morris said. "Who needs him?"
> "So why *you* didn't have the sense to make out of your grocery a wine and liquor store when came out the licenses?"
> "Who had cash for stock?"
> "So if you don't have, don't talk."
> "A business for drunken bums."
> "A business is a business. What Julius Karp takes in next door in a day we don't take in in two weeks" [9].

Ida is perfectly capable, even anxious, to use the deceptive techniques of the good (in a monetary, if not a moral, sense) businessperson in order to cheat the naive refugee Podolsky if it means ridding herself of the millstone the store has become. That she might be imprisoning Podolsky, who had come to America for the mythical new life as Morris had so many years ago, is not her concern. Nor can she comprehend Frank's willingness to work for nothing in order to pay a symbolic debt to Morris and redeem his own soul.

But the most important factor, for Malamud, in Ida's adherence to this American version of reductive materialism is that it diminishes the value of love. Such an unpredictable emotion threatens the business of marriage, an arrangement, as perceived by Ida, to escape poverty, the only way that a woman can achieve status, wealth, and power. This view of matrimony is her only way of protecting and insuring what future Helen might have: "'Helen,' she said, holding back her tears, 'the only thing I want for you is the best. Don't make my mistake. Don't make worse and spoil your whole life, with a poor man that he is only a grocery clerk which we don't know about him nothing. Marry somebody who can give you a better life, a nice professional boy with a college education. Don't mix up now with a stranger. Helen, I know what I'm talking. Believe me, I know'" [146].

Ida, therefore, measures potential husbands not by their inherent value as human beings, not by their ability to love, but by the money they have or might have: Nat Pearl will be "someday a rich lawyer" [4]; even "the stupe" Louis Karp is acceptable since he can offer financial security. And any quality in Helen, particularly her intelligence—"Some people want their children to read more. I want you to read less." [115]—that reduces her marketability is to be decried and condemned.

What has so embittered Ida is not simple nagging dissatisfaction but guilt, "her guilt that she had talked him into a grocery store when he was in the first year of evening high school, preparing, he had said, for pharmacy" [8]. She had settled for the immediate gratification of ownership and possession rather than wait for long-range possibilities, withheld fulfillment, and postponed satisfaction. It is only when Morris is dead (living he was a constant reminder of that guilt) and she no longer fears starving because of Frank's rent and Helen's salary and Rubin's job that she softens into humanity.

Helen Bober is a more complex character, a mass of American and old-country contradictions, whose perceptions, ambitions, and desires have been conditioned by the hard American materialism of her mother and the otherworldly, inappropriate wisdom of her father. Helen tends to see herself, as do Ida, the Karps, Nat Pearl, and even Frank Alpine initially, as merchandise upon whom a price has been set. Although she is concerned with abstract goals and impractical notions of morality, preoccupied with philosophy, an idealist believing in the something more beyond the material that gives life its meaning (symbolized by her addiction to literature), she nevertheless thinks of Helen Bober as a commodity to be judged by some sort of externally devised concept of worth. And that standard is a social one contingent on her lack of prospects, "as poor as her name sounded, with little promise of a better future" [14]. Therefore, in spite of her obvious intelligence, sensitivity, and capacity for love, she is constantly worried at being valued under her expectations, certain that she is worthless even to a man like Nat Pearl, whose ambitions she derides and suspects. As she says, she loves before she is loved, perhaps inviting the expected rejection because of her fear she is not worth the loving. Perhaps that is one of the reasons why Helen chooses Frank, so clearly less than she, an alien, a wanderer, a non-Jew, without position or stability.

As a true child of her parents, Helen romanticizes the power of education, placing her faith in it as the key to realizing her sense of potential, becoming American in the best sense of the word. She does not wish to use education simply to acquire a marketable skill, because such is not the true function of learning. To be educated according to Helen (and to Malamud, no doubt) is to possess wisdom and understanding of life. Helen desires education so that she may become a better person, hardly a useful talent, much less an appropriate one for the national economy. It is this deprivation that Helen feels most strongly, and Frank Alpine ultimately recognizes that it is the one gift he can offer that Helen cannot return.

At this point, we must examine Helen's curious ambivalence toward the act of gift-giving, a persistent motif throughout the novel. She is able to give *things*—her salary to her parents, for example—as an expression of her feelings, but she cannot, in the course of the novel, give her body because it is the concrete form taken by the self, the physical essence of the soul. To offer so precious a gift and to have it rejected or misvalued is to destroy the integrity of the person that is Helen Bober. Even Helen, in a subtle fashion, uses the external, the physical, the concrete, as a source and standard of individual worth. However, Helen is most reluctant to accept gifts for a number of reasons. First, to accept a gift is to acknowledge another's judgment on Helen-as-object, whose value is instantly visible by the quality of the gift: "Nat, at his best, had produced a half-dozen small pink roses" [112], while Frank had given her an expensive scarf and a leather-bound copy of Shakespeare. Second, to accept a gift is to incur debt and obligation, is to become a human IOU, a particularly uncomfortable situation for the insecure. Says Helen, "for gifts you pay" [112]. And finally, to accept a gift is to put a price on love, to admit that affection can be bought for things, an idea that Helen instinctively knows to be false in spite of a culture that has made it a truth. Although Helen wants no part of Nat Pearl's materialism, admiring instead the intangible and impractical qualities of sensitivity, perception, and depth, and resents her treatment as a commodity, she nevertheless chooses to treat Frank Alpine as such a vehicle for the realization of a future.

Yet it is only when Helen realizes that gifts are merely an

outward sign, an honest expression of true emotion, when she
learns to take gracefully as well as to give generously, when she can
thank Frank for his unselfish help, that Helen can become truly
loving.

Because of the limitations placed on her needs and ambitions
by economics and her own psychology, Frank, who has traveled,
moved, *lived*, is transformed into the embodiment of her unfulfilled
possibilities. Since she resents her loss—"The world has shrunk for
me.... I want a larger and better life. I want the return of my
possibilities" [43]—she makes Frank the *tabula rasa* on which to
write her dreams:

> And if she married Frank, her first job would be to help him
> realize his wish to be somebody.... Frank...was struggling to
> realize himself.as a person, a more worthwhile ambition. Though
> Nat had an excellent formal education, Frank knew more about life
> and gave the impression of greater potential depth. She wanted him
> to become what he might, and conceived a plan to support him
> through college. Maybe she could even see him through a master's
> degree, once he knew what he wanted to do. She realized this would
> mean the end of her own vague plans for going to day college, but
> that was really lost long ago, and she thought she would at last
> accept the fact once Frank had got what she hadn't [133].

When she discovers that Frank is anything but a paragon, a mere
man with considerably more than his share of human weaknesses
(as thief and rapist), she hates him for being less than her fantasy of
him, a deception using her body as a possession; and she hates
herself for so radical a misjudgment and for once again being
valued under her expectations. Helen can only accept her own
flawed humanity when she recognizes the real humanity in Frank,
acknowledging that he has in fact changed, that he has become that
better person, not through a college education but through
suffering. Hardly the American dream, Malamud believes, but it
will do.

But it is in the creation of Morris Bober and his encounters
with the world that Malamud offers his disapproval of aspects of
the American dream: the expectations and promise defined, the
defeats and loss explored. Morris's immigrant history may be seen
as disappointment. First there is an escape from tyranny and
persecution which was life in the old country. "They were poor and
there were pogroms. So when he was about to be conscripted into
the czar's army his father said, 'Run to America'" [81]. Then comes
a taste of freedom, the opening of possibilities. "After I came here I

wanted to be a druggist. . . . I went for a year in night school. I took algebra, also German and English. 'Come,' said the wind to the leaves one day, 'come over the meadow with me and play.' This is a poem I learned. But I didn't have the patience to stay in night school, so when I met my wife I gave up my chances" [83]. And finally, immobilizing entrapment in a dying economic venture, "He had escaped out of the Russian Army to the U.S.A., but once in a store he was like a fish fried in deep fat" [83]. Why then did a man who risked the wrath of the czar's sergeant fail when confronted with America's multiple opportunities? What spoiled the hope? And how could such a failure, with so many lost chances in a society that offered so many futures, become the moral center of *The Assistant?*

Josephine Zadovsky Knopp defines Morris's ethical beliefs as the concept of *mentshlekhayt* which

> has as its fundamental premise the innocence of man, man free of the sins of the Fall. It recognizes that within man run opposing tendencies toward good and evil, and that within this context man is completely free to choose. It rests its ultimate faith in man's basic goodness and the implicit assumption that, in the final analysis, he will always choose what is morally and ethically right. It believes in action as the path toward moral redemption. . . . It is an ethic concerned with improving man's lot in this world. . . . To those who accept, perhaps even unconsciously, the ethical code of *mentshlekhayt*, the concept of an "absurd" universe is foreign; to them the universe has a definite structure and meaning. . . . At least a part of this meaning resides in the code's implicit faith in the moral significance of man's action, . . . and that he has the obligation to apply this power in the cause of good.
> *Mentshlekhayt* also encompasses the very strong sense of community that has traditionally been a feature of Jewish life. The paramount characteristic of this community feeling is the moral imperative of man's responsibility to his fellow man. . . .
> The code . . . is an order, a Law in a world of chaos and suffering, and thereby brings sanity and significance to life.[23]

While this clearly describes elements of Morris's credo, Knopp does not appear to appreciate the irony of assigning such an ethical system to a man who inhabits a society that makes adherence to such values a sure sign of failure. Given American culture as it is portrayed in *The Assistant*, this admirable moral structure appears to be a source of passive endurance, rather than an active commitment for change.

Morris collapses into prisoner and victim because the national community that Morris has chosen as refuge and affirmation no longer uses or finds valuable the virtues of a truly good man. And while it is true that even Karp keeps returning to Morris for approval and spiritual sustenance, it does the liquor store owner no good, for he continues to denigrate, mock, and betray the values Morris subscribes to. In Morris's decline, embodied in his inability and unwillingness to adapt to an increasingly opportunistic culture, we witness the triumph of the dream as nightmare. The memories that haunt Morris throughout the novel are not, ironically, of an American paradise but of an Eastern European one: "No, not for an age had he lived a whole day in the open. As a boy, always running in the muddy, rutted streets of the village, or across the fields, or bathing with the other boys in the river; but as a man, in America, he rarely saw the sky. In the early days when he drove a horse and wagon, yes, but not since his first store. In a store you were entombed" [5-6]. The world of persecution has become a remembered Eden of open spaces, while America, the new land, is a closed box, a coffin.

In an environment where every penny is important and money an icon (notice how carefully Malamud accounts for the store's income before the robbery), Morris trusts and gives trust:

> "My mother says . . . can you trust her till tomorrow for a pound of butter, a loaf of rye bread and a small bottle of cider vinegar?"
> He knew the mother. "No more trust."
> The girl burst into tears.
> Morris gave her. . . . The total now came to $2.03, which he never hoped to see. But Ida would nag, . . . so he reduced the amount. . . . His peace—the little he lived with—was worth forty-two cents" [4].

A Lincolnesque figure, his honesty is only the stuff of legends and eulogies, and about as relevant in this civilization: "Helen, his dear daughter, remembers from when she was a small girl that her father ran two blocks in the snow to give back to a poor Italian lady a nickel that she forgot on the counter" [228]. He is a man of responsibility in a culture of the irresponsible, who wakes early, morning after morning, to insure that the Poilisheh gets her three-cent roll.

In a society that elevates transience and prizes mobility, Morris, especially after the death of his son and future, remains frozen and immobile, actually as well as metaphorically *going nowhere*. He does not cheat. He will not steal, even in a business situation where such behavior is not only commonplace and justified but also necessary to insure that magic word—profit.

"It's easy to fool people," said Morris.
"Why don't you try a couple of those tricks yourself, Morris? Your amount of profit is small."
Morris looked at him in surprise. "Why should I steal from my customers? Do they steal from me?"
"They would if they could."
"When a man is honest he don't worry when he sleeps. This is more important than a nickel" [84].

And in spite of his admiration for the greater efficiency and practicality of the modern, Morris is, not surprisingly, attached to the old ways. He teaches Frank the skills he possesses with a mixture of pride and embarrassment, remembering when it required real ability to be a grocer: "As if ashamed somebody could learn the business so easily, Morris explained to him how different it had been to be a grocer only a few years ago. In those days one was more of a macher, a craftsman. Who was ever called on nowadays to slice up a loaf of bread . . . or ladle out a quart of milk?" [83-84]. But since "the chain store kills the small man" [33], of what significance are those abilities in a packaged culture valuing speed not technique, convenience not aptitude, and the plastic rather than the authentic: "Now is everything in containers, jars, or packages. Even hard cheeses that they cut them for hundreds of years by hand now come sliced up in cellophane packages. Nobody has to know anything any more" [84].

As that traditional but impossible American paradigm—the small business where "at least you're your own boss" [33]—Morris is a failure. Perhaps the ideal has become mendacious—"To be a boss of nothing is nothing" [33]. Certainly Ida and even Helen, trapped in a civilization that has divorced success from human worth, ethical conduct, and morality, condemn or minimize the quality of Morris's true achievement.

I said Papa was honest but what was the good of such honesty if he couldn't exist in the world? . . . Poor Papa; being naturally honest, he didn't believe that others come by their dishonesty naturally. And he couldn't hold onto those things he had worked so hard to get. He gave away, in a sense, more than he owned. . . . He knew, at least, what was good. . . . People liked him, but who can admire a man passing his life in such a store? He buried himself in it; he didn't have the imagination to know what he was missing. He made himself a victim. He could, with a little more courage, have been more than he was [230].

Morris's final judgment is also one of regret, loss, and disappointment: "He thought of his life with sadness.... His mood was one of regret. I gave away my life for nothing. It was the thunderous truth" [226].

Ida, Helen, and Morris are to a limited degree correct in their assessment of Morris's accomplishments or lack of them. Unfortunately, the paradox (according to Malamud) is that, given the kind of man Morris Bober was, his future in America was inevitable. The essential characteristics that one must acknowledge and admire in him are those very characteristics that made financial success in the world impossible.

The America that has diminished and defeated Morris Bober accords respect, admiration, and power to the insensitive Karp who seizes the main chance at the expense of honor, loyalty, and friendship, and rewards with success and wealth the corrupt Charlie Sobeloff, "a cross-eyed but clever conniver" [204] who cheated and defrauded the innocent and trusting Morris.

> Arriving at Sobeloff's Self-Service Market, Morris... was amazed at its size. Charlie had tripled the original space.... The result was a huge market with a large number of stalls and shelved sections loaded with groceries. The supermarket was so crowded with people that to Morris... it looked like a department store. He felt a pang, thinking that part of this might now be his if he had taken care of what he had once owned. He would not envy Charlie Sobeloff his dishonest wealth, but when he thought of what he could do for Helen with a little money his regret deepened that he had nothing [207].

As Morris joins that "silent knot of men who drifted along Sixth Avenue stopping at the employment agency doors to read impassively the list of jobs chalked up on the blackboard signs" [208], he sees an America that has discarded the poor, the old, the sick, the uneducated, and has rendered them useless, unfit for participation in a society that popularly believes that "God loves the poor people but he helps the rich" [211].

It is an America that has betrayed its symbolic promise and traditional ideals. For Morris, "America had become too complicated. One man counted for nothing. There were too many stores, depressions, anxieties. What had he escaped to here?" [206]. A good man can retain his soul only at the expense of a freedom too easily become opportunism, and an opportunism too easily become deceit, trickery, corruption.

Frank Alpine enters the story like a dingy American Lochinvar "lately come from the West, looking for a better opportunity" [29].

Like Helen, Frank is a divided personality, one who steals yet yearns for goodness, who wanders yet yearns for stability, who rapes yet yearns for love. He wants "money, nightclubs, babes" [92], and at the same time wishes to be like St. Francis, for whom "poverty was a queen" [31]: "Every time I read about somebody like him I get a feeling inside of me I have to fight to keep from crying. He was born good, which is a talent if you have it" [31]. Frank is a man ensnared by the corruption of his culture, as well as by his own inner drives and compulsions; he is looking for a model to provide an alternative mode of being. Not finding St. Francis, he discovers the next best thing in contemporary America—Morris Bober— and becomes his surrogate son, and spiritual heir, giving up the opportunities of the world, the flesh, and the devil for the ascetic discipline of the imprisoning grocery store.

Frank is that not uncommon American phenomenon, the wanderer, the mover, the man without roots who leaves when things do not work out or disappears when responsibility weighs too heavily and commitments become too demanding. "I am too restless—six months in any one place is too much for me. Also I grab at everything too quick—too impatient. I don't do what I have to. . . . The result is I move into a place with nothing, and I move out with nothing" [37]. And like so many of his fellow citizens, he rationalizes this particularly American brand of irresponsibility as the testing of freedom, a trying of opportunities, the correct use of his country's promise. It is hardly surprising that Helen, who longs for such motion and such possibilities, is seduced by Frank's words:

> "The way I figure, anything is possible. I always think about the different kinds of chances I have. This has stuck in my mind—don't get yourself trapped in one thing, because maybe you can do something else a whole lot better. That's why I guess I never settled down so far. I've been exploring conditions. I still have some very good ambitions which I would like to see come true. The first step to that, I know for sure now, is to get a good education. I didn't use to think like that, but the more I live the more I do" [98].

An excellent statement of the national credo. That he may be using this pronouncement to seduce Helen does not obviate the fact that a portion of Frank's personality believes it.

Frank wants to be better than he is in both the financial and moral spheres of the American experience without perceiving that he cannot achieve both ambitions in the kind of driven, materialistic culture America has in fact become. He is particularly concerned with the acquisition of wealth, power, and importance;

he is possessed by the sense that "he was meant for something a whole lot better—to do something big, different" [91-92]. Daniel Bell has indicated in his essay "Crime as an American Way of Life" that for a man with no skills, the American dream may be achieved through crime.[24] Thus Frank thinks that:

> At crime he would change his luck, make adventure, live like a prince. He shivered with pleasure as he conceived robberies, assaults—murders if it had to be—each violent act helping to satisfy a craving that somebody suffer as his own fortune improved. He felt infinitely relieved, believing that if a person figured for himself something big, something different in his life, he had a better chance to get it than some poor jerk who couldn't think that high up [92].

Frank's dream is only partially influenced by its Dostoevskian counterparts. The Russian's protagonists are, in fact, concerned with the metaphysics of power while Frank wants the external accoutrements of success that can be acquired by crime.

But crime is taking, the way Frank takes from Morris by theft, from Helen by rape. It is simply another variant of the culture's dominating materialism that defines people as things for use, manipulation, exploitation, or expropriation. However, it is only when Frank can learn to give unselfishly, without hope for return or need of payment, that he can achieve moral success. And this education begins when he willingly attaches himself to the Bobers and to the enclosing confinement of the grocery store.

Initially Frank brings into the store the values of the American universe outside. Though improvements are made in the best sense of American business, Frank steals, exploits, uses. He robs Morris, defending his actions as the cause of the store's improvement. He (and Ida) are willing to make changes that the conservative Morris has resisted as a sign of integrity—the change from milk bottles to containers. He suggests, to Morris's horror, that they cheat customers. And perhaps most significantly, Frank is a salesman, a "supersalesman" [67] one of the customers calls him, capable of utilizing all the manipulative techniques of salesmanship Morris disdains: "The customers seemed to like him. . . . He somehow drew in people she had never before seen in the neighborhood. . . . Frank tried things that Morris and she could never do, such as attempting to sell people more than they asked for, and usually he succeeded" [67]. Even the practical Ida wonders if she and Morris had been "really suited to the grocery business. They had never been salesmen" [67].

We can clearly see that use of exploitation in Frank's treatment

THE GOOD MAN'S DILEMMA

A New Life and the Failure of the West as Eden

   A New Life may be viewed as the author's first overt attempt to consider and dramatize questions of social concern, "a definite broadening of Malamud's social horizons,"[1] as one critic has put it, an open examination of problems and issues only suggested or implied in his previous work. It is, therefore, an important book, given the quite specific concerns of this study, and will be examined with thoroughness. Perhaps the most crucial factor in this novel is the multidimensional and ironic use to which Malamud has put setting. The two earlier works occur amid physical surroundings that seem to have been deliberately left vague or purposely generalized. Concrete description has been minimized. And in the case of *The Assistant*, a given environment is presented that is so constricting and limiting as to imprison the body and shrivel possibility. They are settings without true geography or sense of historical time, giving the impression of existing almost by accident, or, at the very least, tangentially. *A New Life*, on the other hand, takes much of its meaning from a particular locale and its ramifications. Here is a territory where nature is omnipresent, where the true population can be named by any literate Adam using *Western Birds, Trees, and Flowers.* In addition, the events of the novel are acted out amid the political scenery of the nineteen fifties, a time in the country's history marked by mistrust, suspicion, and the failure of moral nerve, the reflection of which is to be found on the campus of Cascadia College:

> The country was frightened silly by Alger Hiss and Whittaker Chambers, Communist spies and Congressional committees, flying saucers and fellow travelers, their friends and associates, and those who asked them for a match or the time of day. Intellectuals, scientists, teachers were investigated by numerous committees and if found to be good Americans were asked to sign loyalty oaths. Democracy was defended by cripples who crippled it.[2]

Indeed, S. Levin, former drunk, son of a thief, contemporary heir to the westward-driving pioneer, must come to terms with self and ego by directly confronting and testing those myths that control the meaning of the American experience through the pastoral image of a frontier Eden, "the infinite and the gold/ Of the endless frontier, the deathless West."[3] Leaving the decayed East, New York, the dark *urbs Americanus,* perceived by Levin only as the hell of closed prospects and the trap of a fixed destiny, he, like so many of his fellow countrymen before and since, goes West to find the future, the manifold promises of which are clearly represented by the more spacious landscape of Marathon, Cascadia (no doubt the national version of the ancient Arcadian dream). But here Levin finally and inevitably discovers, through a series of mock-heroic encounters with the inhabitants of this brave new world which serve to puncture the comically inflated sense of his role as teacher, that the landscape provides only limited absolution. He recognizes that to recover Eden is an impossibility and that a new life is invariably built on pieces of the old—"how past-drenched present time was" [25]. He learns, as do Roy Hobbs and Frank Alpine, that success American style is corrosive. Levin further learns that the freedom proffered by the West is illusory, bought at the price of smug, small-minded self-righteousness. His experiences teach him that reality in both personal and social contexts consists of the acceptance of duty and the assumption of responsibility, even though such actions cause dreams to shrink to an old car and a new family returning to the ambiguous complications that signify human relationships.

This motif of the necessary re-entry into human society after a sojourn in "the green world" indicates that the form taken by *A* power of Nature and the moral strength of the West.

There is more than one variant of the Western myth that Levin must encounter, modify, or reject before he can acknowledge, much less accept, the notion that the limitations on freedom inherent in the ideas of responsibility and duty are necessary in order to create a moral self. But a concept of self-formation based upon the acknowledgment of such limits is hardly a favored one in the society Malamud offers as a model of our America. Levin's task is made even more difficult because he is asked to question certain basic ideals that are fundamental components of the national ethos, ideals that Levin himself thoroughly endorses, at least at the outset of his sojourn. He is forced to discount, as we are, not only those attributes which condition the behavior of the Cascadia College community, but he also must come to recognize and understand the environment of Pauline Gilley's discontent. And finally he is forced to test his own preconceptions and convictions against the facts he finds in Easchester.

The physical topography of this Western community, an abundant, fertile, natural world, brimming with life, is usually described in Edenic or redemptive terms. As C. D. Fabrikant, the English department's self-proclaimed "liberal," says with unintended irony that grows sharper as the novel unfolds (and which the last fifteen years of American history reinforces), "I've often thought if the capital of the United States were located out here we'd have a lot more sanity in our national life" [108]. Cascadia is explicitly called paradise; it is perhaps *the* American paradise to which most of the major characters have come to establish new and materially successful lives: "There are people here, originally from the Plains states or the Midwest, who swear Easchester is paradise. Gerald is one of them. Wherever he goes he wants to come home" [19-20], explains Pauline Gilley of her husband and, by extension, all the inhabitants of Easchester. We ought to note at this point the significance of the town's name—EASCHESTER. First, the environment is clearly not the EAST, so says the absence of that *t*. Second, such a designation defines a world of EASE, where achievement, success, happiness are meant to come EASY and without pain. Third, the word CHESTER, derived from the Latin word *castra* meaning camp or fortress, and the Old English word *ceaster* meaning walled town, describes, in fact, what the town really is, armed against the complexities of the world beyond Cascadia. This symbolic location may indeed be the paradisal garden, or it may be another representation of the land of the lotus-eaters. Or it may conceivably be both, depending on whether one is an insider, an approved member of and participant in the society, or an outsider, different and complex, a stranger who does not quite belong nor is wanted.

But the meaning of this utopian terrain is not so simple as would first appear, even to the receptive Levin. For there are those who have come not only for the fulfillment of new lives but also to escape the wearying demands made by the intricacies of human existence. Levin himself comes in part to hide from an increasingly frightening America as well as to evade the burdens of his own fearful past:

> The cold war blew on the world like an approaching glacier. The Korean War flamed hot, although less hopelessly for America. The country had become, in fear and self-accusation, a nation of spies and communists. Senator McCarthy held in his hairy fist everyman's name. And there were rumors of further frightening intercourse between scientists and atomic things. America was in the best sense of a bad term, un-American. Levin was content to be hidden amid forests and mountains in an unknown town in the Far West [95].

Joe Bucket returns from graduate school encumbered with family and failed dissertation to the safety of Fairchild's patriarchal custody. Others have chosen the West as home in order to elude anxious encounters with the world:

> Pauline . . . found Levin and insisted on introducing him to the department wives. . . . None was without a suggestion of experience in the world and glad to be done with it—whatever their experience had been, the world outside Easchester, the unmated life. "We've settled in . . . ," Pauline said [91].

Even George Bullock, the appropriately named jock-sophisticate who would surely be more comfortable in San Francisco, has remained in Easchester in order to dodge the most elementary relationship with his mother-in-law.

Levin also becomes aware very early in his exploration of the town and its setting that they combine to produce a world empty of history, without a significant past other than the mythos of its creation:

> During the day, Levin enjoyed the town though it seemed entirely contemporary, without visible or tangible connection with the past. Nature was the town's true history, the streets and park barren of fountain spray or sculpture to commemorate word or deed of any meaningful past event. Lewis and Clark had not slept here, nor

Sitting Bull, Rutherford B. Hayes, nor Frank Lloyd Wright. After
the covered wagons apparently little had happened that was worth
public remembrance . . . [74].

Like the individuals of Easchester who have sought to ignore, bury,
or avoid the past and the responsibilities for action taken, in order
to maintain the necessary smiling surfaces that signify the West, so
too have the town and the region made the same decision: to escape
a confrontation with the possibly painful, possibly chastening facts
of history, eliminating entirely the need for communal memory by
elevating nature to a force of powerful omniscience. "Nature was
the town's true history," says Levin, without recognizing as yet the
danger of such an evasive rationalization. This would seem a not
untypical national response to the difficult and insistent demands
of Clio. One of the premises of America as symbolic and actual
experience is precisely that an individual can, in fact, obliterate
personal trauma, cultural conditioning, and historical determinism
to begin again, to fashion a new self, to shape a new identity. That
this may be a misconception not only about America but also about
the realities of human behavior, goes without saying. That it has
been, nevertheless, an actual mode of response for generations of
Americans is equally true. While such a belief may be comforting
to Malamud's protagonists, they must learn that the past cannot be
erased. Any attempt to do so breeds irresponsibility, pretense, false
hopes, and, more often than not, the failure of love.

The West as redemptive environment is neither so simple nor
so satisfying an idea or possibility as Levin (and America) might
wish, no matter how important a concept it is in the formation of a
national consciousness. The equivocal nature of this concept may
account for the ironic use to which Malamud puts the Transcenden-
talists who did believe in America's Edenic presumptions. Thoreau
and Emerson, in particular, serve as mentors whose philosophy
frequently prevents Levin from an accurate evaluation of his
adopted community, contributing to the comic romanticism that
makes the New Yorker an American Quixote.[11]

The notion that Eden is possible, can exist, can even be located
as a specific geographical area is a treacherous one, filled with
uncomfortable ambiguities, at least as it has been perceived and
defined by this civilization. Whether it is America's Arcadia,
Gilley's paradise, or Levin's secular utopia, the particular view of
Eden presented in *A New Life* necessarily prizes the superficial and
the external, for to know deeply is to experience pain or cause
anguish, something unacceptable in this Elysium. It values

innocence, long after innocence has become unconscious hypocrisy in the face of objectionable truth. It exalts nature above truth, and freedom without responsibility. And it excuses any and all action, however mean or petty, taken to preserve its Edenic integrity. It is a world described by Pauline as "sheltered . . . landlocked, and bland" [19].

The staff of Cascadia College runs the gamut of professorial types described by John Lyons: the businessman, the philanderer, the opportunist, the educational philosopher, the pedant, the anti-intellectual jock, the radical, the eccentric whose non-conformity emphasizes the flaws of the system—roles that move beyond simple convention or satire because of the paradisal location of the novel's action. The god presiding over this apparently ideal community is neither genial, kindly, nor liberal as one might expect, given the traditional image of the West as an open, hospitable, free society. He is rather the distant Marion Labhart, president of Cascadia College, whose very name—Labhart—reveals the essential character: a cold, miserly administrator whose allegiance is to the pragmatic materialism of technology, not to the emancipating skepticism of the humanities. Labhart is an unforgiving deity meting out angry punishment, quick to expel those few, Leo Duffy and Seymour Levin especially, who have eaten of the tree of knowledge and can see the town and the college as less than Eden. Because the inhabitants believe they have attained social perfection, and therefore do not require criticism or want change, they are content with this patriarchal tyranny, since the kingdom is paradise. Indeed, perhaps any attempt to make real any vision of a particular social system as paradise must result in a closed, controlled environment from which are excluded risk, discontent, and human unpredictability, for these are forces that bring innovation, clearly unwanted by the populace of Easchester.

If President Labhart is a remote Jehovah, whose occasional but vengeful presence is necessary only when those few recalcitrants who explicitly break the rules and upset the established order require discipline, his most important apostle, his spiritual heir is the more approachable and more dangerous Orville Fairchild (who is anything but fair, and only a child insofar as all residents who remain in Eden are children), chairman and guiding spirit of the English Department, author of the much revised *Elements of Grammar*, and arch defender of the *status quo*. His fatherly concern masks a will of iron. In spite of the framed motto, greeting newcomers—"'Strangers are welcome here because there is room for all of them, and therefore the old inhabitants are not jealous of them—' B. Franklin"—Fairchild is wary of difference, suspicious of any idea, emotion, or experience that undercuts his position, threatens the Edenic design, and liberates the human spirit.

As a teacher, Fairchild is preoccupied with the many editions of his textbook. Dulling repetition, memory, and rigidity are the crucial factors in the good chairman's educational philosophy, rather than encouraging the free play of the mind and releasing the spark of intellectual inquiry. Art has no value because it serves no practical function in creating a materially successful society:

> Ours is a land economy based on forestry—the Douglas fir and ponderosa pine for the most part; and agricultural—grains, grasses, flowers and some fruit. Our fishing industry is important too. We need foresters, farmers, engineers, agronomists, fish-and-game people, and every sort of extension agent. We need them—let's be frank—more than we need English majors. You can't fell a tree, run a four-lane highway over a mountain, or build a dam with poetry [40].

Indeed, this strain of utilitarian anti-intellectualism has been endemic in American life, and a crucial factor in the growth of a national culture.[12] Furthermore, Fairchild distrusts students, seeing them as potential cheats. And even his death is clothed in the irony of grammatical structure:

> "The mys—mystery—of the in-fin—in-fin—in-fin—"
> "Infinite."
> "In-fin-i-tive. Have—you con-sidered—its possi-bil-i-ties? To be—"
> [304].

Fairchild is also very particular about what constitutes a teacher and what does not: "There are two kinds of people I deplore in the teaching profession. One is the misfit who sneaks in to escape his inadequacy elsewhere and who ought to be booted out—and isn't very often; and the other is the aggressive pest whose one purpose is to upset other people's applecarts, and the more apples, the better" [41]. While these strictures may have merit, in the hands of a chairman such as Fairchild, or later Gerald Gilley, they are used to stifle creativity and unorthodoxy, to rid the community of such men as Duffy and Levin whose idealistic activism so clearly menaces the stability of utopia.

As an administrator, Orville Fairchild is intent simply on economy. If money is unavailable, then little innovation can be accomplished. The old way turns out not only to have been the best way, but also the cheapest. His pride is invested in the pennies saved, not in the establishment of an imaginative and humane department. "We've had hard times, when the administration gave us almost nothing to live on. I scrimped to save. I had to pare down salaries, occasionally causing friction, I confess.... At one time I ran about the cheapest department on the Coast, and frankly I was proud to help keep the college solvent and functioning during times of crisis" [53].

As a man, he is antagonistic to "creeping socialism, where it crept, the tyranny of the New Deal, which Easchester had four times voted against, and the evils of federal aid to education" [100], all political movements that are interested in the extension of freedom and the democratization of opportunity. He fears sexuality, cautioning Levin the bachelor to marry, and believes that liquor causes irresponsibility. It can hardly be surprising, then, that Fairchild's vision of the West is anything but expansive. Instead, it is narrow, limiting, and provincial: "You might keep in mind that this community . . . was founded a hundred years ago by missionaries from the East, hard on the heels of the forty-niners; almost overnight they established temperance societies" [50].

Fairchild, it would seem, sincerely believes that he can protect and sustain his puritan's version of America's Edenic experience through an act of closure: by eliminating the sources of and reasons for temptation, there can be no possible recurrence of the American Adam's Fall. He exhorts Levin, as a father to a son, explaining that if he wishes to remain in Arcadia that he must

> show a decent respect for the opinions of mankind. . . . And I advise you . . . not to have anything more to do with the wives of your colleagues. They're married women. . . . I warned you very strongly against that sort of thing and I renew my warning. I am being tolerant only out of charity, to keep you from destroying your career at its inception. To subdue your passion to interfere with others as well as criticize everything in sight, you might profitably begin with some much-needed reforms of yourself. . . . Be humble. We must all be, especially those who teach others. . . . Be good—" [303].

His unctuous advice makes him sound like an academic version of Judge Goodwill Banner. Nevertheless, it is clear that the destructive capacities of passion are, to Orville Fairchild, the greatest threats to the perpetuation of Eden.

Gerald Gilley, director of composition when the novel begins, is Orville Fairchild's chosen inheritor, and had the job continued to be an appointive one, would have assumed the chairmanship as a matter of course. Although as fiercely protective of the region's idyllic reputation as his predecessor, Gerald possesses neither Fairchild's authoritarian personality nor his puritan disposition, perhaps because he wishes too intensely to be liked. It is possible he senses that to incite hostility and induce anger bespeaks a discontent that vitiates the Arcadian reality. Gerald, however, for reasons that he cannot willingly acknowledge, is ambitious, hardly an appropriate emotion in what is ostensibly paradise, where all is presumably without flaw. The only way, then, to legitimize such an unsuitable drive for power and privilege is by making his personal successes as teacher and soon-to-be department head, as politician and democrat, as family man and caring human being, direct and unequivocal reflections of the Edenic identity of this Western community. But before Gilley can acquire the authority and confidence inherent in the office (albeit absent from the man), he must face an unnerving election—the brainchild of the new dean, an interloper "dug up... from the cornfields of Iowa" [122]— in an ironic attempt to liberalize the totalitarian structure of utopia's academy. It should be noted how disturbing to this society, which regards itself as the only true begetter of American idealism, is the notion of the departmental election, in this case a clear symbol of the democratic principle that has always been an essential component of Western mythology. If Eden signifies that which is faultless, and democracy that which is choice and change, then there may very well be an intrinsic contradiction within American culture, believing that one may inhabit Eden at the same time that one dwells in a democracy.

The election is more than an unnerving event in the lives of the Cascadia College English department. For Gerald Gilley (as for Seymour Levin), it possesses the aura of primal confrontation, demanding that he participate in just those situations designed to threaten his security and self-esteem within a model social order. But the conflict inherent in the idea of an election also attacks and undermines the premises upon which that seemingly perfect system is based. Gilley must face the possibility that the exemplary world of the American West is false, and that the values embedded in that symbolic geography are illusory. That in the end he chooses to accept the rightness of his own cultural perceptions can be ascribed to the strength of the nation's Edenic commitment, and the decided preference exhibited by so many Americans to believe in the ennobling ideal, rather than to acknowledge, or even to recognize, a more painful concept of reality.

Gerald values his profession, "feels anyway that at Cascadia College—the kind of place this is—the emphasis should be on teaching" [15], but he measures an instructor's achievements (and his own, for that matter) by how quickly the departmental examination is graded, by how few failures there are, by how popular an instructor is, and by how little he disturbs the placid surfaces of the department. His attitude toward students is markedly ambivalent, although Gilley proves to be incapable of seeing the incongruities in his outlook. He claims to trust those whom he teaches, and frequently insists to Levin on their worth as individuals; yet he speaks of their treacheries with undisguised contempt and unbecoming rage, as if their betrayals were personal insults to his tolerant, easy-going good nature:

> I wonder if you have any idea what we're up against in cheating these days? Not only cribbed papers but all kinds of cheating. Students break into offices for exams. They steal Milly's wastebasket regularly to see if there are any copies of tests she might have mimeographed.... Girls pin notes under their skirts.... They hide answers in their brassieres. Some of the boys come with sentences diagrammed on their palms and definitions printed all the way up their arms. They keep notes in their cuffs and socks. One kid even had a kind of invisible ink he used to write with on his shirt cuffs, and a pair of dark glasses he could see the writing with. It's a regular industry and the only way to lick it is to stamp it out without mercy wherever we find it" [176].

Genial Gerald transformed into an academic Savonarola with no awareness of the conflict in perception. Education, to Gilley, does not encourage questions nor does it challenge conventional assumptions; instead, it enforces the excellence of what is.

Gilley has also ceased to be concerned with any form of intellectual growth or accomplishment. Pauline sadly says of him, "Gerald was the only person of his year to have an article in *PMLA*, during his graduate career. I hoped he'd go on with scholarly papers, but he says they're a bore. . . . He's done a few textbook reviews here and there, but not much else. Gerald is an active type, too much so to write with patience. And there's no doubt he's lost some of his interest in literature" [15]. In fact he prefers composition, no doubt because it is simpler to inculcate the mechanics of writing as taught at Cascadia College, more satisfying to the professorial ego to be able to measure obvious improvement, and certainly much easier than teaching the judgment, under-standing, and sensitivity demanded by literature. Indeed, the height of Gilley's scholarly ambition is the preparation of a picture book of American literature that would concentrate on the presentation of the observable externalities of an author's existence: "I thought the students would want to see what some of our writers looked like, the houses they lived in and such. Most of them can't tell Herman Melville from the Smith Brothers on the cough drop box" [31]. Perhaps Gilley no longer finds such cerebral fulfillment necessary. As his wife astutely observes, "Nature here can be such an esthetic satisfaction that one slights others.... Life is so varied and what happens so often unexpected.... There's so much to do—to be done" [15].

The utopian impulse and the Western sensibility added to the Edenic geography apparently obviates the need for any real life of the mind. This quality of mental stagnation ironically undercuts what limited validity Gilley's opinions possess, comically deflating even further the character's sense of self-importance. Only those who are not full participants in the experiences of life as defined by the self-satisfied inhabitants of Easchester's academic groves, such as the sexually repressed Fabrikant, the discontented radical Leo Duffy, the unfinished Joe Bucket, or the Easterner Levin, find the active uses of the intellect an imperative requirement.

As a politician, Gilley is an ambiguous success. It is true that his native affability and his position as acting head of the department seemingly permit him to campaign effectively, winningly, and effortlessly for the chairmanship, while Fabrikant sits stonily behind closed office doors, and Levin becomes a distasteful nuisance:

> He [Gilley] was healthy, happy, flourishing.... For hadn't the mantle of office fallen smack on his shoulders? He strove less yet managed to campaign without seeming to do so.... Wasn't it politicking when Gerald sent out, more often than necessary, notices signed "Gerald Gilley, Acting Head"? ... Things were the same only more so.... He put in the usual time in the coffee room ...joking with instructors; or discussing the college baseball picture with Marv Beal or Doug Womack.... Gerald was friendly as ever to anyone who approached him ... [306-307].

But Gerald's honest friendliness hides an equally strong opportunism, no less an important factor in his character for being unacknowledged. The job offer to Levin, the subsequent generosity with supplies, a private office, and time, is clearly a function of his need for allies and guaranteed, committed votes. In matters of principle, Gilley raises sophistry to a moral imperative and a high art. During every significant crisis where the defense of academic freedom is an issue, the maintenance of intellectual integrity a problem, and the support of educational probity mandatory, Gerald takes the easiest, least troublesome course—hardly surprising, given the paradisal environment—coming down on the side of a provincial, narrow, conservative majority whose beliefs, in this utopian democracy, are invariably correct. Furthermore, using a series of elaborate, casuistic rationalizations, he transforms this surrender to the forces of illiberalism into the only possible right stand to have taken. Justifying the elimination of a short-story anthology containing Hemingway's presumably objectionable "Ten Indians," on the complaint of a dissatisfied parent, the good-natured, ever-amenable director of composition first asserts that he must not antagonize any citizen with a grievance because "the townspeople are just as good as we are, Sy" [225]; then, that the college's budget would suffer if such a complaint reached the state legislature; next, that the institution's reputation would incur harm; finally, as if to prove that the withdrawal of the textbook is not a problem of censorship, Gerald claims in the voice of a man convinced of his own unbiased rectitude: "Suppose we kept on teaching the story and one of our Indian students, or somebody with Indian blood in him, objected to it as degrading the American Indians? They're pictured as drunks, even if there was a Fourth of July celebration in the story. It wouldn't be long, I bet, before we'd have the Un-American Committee here investigating us and making all sorts of nasty charges. Then where would we be?" [227].

This kind of transformational morality recurs in the matter of Bullock's list containing the names of instructors unsympathetic to athletes, as Gilley follows a not unsimilar line of reasoning, culminating in an outburst of genuine, if self-serving indignation:

> "I may not be for that kind of list, Sy, but I'll tell you this. I frankly don't see anything wrong with anybody wanting to look out for the boys on our teams. They have their place in college as well as anybody else.... Athletes set certain standards of perfection which is part of your liberal education. Sports mold character. Besides that, practically speaking these boys bring us a lot of exciting games and keep the town interested and grateful to the college.... You could say they're really playing for America.... Don't kid yourself that spectator interest in athletics doesn't influence legislators. The fact of it is that our athletes do a lot for all of us and we ought to admit it and be thankful.... Let's face the facts ... people *should* be doing things for these boys who break their backs for Cascadia" [283-284].

Yet in spite of his obvious antagonism toward Levin's political opinions and departmental activities, Gerald is psychologically unable to sustain his anger, until that point in the novel when all the blame for the turmoil that has occurred can be assigned to the alien Easterner's behavior, and Gilley himself can be absolved of all responsibility as a causative factor. Instead, after each tense encounter, Gerald feels compelled to apologize for such a show of overt animosity, or to say a few words that might mitigate the hostility of confrontation: "We may disagree here and there, Sy, but I think we value the same thing" [291]. Even the disturbing Levin cannot be turned into a permanent enemy. Levin condescendingly says of his foe and the man he has cuckolded, when he has ceased to be impressed by the idyllic images of Easchester life and the beauty of the terrain, that Gerald is a "congenial democratic soul, five-eighths affection . . . three-eighths fear, as though his well-being depended on *everybody's* good will" [307]. Levin is quite correct in his assessment, but has not recognized the reason for this all-encompassing need to be liked. To accept the Edenic presumption which defines the quality of this Western environment is to assume not the possibility, but the actuality of a perfected existence which denies rage, pain, defeat, or failure. To acknowledge the presence of such negative and destructive emotions is to crack wide-open the intact paradisal vision. And this is something no one but Pauline, the Eve figure, cares to do. As Gerald says, "One thing you so-called liberals can't get into your heads is we *want* it that way" [287]. Of course—if the ideal is possessed, why make changes? There is just no need.

In his personal life, Gerald exhibits the same behavioral patterns and unconscious sophistry that mark his professional existence, and for precisely the same reasons. Gilley is a man necessarily concerned with the surfaces of things and people, for in this American Garden the surface is the reality; hence the picture book, the interest in photography, his last act snapping a picture of his departing wife and her lover, since these capture and preserve the outer truths, the only kinds that have legitimacy in this world. And it is this reflex that ultimately wrecks his marriage. When Levin first sees the Gilleys and their children, he comments, "Nice people...a real home" [22]. Gerald wants nothing so much as to preserve this ideal. That there may be weaknesses in the marriage— Pauline's discontents; Gerald's sterility, originally ascribed to Pauline's tipped womb (after all, she is the dissatisfied one, and so must be punished); *l'affaire* Duffy; the contemplated divorce. But that the marriage may be a sham cannot be acknowledged by Gilley

or the community, which does its helpful best to maintain the air of
secrecy surrounding Pauline's relationship with Leo Duffy.
Therefore any action taken to protect the external face of happiness
is justified, from taking surreptitious photographs to tape-
recording conversation: "'She drove me to it,' Gerald said heavily.
'First she took up for him, then with him. I suspected something
was fishy and watched her, as I ought to have done with you
around.... One day I got wind they were going to the coast and I
followed them. My Leica was in the glove compartment of the car. I
always keep it loaded—' 'It was loaded so you snapped'" [343-344].
Gerald readily accepts the photographic evidence without understanding the demands and pressures that might have provoked a
sexual link between his wife and another man because it validates
his own innocence. The failure of the marriage, then, is not his
fault. That responsibility belongs to Pauline, to Levin, even to the
dead Leo Duffy. It is significant in this regard that Gilley initially
wishes to keep Eric and Mary, children who are not his, whom he
did not really want to adopt, whom he does not even quite like. To
assume custody would publicly brand his wife an adulteress and
serve as a constant reminder of his status as the injured party.

Gerald's responses to Seymour Levin are also conditioned and
complicated by the Edenic justification that shapes the community.
It is appropriate for Gilley to use Levin in order to insure his
election as department head, since that would presumably certify
the continuation of things as they are. But when Levin comes to
doubt the utopian definition of the West, becoming first critical,
then hostile, and finally a political antagonist, Gerald becomes
resentful of the services rendered the New Yorker. "I assume that's
in the nature of thanks for all I've done for you.... I got you this
job—I gave you your office and other privileges" [285-286]. He
becomes angry at the arrogance of this stranger questioning the
validity of the dream:

> "You have a rare nerve to criticize, with no experience to speak of
> to back it up. You haven't even taught a full year in a college. How
> knowledgeable do you think you are, for instance?... What's your
> big hurry to give out advice about changes *you* think we ought to
> make?... You know... one thing I have never liked about you is the
> way you look around with an eye that says 'I've seen better.'... Our
> literacy rate is one of the highest of all the states. I didn't expect you
> to know that because you have the New Yorker's usual cockeyed
> view of the rest of the country. You are still an outsider looking in"
> [287-288].

And when he proves to be the reason for Gilley's disintegrating marriage, Levin must be banished in order to protect the integrity of the paradisal vision.

C. D. Fabrikant, bachelor, malcontent, Harvard graduate brought West to the golden land by the Depression, is another important character whose conduct exposes the dangers inherent in the American attempt to realize Eden as fact. It is worth observing how effectively this character's name reveals the inadequacies of the man, even before the reader becomes acquainted with his actions: Fabrikant—the maker who can't as well as the maker of *cant*. An associate professor, Fabrikant is both department scholar and department liberal in a setting that values neither, as attested to by the length of time he has been made to wait for a long-deserved promotion. He is a soured romantic with just that interpretation of symbolic Western experience:

> "This corner of the country was come upon by explorers searching for the mythical Northwest Passage...and it was opened by traders and trappers in their canoes trying to find the Great River of the West, the second Mississippi they had heard of. Then the settlers came, fighting the Indians, clearing the land, and building their homes out of their guts and bone....There were giants in those days....Their descendants are playing a defensive game. Their great fear is that tomorrow will be different from today. I've never seen so many pygmies in my life" [108].

That he is among the pygmies he does not understand, for he views himself as the last, lonely representative of those noble, strong, adventurous men.

Though dissatisfied, Fabrikant will not move to try his abilities elsewhere, "he'd rather not move to any place that might turn out worse than this" [69]. If one cannot succeed in the ideal environment, then defeat elsewhere is assured. Clearly, and perhaps deliberately, an atypical Westerner (from Montana, via Harvard) whose behavior runs against the mythic grain, he prefers privacy and isolation to hospitality and friendship. He lives behind closed doors, only reluctantly allowing another to enter. And when he runs for the chairmanship, these attitudes are a distinct liability: "Almost everyone complained Fabrikant was not very sociable. He never went to anyone's house and invited no one to his; he never appeared in the coffee room; he practically lived in his office. 'How the hell am I supposed to vote for him,' Scowers said, 'if I'm not even sure what he looks like?'" [293]. Moreover, Fabrikant, unmarried by choice, is not simply a prude, ashamed or afraid of the physical; he seems, rather, to be repelled by human sexuality. Declining Levin's invitation to the movies, he says, "Thank you, no...I don't go to the movies, too darn much sex" [113]. And it is this disgust that is a crucial factor in negating the intent of Fabrikant's already weakened liberalism.

Unlike Gerald, C. D. is committed to scholarship—"He's the only one of the whole department here who will take the trouble to read up on an idea and write it out. He's had more than twenty different articles and essays published" [69]—and he encourages scholarly ambitions in others. But it is equally true that Fabrikant is an unimaginative pedant:

> "Have you read any of his stuff?" Bullock asked.
> "Fabrikant's?"
> "Yes."
> "I expect to."
> "Be sure to go over it with a vacuum cleaner."
> "It's dusty?"
> "You'll die sneezing."
> "No good insights?"
> "They were decrepit when he came on them.... Goddam, imagine bibliographing Civil War fiction" [120].

It is most important for the purposes of this study, however, to evaluate Fabrikant's reputation as a liberal, to examine the content of his beliefs, and perhaps to account for his failure. Since the ideal society has no real need for criticism questioning first principles, Fabrikant has become a reclusive eccentric not to be taken seriously, rather than the outspoken man of conscience he perceives himself to be. And what passes for liberalism has declined into crochets and petty squabbles over prerogatives and perquisites. George Bullock's description is appropriate:

> "Okay, he's got good marks for plugging for salary increases, more promotions, freer sabbatical rules, and a better retirement system than we have on the books. He's also for academic freedom, but who isn't outside of Congress? . . . If you want to know what's mostly on his mind, read some of the letters he's written. . . . On campus he's against reports in triplicate, fraternities, and student apathy. . . . His letters to the *Commercial Budget* protest the inefficiency of county government. He's against indiscriminate garbage dumping and dogs that run loose and murder his chickens. He's also got no use for chlorine and fluorides in the drinking water. . . . Do you call that a record?" [231-232].

When the campaigning for department head begins, the responsibility for promoting Fabrikant's candidacy belongs to

Levin, while C. D. remains in the shadows, not only because such vulgar politicking is beneath the scholar's dignity, but also any overt political activity might jeopardize his promotion. Besides, since Levin, as the outsider in Eden, has so much less to lose, it is fitting, according to Fabrikant's notion of decorum, that Levin be the visible focus of blame should the campaign misfire. Fabrikant is, in his way, as much of an opportunist as is his antagonist Gilley.

A more pointed indication of the impotence of Fabrikant's position as a purported liberal in a utopian community that regards his presence as useless is his reflexive response when his support is needed on matters of principle. He refuses to become a public advocate ostensibly because no one issue is sufficiently important or dramatic enough to force the necessary changes: "One battle isn't the war. . . . This isn't the time to fight each petty tyranny or idiocy that comes along but to wait and overthrow the tyrant" [233]. And on another occasion, he claims: ". . . the way to fight this is not piecemeal but by getting at the source of a rotten situation. In the meantime let's not tip our hand but keep our powder dry" [278-279].

It is more likely, however, that Fabrikant is reluctant to be tied to an unsuccessful cause, or to lose that full professorship. Yet to reject action because it might be construed as an inconsequential gesture offers the perfect moral justification for doing nothing, Fabrikant's habitual stance regarding major questions of conscience. Fabrikant's version of liberalism comes a cropper when he confronts a public situation—Leo Duffy's dismissal—whose complexities are rooted in private antagonisms and infidelity. Although Duffy's discharge clearly has been conducted contrary to accepted university policy, C. D. Fabrikant nevertheless drops the legitimate "AAP" defense when he is shown proof of adultery. Personal revulsion at the possibility of sexual license betrays the obvious demand for justice. So much for courage; so much for commitment; so much for the role of the liberal in Arcadia.

Some additional problems to be faced by this effort to reclaim Eden as actuality can be seen briefly in the lives of two other men in the department—Joe Bucket and George Bullock. Joe Bucket, the uncompleted man, is as much a character out of *Tristram Shandy* as he is out of Malamud. His existence is complicated, as is Tristram's, by Life: a continually rejected dissertation on "Disorder and Sorrow in Sterne," too many children, too little money, a forever unfinished house. But he is sympathetic to Levin because he recognizes the accuracy of much of the New Yorker's criticism levelled against the department, the town, and the mythic West. It is evident that Bucket must be passive and remain silent out of necessity. He can neither afford his discontent nor voice his dissatisfaction since this enveloping paradise offers him the security and safety and protection not to be found elsewhere. On the other hand, George Bullock, jock and man of action, is scornful of Bucket's ineffectuality: "I have nothing against the guy even if he does talk like the *New York Times*, but what makes me uncomfortable is the futility he gives off" [119-120]. Yet in spite of the relative flexibility conferred upon George by independent wealth, a finished degree, and a soon-to-be-published anthology, he too remains. Surely it is not simply to escape his mother-in-law. By becoming close to the athletes he tutors, George may satisfy his heroic ambitions, his paternal instinct, and his self-made image as a winner. Perhaps this Eden allows George to reaffirm his definition of masculinity. Easchester as idyllic community, and the West as the new golden land, are sustaining and life-preserving conceptions for the likely and the unlikely.

The remaining members of the English department offer a study in the effects of the egalitarianism that has always been an ideological characteristic of Western democracy. Young men, seemingly indistinguishable from one another, cluster together in friendship as if to mitigate the loneliness that Tocqueville claims to be the essential outgrowth of American notions concerning equality. Initially, Levin appreciates their apparent normality: "His colleagues... were amiable people, sociable, unpretentious, several well-educated but no one eager to show it.... Every man, no matter his rank, was every man's assumed equal, very relaxing. Competitiveness, if it existed, was hidden: no visible back-biting or in-fighting, promotions came when they came and nothing could be done about it. No jackdaws crowed... [98].

But Levin is quick to learn that among such men there can be no drive for excellence, nor any need for outstanding achievement, nor even real excitement about ideas. Their pleasures are active and non-cerebral with a vengeance: "The men... talked about flying saucers, five percenters, TV, Ben Hogan's golf come-back ... hunting, fishing, their army experiences.... Although books were mentioned they were rarely discussed" [100]. Neither can there be passionate commitment nor a recognition that their lives

may be flawed, that things could be better; as Levin discovers
when he begins his involvement in the departmental election:

> Most of the other men seemed no more than mildly interested in
> what was going on. Either they hid their interest for reasons of
> their own, or it was a case of "whoever wins is good enough for
> me," equalitarianism at its most desperate.... It astonished him
> that several of the men wanted to know what was wrong with the
> way the department was being run.... He expected hot commitment
> but would have to get used to commitment withheld. He felt
> heavy-handed and big-booted among them, shaken by their
> blandness and reticence [292-293].

Malamud is describing a generation that has settled for
equanimity, self-concern, and an even contentment. They seek to
be not simply normal, but ordinary—professors who "looked like
the Rotarians downtown" [98]. Fearing controversy and hiding
from difference, forces that threaten to shatter their complacent
satisfaction, these men have the capacity, by their very indifference
to criticism, to destroy those who wish to dislocate their idyllic
world. Levin finally acknowledges the dangerous power of such
apathetic blandness as it denies the necessity for change: "He
feared the name-callers, satisfied with what they had, wanted
more of the same, three cars in every garage. Anyone who
suggested that to be too contented with one's life or society was a
subtle form of death, was clearly off his rocker, alien, without
doubt a Red" [318].

What brings together such disparate figures as Fabrikant and
Bucket, Fairchild, Gilley and Bullock, as well as those un-
questioning young instructors, is the shared belief that their
western community is Eden in fact, that their comfort and ease are
real, that the utopian myth has become actual; therefore, their
resistance to innovation is justified. Says Pauline, "People here
are satisfied. I blame it on nature, prosperity, and some sort of
laziness" [19]. They cannot risk admitting to discontent or
dissatisfaction, to anguish, despair, or failure. To do so would be
to confess the defeat of the paradisal dream, and to reveal the
society and their lives as shams. As Gary Wills has written of the
symbolic significance of the golden West Coast, in another but no
less valid context:

> The land promises escape; since it cannot (nor can any place) *keep*
> that promise, men live in fear. An embittering dawn of reality
> impends, always, over professionally chipper Californians. Their
> resentment is easily triggered—by someone who came to the state

after them or just before, crowding new kids into schools or trying
to keep new kids out. . . . By a man in flight from things they want
to retain, or one trying to preserve a thing they came west to
escape.[13]

If an individual cannot find success, happiness, love, or freedom
in this mythic place, there is nowhere else. We have run out of
continent.

Pauline Gilley is the emblematic, ambiguous, complex Eve
in this American Eden, tempting not one but two reluctant
Adams into a necessary, but not entirely welcome knowledge of
life: Gerald Gilley, the husband who resists, keeping his
uncomfortable and pernicious innocence, thereby losing a wife;
and Levin, who learns through her agency that to live in Eden is
to cripple one's humanity, and in so doing acquires a ready-made
family, a pregnant mistress, and imprisoning responsibilities.

Others, content in Arcadia, clearly perceive, and may even
fear her difference, since it functions as a reminder of how
equivocal the paradisal vision might be. Although native to the
environment in a way Levin is not, she is as unwanted, set apart
by her acknowledged dissatisfactions, intensities, confusions, and
unhappiness. Her mere presence serves as an ironic commentary
on the imperfections of Eden.

Her liberal political opinions, derived like Levin's from
experience, are not her husband's, and Joe Bucket cautions, "I
wouldn't judge him by her" [118]. It is Pauline, more than
anyone else, who attempts to educate Levin's naive, romantic
perceptions about the West. As we have already seen, she seems to
recognize the difficulties inherent in living in paradise, and she
tries on the very first night of his sojourn in Easchester to warn
the Easterner of the town's narrow, hermetic quality: "I hope you
won't be disappointed in us, Mr. Levin. In the College and the
town. Easchester can be lonely for single people—I don't mean
college students, their world isn't real. Someone from a big city
might be disappointed here. You have no idea how sheltered we
are, landlocked, and bland. . . . We miss a lot through nobody's
fault in particular. It's the communal sin of omission" [18-19]. As
the symbolic carrier of knowledge, she even must tell Levin of the
one drawback that mars the beauty of nature in this ideal
territory—rain, perhaps a mocking inversion of "The Waste
Land": "Didn't Gerald write you about the rain? . . . He ought to
have. It rains, for instance, most of the fall and winter and much
of the spring. It's a spongy sky you'll be wearing on your head"
[19].

The disaffection with her personal life is equally evident even to the usually insensitive Bullock: "Pauline can be a moody dame" [184]. Since all judgments made by this community are based on the appearance of relationships, and because Pauline possesses all that a woman can desire by Easchester standards, her discontent is resented by those who want what she has, like Avis Fliss:

> "Well . . . she strikes me as the sort of person who can't always be depended on to strengthen a man's rear when he's on the march. . . . Please don't misunderstand me, Seymour, I have nothing against Pauline. She's been nice to me, especially when I first came to Easchester, kind with invitations to their house, though I suspected Gerald had to ask her to ask me. What I have reference to is that she gives the impression of being dissatisfied in the midst of plenty. . . . She can also be absent-minded about her social responsibilities, which rather disturbs him" [128-129].

But Gerald needs Pauline in order publicly to preserve the belief that all is well: happy marriage, delightful children, stability, serenity—the necessary familial virtues as determined by the town. That the marriage is disintegrating, that Erik and Mary are always ill, that stability and serenity are an illusion, must remain unspoken, even though the community knows and willingly hides the truth: "A curious thing about a small town: if it didn't destroy you, it protected you" [281]. However, Gerald is not above using his wife to further his ambitions (compensatory drives to mask *his* sterility and *her* adultery): "'We've got to get started entertaining again,' he was saying with emotion. 'It's hurting me in the department'" [127]. And he unleashes a final tirade minutely informing Levin that living with Pauline will be no paradise. It should not surprise us that much of what Pauline wants for herself echoes Levin's desires:

> "I've already told you she is never contented. . . . She was born dissatisfied . . . or maybe she was brought up that way. Whatever it is . . . she was never satisfied. She always said she felt she should have done better. Not that she *could*, mind you, but that she *should* have, as though all you have to do to execute a better performance is to wish for it. . . . When you ask her what she had expected, all she can tell you is that she wanted to be a better person than she is" [352-353].

Gerald further points out with considerable self-righteous anger that Pauline is reluctant to inhabit totally and contentedly traditional feminine roles. She has failed as wife, housekeeper,

mother, sex object, and biological woman, for Pauline even has
an irregular, anovulatory menstrual cycle. The reader comes away
with the strong sensation that Gerald relishes this outpouring as
an act of vengeance on both Pauline and Levin. He, of course,
does not realize that Levin has already confronted and experienced
a great deal of her neurotic behavior in the intense psychological
space that has characterized the relationship. Perhaps Gerald
believes that Pauline deserves the pains of her discontent as
punishment for criticizing and then rejecting the Eden he has
offered.

What is particularly significant about Pauline Gilley,
although not unexpected given her equivocal position in the
community and the sibylline function she performs in the novel,
is the self-knowledge that she possesses. It would seem that only
the deeply dissatisfied become inward-looking; the contentment
and complacency of paradise do not encourage such wisdom.
What is also important, and will be explored at greater length in
Chapter Four of this study, is the extent to which Pauline's
judgments about self and identity parallel Gerald's criticisms:

> "I'd be nicer if I were less superficial and more accomplished. . . . I
> am too conscious of the misuses of my life, how quickly it goes and
> how little I do. I want more from myself than I get, probably than
> I've got. Are we misfits, Mr. Levin? . . . Gerald suffers from my
> nature . . . though he's a patient man. With a woman more satisfied
> with herself, less critical and more appreciative of his good
> qualities, maybe he would have been a different person. . . . If
> you're a married woman past thirty you have at that age pretty
> much what you're going to have. Still, I blame myself for my
> compromises, and I resist the homogenization of experience and
> . . . intellect. I wish I could do more myself, I really can't blame
> Gerald for not wanting to make a career of shoring up my lacks"
> [188-190].

Her emotions concerning what constitutes her womanhood
are clearly ambivalent. On the one hand, she is uncomfortable in
the roles provided by society, yet on the other, she needs them in
order to define herself as an individual because her environment
has given her little else. But she knows, valuing that very
uncertainty, that Easchester is no utopia, and if it should be, it is
one in which she does not belong. Drawing on her experience,
Pauline recognizes that existence is more complex, more
anguished, more ambiguous than the town believes it to be. She
also is aware that love is more than fitting successfully into
acceptable stereotypes. And she understands that if she is to

survive with her humanity intact, this Eve must willingly leave
Eden with an Adam who shares her perceptions about what is real
in life.

Her relationship with Leo Duffy is the result of these
multiple insights and Pauline's first "extra step to make
something happen" [211]. In choosing Duffy, she selects someone
completely antithetical to the smug, complacent populace of
Easchester: "Leo was different and not the slightest bit fake under
any circumstances. He was serious about ideas and should have
been given a fair chance to defend his. People were irritated with
him because he challenged their premises" [190]. But Duffy was
not strong enough to confront the world with his wisdom, and he
committed suicide: "The time is out of joint. I'm leaving the
joint" [334].

Pauline then uses her wisdom to help teach Seymour Levin
the meaning of love and the nature of responsibility, because she
sees in him the capacity for vision and experience, affection and
despair, delight and suffering, and what Duffy lacked, the
strength of commitment. With the apple eaten, paradise is too
simple, too easy, too infantile a conception to encompass the
complex range of human feeling, and too hostile a locale to
contain such a pair of malcontent lovers. (Pauline will be dealt
with more extensively in conjunction with Malamud's other
women in Chapter Four.)

Malamud's most important comments on the failure of the
Edenic design as an achievable as well as a desirable American
ideal and the human results of such exalted ambition can be seen
in the western journey and abortive professorial career of S.
Levin, Natty Bumppo as schlemiel, the urban Adam, as he
gradually discovers, much to his regret and embarrassment, that if
Cascadia is indeed paradise, he wants no part of it, even though
he must exchange his liberal, but naive utopianism for the
entrapments and limitations of responsibility, duty, and perhaps
even love. He has come, as others before him, to shed a destructive
alcoholic past, to escape an implacable, downward fate, to evade
confrontations and to find renewal, the liberated spirit, and the
expansion of possibility. The punning changes of name—
Seymour (see-more), Sy (sigh), Lev ("Lev is closer to love" [220]),
and Sam (as in Uncle?)—reflect the changes in Levin's personality
as he casts off layers of illusion, betrayed promise, and false
romanticism.[14] It is clear that Levin has come ultimately to test
two related propositions: first, his newly found revelation that life

is holy; second, that it is in Easchester, the frontier as paradise, nestled in the mountains, surrounded by the extravagant fullness of nature, inhabited by America's true democrats, where that new consecrated life is to be truly lived: "'My God, the West,' Levin thought. He imagined the pioneers in covered wagons entering this valley for the first time, and found it a moving thought. Although he had lived little in nature Levin had always loved it, and the sense of having done the right thing in leaving New York was renewed with him. He shuddered at his good fortune" [4-5].

Levin begins as a romantic, believing intensely in the feasibility of his very American quest. He knows with the certainty of the idealist that his lofty expectations will be realized given the Edenic presuppositions that are central to the national consciousness. Like his colleagues, he is enamoured of the surfaces that reflect back the perfection he wishes to see. Yet whenever Levin too innocently accepts the superficial as true, whenever he becomes too awestruck, or pompous, or self-righteous, he is immediately and comically undercut by the less than perfect environment—Pauline drops a tuna casserole in his lap, Erik urinates on him, his trousers are stolen by an angry Syrian at the moment of sexual consummation, he gets lost on his way to an erotic tryst, Mrs. Beaty's cat falls in love with him, and so on throughout the novel—as a reminder and a warning for Levin and the reader to look harder and see deeper, to observe below the external. In fact, this deflationary technique, with its mock-heroic satire and slapstick events, is the source of the book's humor. The action in *A New Life*, then, becomes the process by which Levin learns that the freedom from history and the individual past, from the demands of the self, from the responsibility to others which he presumed not only desirable, but possible, even encouraged in this Western Arcadia, is a destructive dream as well as a prophetic vision.

Ostensible proof of Eden (hence the unusually high frequency of detailed descriptions of actual geography and landscape, rare for Malamud) lies in the beauty of the natural environment that the city-bound Easterner encounters: "Nature was the town's true history. . . . What Easchester lacked in communal memory . . . it made up in beauty of natural setting, trees and clouds, cleanliness and quiet. Roses and ivy grew up some of the phone poles. . . . The new instructor's spirit was eased. He did not mind the smallness of the town. Had not Concord been for Thoreau a sufficient miniature of the universe?" [74]. Levin, remembering

only too vividly the meagerness of urban nature, reflecting, no
doubt the meagerness of his derelict's existence, is dazzled by such
fecundity, promising by contrast an explosion of possibilities.
Here there can be no sterility, no empty deserts for the "thick,
thin, fine, ubiquitous, continuous, monotonous, formless" [162]
rain insures an almost perpetual fertility, a deliberately ironic
fact, considering Gerald Gilley's difficulty. These open surroundings reinforce Levin's naive conclusion that his life has
undergone a radical and permanent change because he has had to
learn new skills and acquire new habits: ". . . mowed frequent
lawns, the grass still green and growing in December; raked a
billion leaves, fifty percent from neighboring trees, gathered
walnuts in October; . . . regularly attended and even cleaned Mrs.
B's rumbling sawdust furnace, and so on and what not. Last week
he had washed and waxed his car. Levin the handy man; that is to
say, man of hands" [143]. Eden is curative because it modifies
Levin's self-absorption. This idyllic terrain draws him out of his
customary isolation, his emotional solipsism, and an often
paralyzing sense of insecurity: "The sun had sunk behind the
mountains but the sky flamed rose. Clouds in surprising shapes
and colors floated over his head. One looked like a fat red salmon.
Another was a purple flower. One was a golden-breasted torso out
of Rubens. . . . His misery had exhaled itself. He was once more
the improved Levin" [165].

More important, however, the always fruitful landscape
allows Levin to escape, at least momentarily, the cycle of time
that ordains "today's spring, tomorrow's frost, age, death, yet no
man's accomplishment; change that wasn't change, in cycles
eternal sameness" [195]: primroses in winter; daffodil shoots at
Christmastime; jasmine at the New Year; camellias budding in
January. In paradise, nature is a denial of death: "just when he
[Levin] was about to take the loss, the yearly symbolic death of
nature, to heart, he discovered that many of the recently harrowed
fields were touched with bright green grass that turned out to be
winter wheat" [123-124].

Here, too, with nature as a model, is to be found the real
America where "you learned as you lived" [145], democratic, free,
humane, liberal. With his Thoreauvian preconceptions (one is
tempted to say misconceptions or delusions, considering
Malamud's attitudes in this novel), Levin expects geography to
function as a positive moral force, granting possibilities and
encouraging individual fulfillment. Moreover, those who inhabit

such a golden land cannot be other than good, happy, and content.

But the New Yorker must learn that the seductive redemption offered by nature is not simply incomplete, but often illusory. He is warned by Pauline, that the esthetic, physical, and emotional satisfactions to be found in the natural world produce a dangerous, limiting sameness that diminishes the importance of introspection, critical awareness, intellectual accomplishment and any kind of striving beyond the seeming perfection of what already is. Although the residents of this American Garden remain appropriately close to the land, this proximity has made them neither better, freer, nor more open, as the myth would have it; rather they are narrow conservatives fearfully eager to hold on to what they already have. As Gerald sardonically reminds the would-be naturalist-philosopher, there is more to nature than the admiration of an outsider: "You have seen almost nothing of this country. In the winter and spring vacations you stayed home. . . . I'm not talking about what you can see in the city parks, . . . I'm talking about *nature*. I mean *live* in it. Camp *alone* in it. I mean *climb* a real mountain. Then you'd know what this country means" [290]. If nature is also a projection of consciousness, it can reflect pain as well as delight, as Levin discovers when his affair with Pauline comes to a temporary end: "Levin cursed his particular body, inept apparatus; nothing brought relief. He prayed the night would, but it appeared in profuse beauty, a perfume of new flowers stirring pain. . . . Was a man no more than a pawn to the season's mood?" [259]. He has grown to resent the romantic's belief in the pathetic fallacy. Interestingly enough, landscape even ceases to be a necessary preoccupation while he is involved with Pauline, perhaps because human connections are ultimately more important than the moral virtues revealed in paradisal nature.

Finally, the Edenic distortion of time's natural cycle, which weakens death's dominions and permits Levin a brief escape from the fact of mortality, may well be a symptom of disorder: seasons lose their significance, the ability of the senses to know intensely how the world decays—"the Northwest cool cheated scent, the throb of emotion in the wake of warm fragrance" [194]—and the ordinary patterns of human expectation conditioned by the relentless movement of time no longer seem to exist: "He missed the smell of change and its associations, the sense of unwilled motion toward an inevitable end, of winter coming and what of

one's life in a cold season?" [60]. Those who populate this utopia
measure their certainties by the grace, beauty, and inexhaustible
profusion of nature, therefore they are unable to acknowledge
that Levin's hard-won perceptions and painful recognitions may
have merit.

Levin has journeyed to the West, the geographical locus of
the American dream, the spiritual embodiment of the Edenic
promise, the living source of egalitarian democracy, because it is
there, he believes, that his humane liberalism has the best
opportunity to function and to flourish. On his first evening in
the community, he is revealingly catechized by Pauline Gilley
who wants to know why he has come so far:

> "When the offer came I was ready to go.... What's to say that
> hasn't already been said? One always hopes that a new place will
> inspire change—in one's life.... My life, if I may say, has been
> without much purpose to speak of. Some blame the times for that,
> I blame myself. The times are bad but I've decided I'll have no
> other.... In the past I cheated myself and killed my choices....
> Now that I can—ah—move again I hope to make better use of—
> things.... I've reclaimed an old ideal or two.... They give a man
> his value if he stands for them" [17-18].

But Levin's optimism, his faith in the possibility of human
growth, change, and perfectibility, his Americanism, if you will,
in the best sense of the term, has been shaped by hard, bitter
experience, not the pleasant vacuum of Cascadia. He was the son
of a thief and a suicide, a failure in love, a drunk who "lived in
self-hatred, willing to part with life" [201]. One day, in a filthy
cellar, he observes his rotting shoes:

> They were lit in dim sunlight from a shaft or window. I stared at
> the chair ... a thing with a value of its own.... Then I thought,
> Levin, if you were dead there would be no light on your shoes in
> this cellar. I came to believe what I had often wanted to, that life is
> holy. I then became a man of principle.... Just when I thought I
> had discovered what would save me—when I believed it—my
> senses seemed to die, as though self-redemption wasn't possible
> because of what I was.... I denied the self for having denied life.
> ... I lived in stone.... One Sunday night ... as I was reading ... I
> had the feeling I was about to remember everything I had read in
> my life.... Sensing an affirmation, I jumped up. That I was a free
> man lit in my mind even as I denied it. I suddenly knew, as though
> I were discovering it for the first time, that the source of freedom is
> the human spirit.... Afterwards I experienced an emotion of well
> being so intense that I've lived on it ever since" [201-202].[15]

So Levin, in the great American tradition, is in the process of becoming, of forging a new and better self in the face of a demoralizing, killing past. However, the paradisal reputation of the West has never been tested; that its values work is simply accepted as a given. (After all, Hadleyburg is still Hadleyburg.) For Easchester, perfectibility is, and the only problem is how to maintain what exists. The community's resistance to Levin's reformist impulse should not surprise.

Levin's revelation brings him to teaching: "I was twenty-six when I realized I wanted to teach, a late insight. One day I thought, What you can do for others you can do for yourself. Then I thought, I can do it teaching" [18]. His romantic idealism has transformed teaching into a messianic vocation with which to liberate the human spirit and an agency for social improvement. With considerable self-importance, he tells his class on the first day that "if they worked conscientiously in college ... they would come in time to a better understanding of who they were and what their lives might yield, education being revelation.... They represented the America that he had so often heard of, the fabulous friendly West.... In Levin's classroom they shared ideals of seeking knowledge, one and indivisible" [89-90]. Levin's Socratic fantasy is punctured, however, and the significance of his words is seriously undermined when the new instructor realizes that it is not the eloquent truth that fascinates but his open fly.

The discovery that Cascadia College is not a liberal arts institution disappoints him, for "the liberal arts ... since ancient times—have affirmed our rights and liberties" [27]. Levin-Quixote is prepared to mount an instant campaign to return the liberal arts to the college because "democracy owes its existence to the liberal arts" [27]. That all he is teaching is composition, bonehead grammar, more composition, the less-than-inspiring essays in *Science in Technology*, discourages him. That he is "not teaching how to keep civilization from destroying itself" [115] worries him. That he cannot in the classroom say "they must understand what humanism means or they won't know when freedom no longer exists" [115] convinces him that he is "engaged in a great irrelevancy, teaching people how to write who don't know what to write" [115]. It takes some time before Levin understands that in Eden few care about the fate of civilization.

The students do not seem concerned that in order to retain their prelapsarian innocence and their untroubled lives, they have not only abdicated a responsibility to themselves to question and

examine, but also to the society that exists outside the boundaries
of their utopia. They do not care for ideas or respect intellectuality;
critical thinking might nullify the premises of Arcadia. They
overestimate the usefulness of the pragmatic, not unexpectedly,
since a how-to education insures the survival of their agrarian
community. They define the good life utilizing standards of
efficiency learned from technology. They fear innovation and
difference. What they want is conditioned by the trivial, almost
infantile demands inherent in this particular paradise: good jobs,
winning teams, and the easy way they've always had. Nevertheless,
Levin teaches, overcoming his disillusionment and the sense of
failure, because his students "were human and possible" [274].
He quotes Mill: "Men are men before they are lawyers or
physicians or manufacturers . . ." [275]. He lends his books,
asking those who borrow to come back for more. He encourages
those with promise to transfer to Gettysburg, where a true
education may be found—a heresy. And he tells them that "the
wealth of life lay within, keeping his fingers crossed because he
hadn't learned all the lessons he taught" [274-275].

The administration, from President Labhart, to Orville
Fairchild, to Gerald Gilley, and the faculty do not want to disturb
the very satisfactory *status quo.* "Cascadia is a conservative state,"
says Gilley early enough in the novel to serve as a warning to the
unheeding Levin, "and we usually take a long look around before
we commit ourselves to any important changes in our way of life"
[29]. No issue is ever serious enough to become a matter of
principle to be struggled over, nor is any opinion to be voiced that
might stir dangerous or upsetting controversy. Whether the
trouble is with an unorthodox textbook, a hostile student
wanting a transfer, or a colleague's list of faculty unsympathetic
to athletes, the instinct in this egalitarian democracy is to avoid
confrontation, to yield to the majority's desire. In such a society
which presumes all ideas are of equal merit, as are those who
affirm them, the majority is always right, especially when that
society perceives itself to be the model of the American dream, and
the tyranny of public opinion is powerful. Alexis de Tocqueville
observed the tendency in Jacksonian America, and his description
is no less apt with the passage of time:

> The nearer the people are drawn to the common level of an equal
> and similar condition, the less prone does each man become to
> place implicit faith in a certain man or a certain class of men. But
> his readiness to believe the multitude increases, and opinion is

more than ever the mistress of the world. Not only is common opinion the only guide which private judgment retains among a democratic people, but among such a people it possesses a power infinitely beyond what it has elsewhere. At periods of equality men have no faith in one another, by reason of their common resemblance; but this very resemblance gives them almost unsounded confidence in the judgment of the public; for it would seem probable that, as they are all endowed with equal means of judging, the greater truth should go with the greater number.[16]

Politics then becomes the art of minimization, of engineering equanimity, of insuring harmony. And it is only an agitator like Levin (and Leo Duffy before him) who warrants punishment because he is an outsider insistent on troubling the waters by fighting for his convictions.

Levin cannot accept the logic of Easchester's quantitative democracy. He recognizes that majoritarianism, the politico-philosophic rationale of the Cascadian ideal, can be an oppressive rather than a liberating force. Quite early he recognizes the accuracy of William James's comment that the function of a college education is to enable one to tell a good man when he sees one. Later he thinks that as a teacher "he would ... do everything he could to help bring forth those gifted few who would do more than their teachers had taught, in the name of democracy and humanity" [230], a potent idea made slightly comic by the fact of its occurrence in a urinal, once again mocking Levin's naiveté. He argues with Gilley when the director of composition seeks to justify censorship with an appeal to equality, claiming that ideas are not equal. He suggests to Dean Seagram the possibility of a Great Books program designed to open a deliberately closed faculty community to the exchange of new attitudes, opinions, and impressions—an implied criticism of old patterns. Levin rejects what John Lyons calls "a wishy-washy broadminded-ness,"[17] an outgrowth of the democratization of education which demands that a professor must not only see all sides of every question, but even defend a student's right to hold a mistaken opinion. And he finally articulates a theory that is bound to set him against the self-satisfied West because it values complexity, skepticism, and nonconformity:

> There is more to democracy, even in the American West, than equalitarianism. Equality means equal justice under law, equal suffrage, equal opportunity through free education; it doesn't mean every man is as good as the next—that there is no such thing as an aristocracy of mind, spirit, attainment.... Equality is not

achievement of the identical average. Nor are "ideas" equal in value because they were thought up by friendly people [317].

Although initially reluctant to jeopardize place, job, the painfully created new self, and temporizing at the thought of complicating, potentially destructive involvements, Levin finds a capacity for commitment that propels him into the departmental election, first as a campaigner for putative liberal C. D. Fabrikant, then, as Fabrikant's liberalism proves a sham in the face of Duffy's supposed sexual immorality, as a declared candidate. But Levin's political activism becomes entangled in his affair with Pauline Gilley, and his rediscovery of love alters Levin's position in Easchester beyond repair and redemption, though by that time Levin wants neither. The interconnections between sexual and academic politics that have become apparent, coupled with the growing intricacy of action, provide a structural correlative which comments on the delusive simplicity inherent in Cascadia's version of the paradisal dream.

Seymour Levin approaches love as it should exist in paradise with the same romantic idealism that had distorted his perceptions of nature, teaching, and liberalism, and which is now transforming his relationship with Pauline Gilley into a grand passion. Levin rejoices at his first sexual encounter with Pauline because it has magically materialized in an idyllic wood, shaped by the spirit of primal innocence. However, the lover's Adamic illusion is modified by the disclosure that his miraculous West is merely a piece of property owned by Cascadia College to train foresters. That Pauline is married further vitiates the notion of societal perfection and familial stability. But the situation suits Levin since he wants neither permanent alliances nor crippling obligations to impair the freedom that is so important a part of Western utopianism, interpreting her reluctances " . . . to mean she wanted pleasure, solace, a momentary change, but no serious involvement with him. . . . The situation suited him. If it made their relationship seem less consequential than it might be, on reflection so much the better. If his affair with Pauline inspired Gilley to respond to her, and she to love him for responding, so much the freer Levin's conscience" [210].

However, Levin's emotions are engaged, and once that has happened, commitment can no longer be avoided. As belief in principle drove him to politics in spite of his fears, so the acceptance of feeling leads him to love in spite of his scruples. Ironically, perhaps to emphasize the immature sentimentalism of this Eden's expectations, Levin's declaration of love is made not because of the delights of liberated sexuality, but in order to stop the physical pain during intercourse caused by his hesitation in confessing his affection.

Given Levin's romanticism, no matter how intense his love, disappointment, not bliss, is inevitable. While there is no doubt that the immediate results of Levin's liaison are a deepening awareness and self-knowledge, the assurance it produces is precarious because it is based on dishonesty and lies, however necessary such fraud may be. The once simple moral universe darkens. Our hero wants openness and ecstasy; he gets secrecy and adultery. Guilt, pain, and ambivalence are the companions of his passion. The relationship has even rendered him politically impotent in the crisis over Hemingway's short story, because Levin no longer sees himself as the righteous man with sufficient ethical authority to defend truth. And when the burdens of adultery become too heavy with deceit and shame, Levin sacrifices: "Out of love he gave her up" [251]. Clearly, as the ambiguities of Levin's existence increase, the once-valued certainties of paradise disintegrate into useless irrelevance. His discovery that Pauline has also been Leo Duffy's lover is devastating, a seeming betrayal of Levin's naive belief in the transformational power of love, calling into question the reality of Levin's new life.

Ultimately, however, this revelation of Pauline's previous indiscretion permits him to regain a limited sense of his own integrity, enabling Levin to return to the departmental election. He incites, he agitates, he pushes. As a candidate, he is a troublemaker, living on the ragged edge of nerve, absorbing others' rage, fear, and hostility: "Levin stirred up, during the last days of the term, a terrible discord . . . the subject of much talk and rancor. . . . Those who agreed with his criticisms and suggestions . . . seemed to be as much annoyed with him as those who disagreed. . . . He was accused of starting trouble and disturbing people's peace. He was accused of exaggerating, lying" [318]. No longer the innocent Adam, he perceives himself to be a snake, "he felt like a viper" [318], the serpent bringing a terrifying wisdom to the inhabitants of the Garden. Furthermore, as the pressures intensify, as the doubts and failures torment and entrap, Levin longs for the East, the city that mirrors the mystery of human experience.

But the politics of sex and school are, by this time,

inseparable, and Pauline, ready to leave Gilley, re-enters Levin's life demanding that Levin act on his promises. In the midst of an election, no longer sure of his feelings for Pauline, Levin's impulse is to flee, evade, to escape the responsibility for another human being that he has incurred by loving, as he ran from his past to the always welcoming West. However, this is a solution he can no longer adopt—he has changed too much. He finds that when he thinks through what has happened, Pauline's affair with Duffy does not diminish or impinge on her love for Levin. Having once loved, he finds he can, with some effort, relearn and recover that emotion as a conscious act of will just as he reinvented his belief in the human spirit as a matter of principle. He knows now that with love goes obligation and duty, not freedom, and certainly not sentimental romanticism. It is a hard wisdom, since the West's seductive irresponsibility is so prevalent within the culture.

Unmasked as an adulterer, his political humanism invalidated, Levin loses the election, is dismissed from his job, is blackmailed by Gilley into giving up teaching, so that Pauline can keep her children—the ultimate sacrifice from the prophet of the Serpent's knowledge. But the Biblical story is given a final American ending: Eden remains intact; it is the once naive Adam, now transmogrified into the Serpent, and Eve who are banished. However, some small alterations have been made: *The Elements of Grammar* is no longer in use, the possibility of additional literature courses, the institution of the Great Books program, and C. D. Fabrikant's reddish whiskers. A minor revolution, but a revolution nonetheless.

It would appear on first examination that *A New Life* is merely an excellent, if flawed, example of "The Novel of Academic Life as Argument," defined by John Lyons in *The College Novel in America*. The protagonist is, indeed, a teacher who acts as the author's commentator, espousing a philosophy full of grand ideas on serving and instructing the young. He is, furthermore, placed in a new teaching position where he must fight stultifying tradition, contend with the equivocations of his superiors, and counter the backbiting of his colleagues in order to restore intellectual and moral sensitivity to the institution. Of course, failure is part of the pattern; so the hero either leaves academia for new worlds, or is driven out as is the case with S. Levin. The form taken by this type of academic novel is, more often than not, satire.

But to categorize *A New Life* in this fashion is to oversimplify its meaning, reduce its significance, and misconstrue what seems to be the author's deeper intent. It is on just this point that Lyons's analysis can be faulted. Although he uses words and phrases like "afresh," "born anew," and "reborn" in his brief consideration of the novel,[18] Lyons does not connect their importance to Malamud's criticism of the West as ideal or his concern with the inadequacies of the Edenic extravagances that underlie much of the national mythology. He therefore tends to take a number of Levin's perceptions at face value—a mistake, given Levin's deluded but typical American romanticism. Nor is Lyons able to see the unity that is achieved through Malamud's manipulation of place and mythos.[19] Levin learns, if Lyons does not, that *both* political liberalism and sexual freedom are circumscribed by the paradisal claims of the Western setting. The comically displaced New Yorker discovers that the libertarian frontier is an illusion, its purported openness decayed into smug, limiting complacency. But because the Edenic assumptions remain seductively alive, Levin's criticisms are rejected by the community as unwanted, unnecessary, and for the most part, irrelevant.

He is also taught by this *rite de passage* in America's Western paradise that sexual freedom incurs responsibility and that love demands discipline more than romantic instinct. Through his experiences, he becomes aware that pain, guilt, despair, and anguish arise whenever individuals attempt to establish significant and meaningful relationships, that life, if it is to be fully lived, must confront all manner of human complexity. Such learning must exclude Levin from Eden, an idea to be regarded with nostalgia, perhaps, but whose actual existence is questionable.

For Malamud, in the last analysis, the best that can be said of the myth of the West as paradise, as redemptive geography, is that such a myth exists; the worst, that it is destructive. It simplifies ideas of human experience. It encourages emotional and psychological escapism. It offers security and perfection at the price of individuality and chance. The myth and its attempted realization have proven to be a comfort and refuge for America's ageless children who continue to light out for the territory. Seymour Levin, however, has grown up.

THE BROADER CANVAS

Malamud, the Blacks, and the Jews

Another important, but not thoroughly examined, aspect of Malamud's interest in social issues is a continuing preoccupation with the facts and emotions of the black-white confrontations that are endemic to this civilization, with particular emphasis on the role assumed by the Jew in this very American drama. It is Malamud's treatment of this particular element in his fiction that would also appear to be most affected by the changes occuring in current history. To be sure, the respective fates of Jews and blacks have been linked since Noah and his sons Ham, Shem, and Japheth built the Ark. But it is only in America that the Jew's fortunes have been so wedded to the black experience, at once so like and yet so unlike his own.

By characterizing the Jew, representing the powers of the intellect, and the black, embodying the threat of violent sexuality, as the villainous participants in the archetypal struggle between evil and good, white Christian America thrust upon them an unexpected, uneasy alliance as perennial outsiders and strangers. "The Jew was seen as the usurer, the castrator, the bad father, the abuser of the intelligence, the icy realist, the cold crafty figure of vengefulness, the anarchist, and the revolutionary. The Negro was perceived as a simple-minded child, as a primitive, a rapist, a

brute, a murderer, a symbol of unbridled emotions."[1] Though
both the Jew and the black have internalized facets of these
externally imposed stereotypes in defining themselves and the
other, the Jew could always regard himself as a member of the
chosen people, hence superior to any local environment he might
temporarily inhabit. However, the black stereotype, rooted as it is
in a stigmatized color permanent and ineradicable, is a degrading
and debasing one. So the union, tenuous at best, began to
disintegrate even as it was forming.

As the Jew became assimilated into a society whose concept
of caste was based on color rather than creed, he moved further
and further from a tradition of suffering and exile, and he looked
to the black as a way of relieving the guilt created by abandoning
his past. "And so, as the WASP used the Jew so the Jew uses the
Negro as a symbol of his own lost misery. This empathy with the
wretched of the earth, this transference of sorrow, this unease at a
certain comfort, all translate themselves into a feeling of guilt and
obligation which have led to the close identification of many
Jews with the Negro. For the Jew, the Black man has become a
kind of stand-in for himself."[2]

The black man, whose enslaved ancestors identified with the
suffering and persecuted Hebrews, increasingly rejects these
Jewish protestations of sympathy, understanding, and innocence
because of the role the Jew has come to play in the economic life
of the ghetto.[3] To poor blacks, the Jewish shopkeeper, landlord,
pawnbroker, welfare investigator, teacher is "the Man," the
visible force of the oppressing "Mr. Charlie." This perception of
the Jewish role in the black ghetto has been described by James
Baldwin, remembering his own experiences: "Jews in Harlem are
small tradesmen, rent collectors, real estate agents, and
pawnbrokers; they operate in accordance with the American
business tradition of exploiting Negroes, and they are therefore
identified with oppression and hated for it. I remember meeting
no Negro in the years of my growing up, in my family or out of it,
who would really ever trust a Jew, and few who did not, indeed,
exhibit for them the blackest contempt."[4]

It is the writers, Mailer, Bellow, and Malamud, who have
charted the shifting ambiguities inherent in this symbiotic
dependency. Indeed, Leslie Fiedler has noted about the Jewish-
American novelist "that at the same moment the Jew whom his
Gentile fellow-citizen emulates may himself be in the process of
becoming an imaginary Negro."[5] We can trace the extent to

which the Jewish psyche has been absorbed by the riddle of black identity by examining varying depictions of this association in Malamud's "Angel Levine," "Black Is My Favorite Color," and *The Tenants*. It is this area of Malamud's social criticism that has been most clearly affected by rapidly changing contemporary events.

"Angel Levine" was published during the bland, self-satisfied decade of the fifties when few Americans were even capable of acknowledging the depth of Negro discontent. The injustice done the Negro (not yet metamorphosed into the black) had not yet been recognized as an issue of sufficient political importance at a time when the Cold War seemed to foreshadow Armageddon, nor had civil rights seized the public imagination as the testing ground for this society's oft-stated belief in equality. Malamud's short story is a fifties parable, suffused with the admirable but optimistic innocence that characterized the liberalism of that good grey era.[6] This hopefulness, based, perhaps, on naive assumptions about what constituted black attitudes toward white society, is concerned with the degree to which a simple verbal commitment to the ideal of brotherhood can effect extensive and permanent changes in the conditions of urban blacks.

The protagonist of this brief fable is a poor, prematurely old Jew, Manischevitz by name. His poverty places him on the same economic level as the blacks whom he must learn to accept; his wife Fanny even takes in laundry, the characteristic occupation of black women. His age and his religion place him within a tradition that fears the stranger, especially the dark stranger. His afflictions are Job's:

> Although Manischevitz was insured against fire, damage suits by two customers who had been hurt in the flames deprived him of every penny he had collected. At almost the same time, his son, of much promise, was killed in the war, and his daughter, without so much as a word of warning, married a lout and disappeared with him as off the face of the earth. Thereafter Manischevitz was victimized by excruciating backaches and found himself unable to work even as presser.... His Fanny, a good wife and mother ... began before his eyes to waste away.[7]

Manischevitz's suffering has been adequately generalized (note especially that the daughter runs away with a lout, not necessarily a Christian) to make him an emblem for stricken, victimized, and fearful humanity.

To alleviate Manischevitz's, and therefore humanity's pain, God sends a black Jewish angel. But Manischevitz is initially too suspicious to honor this historically threatening and alien figure as a savior. Necessity, however, drives him out of his narrow definition of the human family to seek Alexander Levine in Harlem. There he discovers a new, but not unfamiliar world, that is in some ways a black replica of his own. The first person he speaks to is a tailor, a shadowy mirror of himself, "an old skinny Negro . . . sitting cross-legged on his work-bench . . . Manischevitz admiring the tailor's deft, thimbled fingerwork" [49-50]. On a second journey into Harlem, a mysterious congregation of black Jews, inhabiting what was previously a cabaret, reveals through the words of a young boy the eternal wisdom, "God put the spirit in all things. . . . He put it in the green leaves and the yellow flowers. He put it with the gold in the fishes and the blue in the sky. That's how it came to us" [53]. As an act of faith in this newly acquired credo, Manischevitz sees through to the essential Levine and accepts him as a Jew, hence a redeemed member of humanity, in spite of his sharp, new unangelic clothes and the "drunken look [that] had settled upon his formerly dignified face" [54]. This gesture, incorporating the black angel into the race of man, assures humanity's renewal. He returns to Fanny, miraculously resurrected, and well at last, saying "A wonderful thing Fanny. . . . Believe me, there are Jews everywhere" [56].

Although there is much sympathy evident in the story, I wish to suggest an alternative, albeit somewhat controversial, reading of "Angel Levine," one that seems to advance a more equivocal doctrine. It is, perhaps, an uncomfortable assertion of Judaic moral dominance and white humanitarianism, rather than a completely triumphant paean to universal brotherhood, which ultimately subsumes Alexander Levine's blackness into a concept of mankind that would erase ethnic and racial differences. Although Malamud attempts to impose the quality of shared experience by creating a common economic status for Manischevitz and Levine, there is a dramatic difference. In America, where caste is chiefly a racial phenomenon, the Jew is less threatened by the prejudices of society. His position is less precarious because his skin will always be white, insuring the possibility of assimilation. The black, however, is ineradicably black. Therefore his situation is, for the most part, an inescapable factor of his birth.

On a deeper level, however, Manischevitz is a singularly inappropriate metaphor for suffering humanity. He is very much a Jew who accepts the concept of Jewish exclusivity, instead of the belief in the brotherhood of man. Even to consider the idea of a black Jew threatens that insular cohesiveness that permitted Jewish survival. Confronted by the actual probability of a black Jewish angel, Manischevitz regards it as a cruel and bitter joke on a man whose identity has been defined by references to Jewish religious practice: "What sort of mockery was it ... of a faithful servant who had from childhood lived in the synagogues, always concerned with the word of God?" [46-47]. His name is even the brand name of a line of products made specifically for the kosher home.

While his two uncertain journeys to Harlem widen a restricted environment, they are in fact rejections of that black world. Manischevitz is appalled by the raucous sensuality inherent in the aspects of black life he witnesses, "whitefaced," through the window of Bella's nightclub. And he is horrified by what has happened to Alexander Levine, losing his Jewishness as he has descended into what Manischevitz regards as the essence of blackness. But these rejections are reciprocal. Not only is Manischevitz repelled by the black vision of existence, but also the inhabitants of Harlem do not welcome the intrusion of his white Jewishness: "Beat it, pale puss." "Exit, Yankel, Semitic trash" [54]. Manischevitz recognizes only Levine's religion, not his color, nor his significance for the human community. The black feather that falls from his wings as he ascends to heaven turns white before it dissolves and disappears into the imagination.

It is particularly interesting to observe in this context what happens to the figure of Alexander Levine, black, Jewish, and "a bona fide angel of God within prescribed limitations" [46]. It is his Jewish identity, rather than his black self, that seems to endow Levine with his essential uniqueness. And when this is denied him by Manischevitz's suspicion and prejudice, Alexander Levine declines into a vicious parody of what white society assumes the black man is. His language disintegrates into black patois, his face loses its dignity, he consorts with whores.

After his initial rebuff, Levine's appearance and angelic ethics deteriorate; and this visible decay disappoints Manischevitz:

> His derby was dented and had a gray smudge on the side. His ill-fitting suit was shabbier, as if he had been sleeping in it. His shoes and trouser cuffs were muddy, and his face was covered with an impenetrable stubble the color of licorice.... A big-breasted Negress in a purple evening gown appeared before Levine's table,

and . . . broke into a vigorous shimmy. . . . As Bella's gyrations continued, Levine rose, his eyes lit in excitement. She embraced him with vigor . . . and they tangoed together across the floor, loudly applauded by the noisy customers [50-51].

A second refusal sends the angel deeper into this negative stereotype, complete with that most Jewish of fears—drunkenness:

He [Levine] was sitting loose-lipped at Bella's side table. They were tippling from an almost empty whiskey fifth. Levine had shed his old clothes, wore a shiny new checkered suit, a pearl-gray derby, cigar, and big, two-tone button shoes. To the tailor's dismay, a drunken look had settled upon his formerly dignified face. He leaned toward Bella, tickled her ear lobe with his pinky, while whispering words that sent her into gales of raucous laughter. She fondled his knee [54].

And when he is finally acknowledged as an angel, he discards his "nigger" costume and returns to his old clothes, calling the transformation "freshening up." If he cannot be Jewish, apparently his only other choice is to become the white man's version of "the nigger." If there might exist a more positive black identity, it is not considered.

The humane and redemptive elements of "Angel Levine" are undeniable. That Manischevitz is meant to be an example of suffering mankind rather than simply a Jew *sui generis* is clear, but not entirely convincing. As Robert Alter asserts, "the Jew as Everyman is a kind of literary symbol that is likely to wear thin very quickly,"[8] because as he further points out, to universalize the unique history of the Jews can be both an insulting and a sentimental vulgarization of their tragic past.[9] And if such a metaphor might violate the particular Jewish experience, surely it does an equal injustice to the black traditions presented in the story. It would appear then, that some of the unconscious assumptions that control the dynamics of "Angel Levine" serve to undercut the ideal of the brotherhood of man. It is the Jew, identified as such, who is made the moral paradigm with which the black man must identify. And that such an identification is desirable goes without saying. When we examine "Black Is My Favorite Color," we can see the further disintegration of traditional egalitarianism in the face of history.

The idealism concerning the possibilities of racial harmony that dominates the surface of "Angel Levine" is the motive force behind the civil rights movement of the early nineteen sixties. Blacks and whites together ("We shall not be moved") integrated lunch counters, picketed Woolworth's, rode freedom buses South, desegregated schools, were bombed, hosed, bitten by dogs, jailed, beaten, sometimes murdered. Under pressure exerted by both races, the institutions of government and society seemed increasingly responsive to the demands for justice, ready to redeem the pledges of the American Revolution owed to its black citizens. On a hot, steamy day in August, 1963, Martin Luther King told a rainbow gathering of honorable, optimistic people massed before the Lincoln Memorial of a dream as old as hope. And "We Shall Overcome" became the nation's new anthem.

Given this atmosphere, the pessimism of "Black Is My Favorite Color" strikes with the uncommon force of prophecy.[10] It is the story of the sweet-sour existence of the aptly named Nat Lime as he unsuccessfully attempts to counter through love the deepening hostility of blacks to all manifestations of white domination. He is a man who inhabits a black society in which the most preliminary human overtures are often seen as a purposeful extension of the white man's power. However, this unhappy portrait may be regarded as an overt extension of the underlying pressures noted in "Angel Levine." It is also worth observing at this point that while "Angel Levine" is a fantasy whose very form accentuates the implausible but humane conclusion, "Black Is My Favorite Color" is quintessential realism, thereby reinforcing the truth of its unhappy ending.

The title itself does not seem to imply the unconscious sense of Jewish moral superiority of "Angel Levine," but rather a capacity to accept and love human difference. "I got an eye for color. I appreciate. Who wants," says Nat Lime, "everybody to be the same?"[11] But "Black Is My Favorite Color" as a title serves, in fact, to emphasize the ironic discrepancy between desire and reality that so dominates a story which opens in an environment of willed isolation and deliberately blurred identities: "Charity Sweetness sits in the toilet eating her two hardboiled eggs while I'm having my ham sandwich and coffee in the kitchen. That's how it goes only don't get the idea of ghettoes. If there's a ghetto I'm the one that's in it" [17]. And it is the black maid who rejects the idea of community in the ritual act of breaking bread, sensing perhaps not the impulse to equality but the patronizing white employer, for whom she does housework: "The first time Charity Sweetness came in to clean . . . I made the mistake to ask her to sit down at the kitchen table with me and eat her lunch. . . . So she cooked up her two hardboiled eggs and sat down and took a small

bite out of one of them. But after a minute she stopped chewing
and she got up and carried the eggs in a cup in the bathroom and
since then she eats there" [17-18]. Nat Lime's bewildered readiness
to accept "colored people" makes this intentional segregation an
understandable gesture.

In "Angel Levine," the author tries to establish at least the
appearance of brotherhood by creating a similarity of class. Nat
Lime in "Black Is My Favorite Color" is clearly an exploitative
presence in Harlem, no longer a replica of the white milieu, but
hostile territory. He is a Jewish liquor dealer feeding off the need
to dream, the desire to escape, a man who gives discounts to his
better customers, thereby keeping them sedated and desensitized.
In describing the problems caused by the liquor traffic in the
ghetto, Lenora Berson says: "Of all the enterprises that have
exploited the poor, none has encouraged more atrocious social
fallout than the liquor trade, which includes alcoholism, sexual
promiscuity, family instability, violence, brutality and the
improvident use of limited funds."[12] And though Nat asserts that
"personally for me there's only one human color and that's the color
of blood" [18], his vocabulary throughout the story reveals a
preoccupation with the divisions that race creates.

Blackness has always represented for Nat Lime the extremes
of experience unavailable to a nice Jewish boy who at the age of
forty was still dutifully living with his mother, and who can
innocently claim "I'm the kind of man when I think of love I'm
thinking of marriage" [25]. Black lives, in both social and psychic
terms, express the limits to which the human spirit can be
stretched and still survive:

> Any Negro who wishes to live must live with danger from his first
> day, and no experience can ever be casual to him . . . knowing in
> the cells of his existence that life was war, nothing but war, . . .
> could rarely afford the sophisticated inhibitions of civilization and
> so he kept for his survival the art of the primitive, he lived in the
> enormous present. . . . Hated from the outside and therefore hating
> himself, the Negro was forced into exploring all those moral
> wildernesses of civilized life. . . . The Negro chose to move instead
> in that other direction where all situations are equally valid, and in
> the worst of perversion, promiscuity, pimpery, drug addiction,
> rape, razor-slash, bottle-break . . . the Negro discovered and
> elaborated a morality of the bottom.[13]

Although this is surely Norman Mailer's fantasy about black
existence, as James Baldwin points out,[14] it is nonetheless

significant that it is precisely this rhetorical stance that becomes part of revolutionary black nationalism as it evolves in the late sixties and early seventies.[15] Eldridge Cleaver put it succinctly: "The term *outlaw* appealed to me.... I was an 'outlaw.' I had stepped outside of the white man's law, which I repudiated with scorn and self-satisfaction, I became a law unto myself...."[16]

As a child, Nat Lime was poor in a marginal white neighborhood, but the blacks were poorer still, their environment a perpetual reminder of the constancy of death: "the Negro houses looked to me like they had been born and died there, dead not long after the beginning of the world" [19]. And Nat is fully aware of the edge his whiteness confers, feeling a prick of conscience that must eventually be acknowledged: "In those days though I had little myself I was old enough to know who was better off, and the whole block of colored houses made me feel bad in the daylight" [20]. Black existence defines the complexity of human experience, providing for Nat a sense of what life is really like: "brother, if there can be like this, what can't there be?" [19]. This assumption naively and unwittingly exhibits that inherited sense of superiority to *their* poverty, coupled with a fear of the excesses of that black world. But Nat is also admitting an attraction to a world pulsating with vitality, a confession, perhaps, of an absent element in his own personality, a revelation seen by one of life's voyeurs: "Sometimes I was afraid to walk by the houses when they were dark and quiet.... I liked it better when they had parties at night and everybody had a good time. The musicians played their banjos and saxophones and the houses shook with the music and laughing" [20].

Violence, so integral to the black milieu he observes and an inevitable component of behavior under conditions of internal and external stress, horrifies Nat to the point of denying its necessary presence: "I was frightened by the blood and wanted to pour it back in the man who was bleeding.... I personally couldn't stand it, I was scared of the human race" [21]. Yet for the young Nat Lime, it is Buster Wilson's self-containment, his ability to confront his world of blood and to remain apparently untouched by its pain, that is an ineluctable part of his fascination: "but I remember Buster watching without any expression in his eyes" [21].

Blackness also represents the seductiveness of open sensuality, "the young girls, with their pretty dresses and ribbons . . . caught me in my throat when I saw them through the windows" [20]. It is therefore not surprising that it is only a black woman who excites Nat, saying of Ornita Harris' obvious sexual attractiveness and exoticism: "She was a slim woman, dark but not the most dark, about thirty years . . . also well built, with a combination nice legs and a good-size bosom that I like. Her face was pretty, with big eyes and high cheek bones, but lips a little thick. . . . That was the night she wore a purple dress and I thought to myself, my God, what colors. Who paints that picture paints a masterpiece. Everybody looked at us but I had pleasure" [24-25]. Yet the physical presence of her sexuality is described as white: "Under her purple dress she wore a black slip, and when she took that off she had white underwear. When she took off the white underwear she was black again. But I know where the next white was . . ." [25].

Given Nat Lime's complex but ambiguous responses, it is not surprising that his efforts to establish actual relationships with blacks fail, leaving the human contract unfulfilled. His putative friendship with Buster is part envy, part guilt, an effort that barely recognizes Buster as a human being. He envies Buster's independence, "I liked his type. Buster did everything alone" [20]. Nat Lime's underlying attitudes at this point, and through the entire story, resemble those which Norman Podhoretz described in his famous essay, "My Negro Problem—And Ours":

> What counted for me about Negro kids of my own age was that they were "bad boys." There were plenty of bad boys among the whites . . . but the Negroes were *really* bad, bad in a way that beckoned to one, and made one feel inadequate. *We* all went home every day for a lunch of spinach-and-potatoes; *they* roamed around during lunch hour, munching on candy bars. . . . *We* rarely played hookey, or got into serious trouble in school, for all our streetcorner bravado; *they* were defiant, forever staying out (to do what delicious things?), forever making disturbances in class and in the halls, forever being sent to the principal and returning uncowed. But most important of all, they were tough; beautifully, enviably tough, not giving a damn for anyone or anything. . . . To hell with the whole of the adult world that held *us* in its grip and that we never had the courage to rebel against. . . .
> This is what I saw and envied and feared in the Negro. . . . [17]

Nat is ashamed of his whiteness, the sign of his responsibility for the conditions which determine the contours of Buster's life. But when Buster invites him into his home, Nat only wishes to escape the impoverished reality of what he sees there,[18] "it smelled so heavy, so impossible, I died till I got out of there. What I saw in the way of furniture I won't mention—the best was falling apart in pieces" [22]. So Nat mitigates his guilt by giving Buster those fragments of whiteness he can afford to part with, assuming, of course, that Buster wants those emblems of conscience: "I stole an extra fifteen cents from my mother's pocketbook and I ran back and asked Buster if he wanted to go to the movies . . . which includes my invitations to go with me, my (poor mother's) movie money, Hershey chocolate bars, watermelon slices, even my best Nick Carter and Merriwell books that I spent hours picking up in junk shops, and that he never gave me back" [21-22].

His affair with Ornita Harris, however, seems an honest attempt to accept her blackness and to love at last. Yet strain and ambivalence are always present. His initial rebellion is a pallid one, minimizing risk and courting safety. On their first date, he takes her to Greenwich Village, a bohemian environment which willingly tolerates interracialism. He will not take her home to meet his dying mother—that is too great a chance to take. They have their first sexual encounter in a rented room. Only when his mother and the tradition she embodies ("Nathan," she said, "if you ever forget you are a Jew a goy will remind you" [26]) is dead, can his rebellion become more overt and seek society: he sells his mother's bed; he invites Ornita into his home; he takes her to meet carefully chosen, *liberal* friends; he proposes marriage.

But this time it is the black community that will not sanction such a union because it is a relationship that seems to reenact the sexual pattern of slavery: the black woman considered only as an object to be manipulated by the white man's lust, no matter how strong are Nat's protestations of love and affection.[19] Significantly, it is at this juncture that the young black men, serving as the active agents of community disapproval, choose to remind Nat of his position as economic exploiter:

> "You talk like a Jew landlord," said the green hat. "Fifty a week for a single room."
> "No charge fo' the rats," said the half-inch brim [28].

In this atmosphere, shaped by overt hostility, unspoken anger, and unconscious ambivalence, the reassuring notion that love can solve all problems seems unworkable.

Nat is incapable of understanding the continued refusals his giving impulse has met with, because he is trapped by the complicated ambiguities of his own responses. He cannot see that to be defined solely in terms of the experiences inaccessible to the white man, to be wanted only as the complement to an incomplete self, is sufficient cause for rejection. Nor is he conscious of his social and political situation in an environment that regards him as the enemy, where even a blind man senses his whiteness and spurns his help. Nat Lime is finally left in his bewilderment to confront a locked door behind which Charity Sweetness sits in splendid isolation. Indeed the world has become a series of locked doors through which love cannot enter, for "the language of the heart either is a dead language or else nobody understands the way you speak it" [18].

In *The Tenants* (1971), we discover that Malamud has taken further steps into social and personal pessimism. This dark novel explores the extinction of brotherhood, the death of hope, and the final collapse of civilization.

The Tenants not only reinforces the changes that "Black Is My Favorite Color" had foreseen, but it also translates the contemporary facts of black-white confrontation into apocalyptic history. The novel is not simply the product of disillusionment; it is witness to disintegration, terror, and chaos. By the late sixties, the civil rights movement, once dedicated to the principles of non-violence, had turned violent. Perhaps this reversal was an inevitable response to what was perceived as an increasingly repressive society, committed not to justice, but to corruption, the misuse of power, and the wholesale merchandising of death. Between 1964 and 1968, Medgar Evers had been shot, James Meredith wounded, Malcolm X and Martin Luther King assassinated. During these years, from the time Watts exploded in 1965 to the violence that erupted across America as a reaction to Martin Luther King's death in 1968, riots in black ghettos became a familiar response to social neglect; and "the long hot summer" became a season to be feared in Cleveland, in Newark, in Detroit, in Philadelphia, in Washington.

The new voices—Eldridge Cleaver, Stokely Carmichael, George Jackson, Angela Davis, Bobby Seale, Huey Newton, the Muslims, the Panthers—were proclaiming with growing militancy "the fire this time." Blacks confronted whites across barriers too high to scale. It is not surprising, then, that Malamud's *The Tenants* mirrors this transformation. The tenants are Harry Lesser, white, Jewish, liberal, a published writer with something to lose and Willie (Bill) Spearmint (Spear), black, believer in the power of his blackness, writing in order to master existence in a white environment. They inhabit a deteriorating tenement in a white neighborhood, emblem of the collapsing house of history. The two meet, clash, try brotherhood, merge, exchange identities, destroy their respective worlds—and remain strangers still.

Like Nat Lime, Harry is a white man whose immediate encounters with the reality of the world are meager and barren. But unlike Nat Lime, Lesser's deprivation is consciously sought. Living on a self-created island (a fantasy which becomes a repeated motif in the novel), he is engaged in a holding action, erecting walls to protect himself from life's intrusive demands, using his art as the excuse to legitimize his withdrawal. He is the last tenant in a turn-of-the-century building scheduled to be another sacrifice to the sovereignty of progress, an embodiment of twentieth-century rootlessness and *anomie,* a building that has been stripped of civilization but for Lesser's protective carapace.

Into this solipsistic environment comes Willie Spearmint. Initially, he seems to be merely a disturbance to the man who "had gotten used to being the only man on the island."[20] Willie's blackness appears incidental to his very real, competitive artist's presence in Harry's private domain, perhaps another one of Levenspiel's stratagems to be rid of him. Beneath the surface, however, it is Willie's blackness that makes his arrival much more threatening. Even before Willie materializes, the stranger's presence is sensed in language that is an ironic amalgam of brotherhood and the intimidating patois of the street black: "Who you looking for, brother?" "Who you callin brother, mother?" [4]. The name the shadow is given in Harry's imagination is rooted in the theological ambiguity of the black-white relationship. "God since the dawn of man should have made it his business to call out names: Jacob meet Ishmael. 'I am not my brother's brother'" [26]. When they do meet, the customary handshake of fraternal welcome is rejected by the black in explicitly racial terms, as if to emphasize the idea that brotherhood cannot depend any longer on habit, law, or lip service: "No handshake though Harry was willing, in fact had stuck out his white paw. There it remained—extended. He was, in embarrassment, tempted to play for comedy . . . but in the end Lesser withdrew it, no criticism of anyone intended or implied. Who said anybody had to shake somebody else's hand? That wasn't in the Fourteenth Amendment" [31-32]. And it is the shamefaced Jew who is compelled to fall back on the old cliché so often used against him—"some of my best friends are...." "He was tempted then to explain that he had, as a boy, for years lived at the edge of a teeming black neighborhood in South Chicago, had had a friend there ..." [32].

Willie is working in an abandoned apartment that had once belonged to the clean, gentle, civilized Herr Holzheimer, but which has now become a jungle—a dangerous, decaying, carnivorous paradise:

> the bedroom walls defaced, torn by graffiti, bespattered with beer, wine, varnish, nameless stains, blots, a crayon cartoon of A. Hitler wearing two sets of sexual organs, malefemale; in a second bedroom a jungle sprouted—huge mysterious trees, white-trunked rising from thick folds, crowding four walls and into the third bedroom, dense ferny underbrush, grasses sharp as razor blades, giant hairy thistles, dwarf palms with saw-toothed rotting leaves, dry thick-corded vines entangling thorny gigantic cactus exuding pus; eye blinding orchidaceous flowers—plum, red, gold—eating alive a bewildered goat as a gorilla with hand-held penis erectus, and two interested snakes, look on. Deadly jungle [11-12].

Harry identifies Willie with this evil ambience: not the noble savage, but the hulking barbarian at the gates of the civilization that Harry has tried to maintain. Unlike his angelic brother, Alexander Levine, Willie seems to project a persistent sulphurous odor, perhaps a remnant of his satanic origins, an odor that ultimately becomes Harry's at that point when he finally and irrevocably betrays Willie. It should be noted that just as Willie exudes a distinctive odor recognized only by white men, so too does the white man emit a characteristic smell sensed only by blacks:

> Mary forcefully shoved him away. "Split honky, you smell.... Don't hold it against yourself Harry. I like you fine."
> "Then what's this smell you mentioned?"
> "Like you smell white is all I mean."
> "How does white smell?"
> "No smell at all" [46-47].

Like hostile animals given a biological form of self-protection, black and white circle each other warily.

Willie is also frequently portrayed as the necessary Friday to Harry's deliberately marooned Robinson Crusoe, hardly an apt metaphor defining human equality, but undoubtedly an accurate rendering of Harry's version of the human connection. As the reality of his black experiences invade Harry's consciousness and force him to confront the actual rather than the word, Willie becomes a growing menace. To Willie, on the other hand, Harry remains the undifferentiated White Man—the Enemy—until he becomes, typically, the civilizing force, the dispenser of largesse: money, knowledge, skill, as he moves Willie from his deadly, primitive Eden to a monastic room furnished with the rudimentary comforts and tools of a cultivated existence. It is then that the minimal extension toward friendship is transformed into an ambiguous but directed personal animosity that functions to reinforce Willie's generalized hatred of whites. And it grows increasingly clear as the novel progresses that Harry and Willie will continue to be locked into predetermined responses as they attempt to deal with themselves, the other, and the world.

One simple gauge measuring the extent to which Harry and Willie are defined by externally imposed and internally generated stereotypes is their attitudes toward Levenspiel, the landlord, an important traditional figure in the confrontation between Jew and black.[21] Lesser feels that archetypal Jewish emotion—guilt— because Levenspiel's requests are legitimate and his problems human. "Lesser tried to wrestle the incident out of his mind. Clever bastard, he knows I feel guilt. Another dollop on my head and I'll go through the floor down to the cellar. That's his plan, I bet" [41]. Willie, instead, reacts with a combination of genuine black anger at the real economic control wielded by the urban Jew in the ghetto and the traditional anti-semitic demonism concerning the supposed financial power of the symbolic Jew— rationalizations which permit labelling any landlord as The Jew:

> "Fartn Jew slumlord."
> "Willie," said Lesser, "if its news to you I'm Jewish myself."
> "All I'm saying is an economic fact" [41].

Harry and Willie, like Manischevitz and Nat Lime, are filled with all those clichés, prejudices, and preconceptions which serve to drive men apart. Stereotypes notwithstanding, however, it is important to note that Lesser, the Jew, does protect Willie, the black, from the antagonism of the white, Jewish landlord.

Isolated, withdrawn, and anguished, Harry, like the protagonist in "Black Is My Favorite Color," willingly, even willfully accepts that particular white man's fantasy based on the assumption that race and class allow blacks to live fuller, richer, more sensual lives. Lesser (here the name is significant) is worn and colorless, with "tired gray eyes, often bloodshot" [14], and "utilitarian lips, wry, thinning" [14]. But Willie and those associated with him, black and white, are all flash, color, and motion: "she wore . . . a plain white mini with purple tights" [42-43]; "a brother wearing a gold blouse and red fez" [124]; "Irene in an orange mini" [125]; "Bill, in yellow cords, purple silk shirt, short brown boots and a flowered headband" [125]. More important, however, is that Harry repeatedly yearns to be a participant in that flash, color, and motion. First, he imagines, projecting himself into a Harlem seething with vitality:

> He sees himself walking on Eighth Avenue above 135th, drifting uptown alone on the wide dark sea, though the place is alive with many bright-sailed small craft and colored birds, brothers and sisters of all shades and shapes. Anyway, he is walking amiably alone, not even thinking of writing, in love with the sights and sounds of this exotic small city on a warm and sunny day, waiting for somebody, blood or chick, young or old, to say as people once did in the not-so-long-ago-past, "Peace, brother, peace to you" [89].

Then he attempts to enter that reality:

> Lesser, recognizing four of the seven and hearing their laughter, felt longing invade his gut and began to follow them. As he watched Irene with Bill, both enjoying themselves, his feeling turned unpleasant, desire in corrosive emptiness. . . .
> From across the street near a florist shop Bill spied him and whooped "Lesser, man, for Christ's sake, cross over here. I got some people with me. . . ."
> There were about twenty souls at the party, the writer and Irene the only whites. . . . As he [Lesser] listened to the music the writer felt yearning, longing for life. . . . Each of them whipped up an island of sound around himself. They played to each other, saying their music was beautiful and so were they. Over them hung an umbrella of sweet smoke, and Lesser felt high [121-124].

But he confronts only open hostility. "'This is an eye-to-eye confrontation of the force of evil versus a vessel of good,' said Jacob 32 . . ." [130]. Finally, when he appropriates Irene Bell, the white woman who once belonged to Willie Spearmint/Bill Spear, Harry actuates his fantasy by destroying the black man at that point of greatest psycho-sexual vulnerability.[22]

While Harry Lesser defines blackness to mean life lived closer to the bone of human experience, Willie is trying to forge an existence in defiance of what he sees as not simply white opposition, but more particularly *Jewish* white domination over those factors that would establish and confirm his identity: the linked triad of economics, art, and sex. Initially, Willie accepts

the traditional imagery of Jewish financial exploitation, inevitably
utilizing it as the central antagonist in the fiction through which
he seeks to create himself. There are the Jewish landlords who do
not let him write in peace. There are the Jewish shopkeepers who
overcharge. There are the Jewish publishers who have silenced
his voice, closing off his access to the world: "I tried ten of those
rat-brained Jews and they all turned it down for a lot of those
horseshit reasons, because they are *afraid* of what the book says"
[75]. Indeed, Willie's anti-semitism is an ironic and defiant
assertion of citizenship:[23] "It isn't that I hate the Jews. But if I do
any, it's not because I invented it myself but I was born in the
good old U.S. of A...." [220].

But Willie's anger at the Jew has a deeper significance than
merely as a facet of the demonology of historical anti-semitism. It
masks a fear of castration, of emasculation, a reflection of what
that society has already perpetrated through slavery and its
aftermath. Circumcision, the age-old emblem of Jewishness,
represents the loss of manhood in the most profound sense, its
threatening quality revealed only during the psychological
release provided by drugs:

> I know you tryin to steal my manhood. I don't go for that
> circumcise schmuck stuff. The Jews got to keep us bloods stayin
> weak so you can take everything for yourself. Jewgirls are the best
> whores and are tryin to cut the bloods down by makin us go get
> circumcise, and the Jewdoctors do the job because they are afraid if
> they don't we gon take over the whole goddam country and wipe
> you out. That's what they afraid. I had a friend of mine once and
> he got circumcise for his Jewbitch and now he ain't no good in his
> sex no more, a true fag because he lost his pullin power.... None
> of that crap on me, Lesser, you Jewbastard, we tired of you fuckn
> us over [50-51].

Given Willie's sense of powerlessness in a world dominated
by whites, coupled with an insecure masculine self, the role
assigned to Irene Bell is crucial. From the inception of slavery to
the present, the white male has used the black woman as sexual
instrument and economic tool, an indication of the absolute
authority he exercises in society. By taking a white Jewish
mistress, Willie reverses history. Not only does he illustrate his
contempt for Whitey, but he also in a visible way asserts control
over his one-time oppressor. When Harry acquires Irene,
recapitulating once again the manipulative history of white
supremacy, when Willie is robbed of that symbolic token of

ascendancy, it is not surprising that he explodes into destructiveness: "You ought to burn up both of these yourself, Willie, on
account of this cat stole your white bitch and pissed up your black
book. Deprived you of your normal sex life and lifelong
occupation according to the choice you made. Must feel like you
been castrated, don't it? You got to take an eye for a ball it says in
the Good Book" [177-178].

There is first the psychic murder of Harry Lesser by
destroying his manuscript, putting a metaphorical end to Harry's
unfinished self. Then the annihilation of the civilization that
Lesser is seeking to preserve: "The door had been jimmied open.
Crying out angrily, flailing both arms against evil, Lesser stepped
into his flat and switched on the light. With a groan of
lamentation he ran from room to room, searched his study closet
blindly, stumbled into the living room, and frantically hunted
through masses of old manuscript pages, poured over piles of
torn books and broken records" [175]. After the symbolic
mutilation of the immediate and personal enemy, Willie's
writing is increasingly committed to the imagery of communal
revenge, rather than individual violence. In his fiction he begins
to envision and perhaps create the apocalypse—the total
elimination of the Jew (his own final solution), identified in
Willie's imagination as the one who determines, regulates, and
controls the social organism at all levels, as in

> a piece called "The First Pogrom in the U.S. of A." In it a group of
> ghetto guerrillas in black leather jackets decide it will help the
> cause of the Revolution to show that a pogrom can happen in the
> U.S. of A. So they barricade both ends of a business block, 127th
> Street between Lenox Avenue and Seventh.... Working quickly
> from lists prepared in advance, they drag out of a laundromat, shoe
> store, pawnbroker's shop, and several other kinds of establishments
> owned by them on both sides of the street, every Zionist they can
> find, male, female, and in-between.... Working quickly in small
> squads, the guerrillas round up and line up a dozen wailing, hand-
> wringing Zionists . . . and shoot them dead with pistols. The
> guerrillas are gone before the sirens of the pigs can be heard
> [219-220].

Crime has become a political act and violence insurrectionary.[24]

Even art, the most promising sign of potential brotherhood,
becomes another battleground on which black and white
painfully explore old angers and settle new scores. Willie's art is
an act of self-definition, the creation of an identity through the

embodiment of the disorder of life, in which blackness overtakes whiteness as a function of an imaginative "Manifested Destiny" [204]. His writing is concerned with difference, separation, and the limits of understanding:

> "No ofay motherfucker can put himself in *my* place. . . . Black ain't white and never can be. It is once and for only black. It ain't universal if that's what you are hintin up to. What I feel you feel different. You can't write about black because you don't have the least idea what we are or how we feel. Our feelin chemistry is different than yours. Dig that? It *has* to be so. I'm writin the soul writin of black people cryin out we are still slaves in this fuckn country and we ain't gonna stay slaves any longer. How can you understand it, Lesser, if your brain is white? [74-75].

But more importantly, Willie believes that artistic creation is a function of human existence and irretrievably tied to being: "I dig a different drum than you do, Lesser. None of that fuckn form for me. You hurt my inside confidence with that word. On account of you I can't write the way I used to any more" [224]. Willie is what he writes.

For Harry Lesser, art is form, discipline, and design imposed on the chaos of experience in order to illustrate a belief in the unity and wholeness of the human spirit:

> "If the experience is about being human and it moves me then you've made it my experience. You created it for me. You can deny universality, Willie, but you can't abolish it."
> "Bein human is shit. It don't give you any privileges, it never gave us any."
> "If we're talking about art, form demands its rights, or there's no order and maybe no meaning" [75].

The writer is one who wishes to explain the links that draw men into civilization: "If you're an artist you can't be a nigger, Willie" [51]. But for Harry, the price for such humanistic observations is ironically high—he himself no longer participates in life. Harry, in fact, writes what he would like to be.

Yet the rifts and the chasms are bridged in curious ways. By the end of the novel, Harry and Willie have become each other's doubles. Through sharing negative behavior, they have become part of each other. Harry has grown Willie's beard, he exudes Willie's odors, he has adopted Willie's work habits and his treatment of Irene. Harry even creates a final hymeneal fantasy that serves as the first segment in the long, complex ending of

The Tenants, during which black and white join in a cosmic wedding: "Someday God will bring together Ishmael and Israel to live as one people. It won't be the first miracle" [216]. But the fraternal hopes are wish-fulfillment, and the vision of mankind's unity, presented as "the end of my book, if I dared" [217], is entirely equivocal. No one participating in these ceremonies seems particularly satisfied. The families who are represented are either unhappy, pessimistic, or hostile. The religious figures who might have spoken for brotherhood are ambivalent, warning instead of the difficulties inherent in interracial marriages. The black chief cautions that integration may be unable to redeem the sins of slavery: "If somebody do bad it do not die. It live in the hut, the yard, and the village. The ceremony of reconciliation is useless. Men say the words of peace but they do not forgive the other" [211-212]. The two couples themselves do not seem to be in love or content with their assigned roles in this humanitarian dream. Harry apologizes to his bride:

> "Mary, I'm short of love in my nature, don't ask me why, but I'll try to give you your due."
> "What's in it for you, Harry?" [213].

And Willie still asserts his blackness in the face of attempted conciliation:

> "Ain't no god been in my house or ever was. ... Like what color is he?"
> "The color of light," says the rabbi. "Without light who sees color?"
> "Except black" [216].

In fact, the marriages appear to be the forced re-enactment of Lesser's remaining liberal beliefs.

Willie, on the other hand, finds Yiddishisms creeping into his language. And Willie's fiction illustrates this fusion of personality and race, as illustrated by

> a weird disturbing story entitled "Goldberg exits Harlem." A Jew slumlord ... come to collect his bloodmoney rents, is attacked in a dark hall. ... The Jew struggles and cries out but they stab him ... then drag his fat body down the stairs to the cellar.
> "Let's cut a piece off of him and taste what it taste like," says the old man.
> "He tastes Jewtaste, that don't taste like nothin good," says the Jamaican woman.

> They remove Goldberg's stabbed clothes and leave his body in
> the cellar.
> Then they go to a synagogue late at night, put on yarmulkes and
> make Yid noises, praying.
> In an alternate ending the synagogue is taken over and turned into
> a mosque. The blacks dance hasidically [203].

Yes, they become brothers, but vengeful brothers.

At last, as form blurs, as metaphor becomes reality, as
narrative gives way to fantasy, the imagery of obliteration
becomes the vocabulary of the penultimate ending. Returning to
the all-encompassing, malodorous jungle, Willie and Harry kill
by destroying in the other the sign of his own vulnerability:
"They aimed at each other accurate blows. Lesser felt his jagged
ax sink through bone and brain as the groaning black's razor-
sharp saber, in a single boiling stabbing slash, cut the white's
balls from the rest of him" [229-230]. Malamud has made a long,
disintegrating journey since the optimism of "Angel Levine." In
this ultimate act of Biblical retribution, it is irrelevant who is
Cain, who is Abel. There is only death, literal and/or figurative.
The final cries for mercy that are the ultimate conclusion of *The
Tenants*, coming as they do from the businessman Levenspiel,
represent the pain of an uncomprehending society which will be
destroyed should the imagined cataclysm become historical fact.

THE BROADER CANVAS

Malamud and the Woman Question

Just as Malamud is interested in presenting the complicated, shifting encounters between blacks and Jews in a society moving toward anarchy and chaos, so too is he concerned, as artist and critic, with describing the roles women are to play in such an environment. Unlike the simplistic, often one-dimensional figures put forward in the works of other male Jewish-American writers,[1] the images of women offered in his fiction reach toward complexity, although not always successfully or consistently. Out of a conservative perception of the importance of women in the social order and the principles they define and embody, Malamud attempts to avoid stereotypes, devising personalities that are multi-layered, human beings that are intricate and independent, subject even to changing authorial awareness as the fictive world he creates continues to evolve. It is, however, worth observing that women appear with decreasing frequency and for shorter periods, albeit in a more autonomous context, in those novels and short stories that precede *Dubin's Lives*. This is, I think, not because Malamud regards women as any less significant. In fact, the contrary is probably true. As the environment in Malamud's fiction continues to be subject to increasing stress, showing signs of further disintegration, exploding in apocalyptic angers, the elaborate value system and complicated psychic design that women have come to represent can no longer function.

Obviously stated in the earliest fiction, more subtly depicted in the later works, but used with flexibility, wisdom, and care throughout, the one persistent idea that seems to underlie and control, to some extent, the variety of women that appear in Malamud's canon is the male's archetypal projection of feminine dualism—life-giver and death-dealer, Lady of the Lake and Morgan Le Fay, Eve and Lilith, Earth Mother and Death Goddess.

> The mythological figure of the Universal Mother imputes to the cosmos the feminine attributes of the nourishing and protecting presence.... She is the world creatrix, ever mother, ever virgin. She encompasses the encompassing, nourishes the nourishing, and is the life of everything that lives.
> She is also the death of everything that dies. The whole round of existence is accomplished within her sway from birth, through adolescence, maturity, and senescence to the grave. She is the womb and the tomb: the sow that eats her farrow.... Woman in the picture language of mythology represents the totality of what can be known.[2]

On the one hand, she is the means by which man is destroyed through his attachment to the world of objects (Memo Paris, Avis Fliss). On the other, she is the agent by which man is redeemed through love and suffering (Iris Lemon, Helen Bober). A man's moral excellence, his sense of positive self is determined by the strength of commitment to the latter. But Malamud's women function in a wider context. As his women become more integrated personalities, rather than simply emblematic icons, Malamud comes to recognize that their discontents, angers, dissatisfactions, and unhappiness are as important to shaping a whole human being able to act in the world as those virtues associated with maternal instincts. Women are no longer just mythic projections by which the male defines his worth, nor the cathectic center of the masculine ethical dilemma. They have their own neuroses to contend with. They have the capacity to change their behavior and revise judgments. And, like the men of Malamud's fiction, they are in the process of creating a self, forging an identity, meeting, and sometimes embracing, what life offers.

   The Natural presents the most primal and schematic model of Malamud's early definition of the feminine. The simplification is, perhaps, an inevitable outcome of the novel's design as a contemporary version of the ancient drama of the quest and its corollary, the myth of the fisher-king, a pattern analyzed thoroughly and brilliantly by Earl Wasserman.[3] The unitary figure of the *magna mater*, the embodiment of the cyclic contraries of life, is fragmented into the two elemental forces that comprise the Great Goddess: easily discernible characterizations of the queen of death (Harriet Bird, Memo Paris) and the earth mother (Iris Lemon). By so dividing the female principle, males are able to reduce and domesticate the apparently unlimited, and therefore threatening, power she possesses. The menacing face of the white goddess can be isolated, her potency recognized, contained, and ultimately devalued, while her beneficent aspect can be acknowledged, exalted, and rewarded.

As befits their black garb, Harriet Bird and Memo Paris are corrosive agents, disintegrative figures, from the province of death. They are specifically identified with Roy's mother, "a whore," who "spoiled my old man's life," who "didn't love anybody,"[4] who drowns cats and abandons sons, whom Roy can speak of only with great reluctance, when drunk, and therefore released from Oedipal repressions. In the larger mythic context, both are facets of the Jungian *mater saeva*, the cruel destructive mother, using sexuality, represented by the succoring maternal breast, to thwart, obstruct, and manipulate rather than fulfill or nourish: Harriet's shooting Roy just as he reaches for her almost naked body; Memo's forbidding Roy her small, presumably "sick" breasts. It is, I think, especially important to recognize that these characters function as primary antagonists shaping the nature and quality of Roy Hobbs's losing struggles with the forces of darkness, first as the naive youth, then as the experienced adult.[5]

The initial encounter with Harriet Bird, who as the "twisted tree" [35], is the human correlative of the sinister and deadly landscape that the young hero must traverse, is Roy's first real test, not his defeat of Whammer Wambold. For Harriet does not challenge Roy's obvious physical prowess. Instead she attacks where he is most vulnerable and least aware, emphasizing his inability to understand. She questions the worth of his actions, the premises determining his values, and the meaning of his conception of the heroic:

"What will you hope to accomplish, Roy?" . . . "Sometimes

when I walk down the street I bet people will say there goes Roy
Hobbs, the best there ever was in the game."
    She gazed at him with touched and troubled eyes.
    "Is that all?"
    He tried to penetrate her question. Twice he had answered it and
still she was unsatisfied.... "Is that all?" he repeated. "What more
is there?"
    "Don't you know?" she said kindly.
    Then he had an idea. "You mean the bucks? I'll get them too."
    ... "Isn't there something over and above earthly things—some
more glorious meaning to one's life and activities?"
    "In baseball?" ...
    "Maybe I've not made myself clear but surely you can see ... that
yourself alone—alone in the sense that we are all terribly alone no
matter what people say—I mean by that perhaps if you understood
that our values must derive from ..." [33-34].

Because he is without experience, because he is unable to translate
the discipline of strength into the discipline of judgment, because
he first defines the heroic ideal selfishly, then materially, Roy
Hobbs fails his first crucial test. The injuries he receives from the
murderous Harriet keep him out of the big leagues until he is
thirty-four.

    Harriet Bird, however, is very much aware of the positive
power that resides in the heroic paradigm, as is Iris Lemon, the
figure representative of the Earth Mother, whose later catechism
on the nature and function of heroism so parallels Harriet's as to
become a sardonic reinforcement of its validity. But Iris wishes to
encourage and enhance Roy's heroic potential while Harriet seeks
to obliterate violently that promise. Her direct and simple
solution to the mythic enigma posed by the presence of this
"natural" seems ironically apt since Harriet's action is the
destructive analogue to Roy's direct and simple ignorance that
masquerades as innocence at this stage of his heroic transformation. He is yet a young man who does not know
complexity, anguish, or the suffering that defines life. And,
according to Malamud, this *necessary* education can be truly
taught only by encountering the various faces of the white
goddess. Nonetheless, Harriet's character, though dramatic, is
flawed. She appears to be an anomalous force, an eccentric agent
of punishment, a dispenser of an odd, not quite comprehensible,
but very personal justice. She is an isolated figure, her strength is
self-generated, she is unattached to the more general corruption
of institutional forms and social structures that constitute an
inevitable part of the hero's trial. This narrowly circumscribes

the extent and exercise of her dark power, thus limiting not only her fictive existence but also the validity of her judgments.

Memo Paris, on the contrary, belongs to the world, a decadent Madonna sharing dominion over a sterile and degraded landscape with the satanic Judge Banner and the supernatural Gus Sands. She does not merely agree with their views, she is an active conspirator with her male cohorts in seducing masculine converts for this new version of an old hell. It is clear that Memo represents a more subtle threat, a deeper, more dangerous aspect of the *mater saeva*; and therefore she is certainly a more suitable temptation for the experienced Roy Hobbs because she carries with her the weight of society's corruption, a force the adult Roy knows intimately.

Throughout the novel, Memo is both committed to and emblematic of the many kinds of death which haunt this version of the waste land. Although she is provided with a Freudian personal history to explain her nihilistic relationships—a sad-eyed, impoverished, weak mother and a dancing, grinning, disappearing Daddy—it is a minimal and largely unsuccessful attempt to give dimension to what is essentially a symbolic power. And the nature of that power is most distinctly revealed if we examine those nihilistic relationships that determine and define Memo's existence.

As Judge Goodwill Banner's deputy, she is linked to a world shrouded in darkness. As we have seen in Chapter One of this study, the Judge signifies the death of the soul through an attachment to an exploitative, corrupting materialism. Ultimately even the self is transformed into an object to be manipulated by the Judge, Gus, and Memo. But before this contemporary Circe can turn men into marketable commodities, she herself must be revealed as chained to the belief that things rule a disintegrating environment in which man is another instrument to be used. Having reduced her own humanity by her commitment to the materialistic American dream, she can now successfully diminish others.

Her life-denying alliance with Gus Sands, the Supreme Bookie who is "just like a daddy" [119] to Memo, results from the related notions that accident can be exploited to acquire money, power, and human souls and that chance can be manipulated to control human behavior. Like the Judge, Gus embodies a reductive philosophy that is dehumanizing, converting men's actions into odds, abstract numbers to be wagered on, disregarding the value of the exercise, the morality of the choice, the skill of the performance. It is not surprising, therefore, that Memo's distorted maternal concern is directed toward Gus; and when Roy attacks the magical gambler, she screams, "Don't touch him, you big bastard. He's worth a million of your kind" [235].

But Memo's deadliest lesson, the final negation, is the futile ongoing connection to Bump Bailey, because that is a covenant with a world drained of love. And that relationship is clearly an extension of her futile ongoing connection to the lost father, as if to underscore that lovelessness has been the essential determinant in Memo's character. Bump, like her Daddy, is the uncommitted man lacking any sense of responsibility, honor, or duty, a seducer and a betrayer, demanding fidelity without giving:

> Oh ... he was carefree and full of life. He did the craziest things and always kept everybody in stitches. Even when he played ball, there was something carefree and playful about it. Maybe he went all the way after a fly ball or maybe he didn't, but once he made up his mind to catch it, it was exciting how he ran and exciting how he caught it. ... To him it was a playful game and so was his life. Nobody could ever tell what would happen next with Bump, and that was the wonderful thing of it" [118-119].

Bump's crucifixion is hardly redemptive. It serves only to remind Memo how little she had of the god's love. She remains still Death's faithful mistress whose companions are grief and emptiness: "The heartbreak was always present—he had not been truly hers when he died (she tried not to think whose, in many cities, he had been) so that she now mourned someone who even before his death had made her a mourner. That was the thorn in her grief" [87]. For Memo, there can be no resurrection because Bump's credo consisted of a greedy egotism, incapable of love. What remains is the repeated obliteration of self, a hollowness filled not with grace but rage and a maenad's cry for sacrifice. Into the arms of this complex goddess, mother of evil and death, walks the adult Roy Hobbs, no less the king of fools his name reveals him to be. Not only is he warned by Pop Fisher about Memo's flaws, but also he ignores the lessons taught by previous suffering and rejects the wisdom of Iris Lemon.

But Memo does have an individual, personal existence, as well as a symbolic one. And her behavior has a more human explanation as well. Out of frustrated unfulfilled love, and in part as an act of atonement for unwittingly giving her body (that most precious possession) to Roy as a result of Bailey's practical joke, Memo is driven to revenge, proof of the intensity and permanence of her ties to Bump and to her father, in order to reassert some semblance of control over her manipulated life. Perhaps since she cannot consciously acknowledge the fact she has been used ruthlessly by Bump nor understand the Oedipal destructiveness of her attachments, she directs her anger at Roy, determined to take an active part in the ruin of the natural, slayer and successor to the father—for any man who actively pursues her cannot be worth much, and therefore must be spurned as unacceptable.

This Lilith seduces by withdrawal and tempts by denial. Feminine biology, generally associated with nurture and fecundity is employed by Memo as an excuse for physical rejection, the most wounding refusal to be suffered by Roy Hobbs, himself a symbol of physicality. Her small breasts and thin body (a doll's appearance, not particularly womanly) are tools used for sexual control, Memo's only real source of power, while menstruation, a sign of childbearing capabilities, is exploited as the negation of that creative gift. When he wants to make love, she denies him by saying:

> "I'm not well," said Memo.
> He was suspicious. "What's wrong?"
> Memo laughed. "Sometimes you are very innocent, Roy. When a girl says she is not well, does she have to draw you a map?"
> Then he understood and was embarrassed for being so dimwitted. He did not insist on any more necking . . . [167].

She nourishes him not with intangibles such as love, sympathy, and affection, but stuffs him to explosion with the material—food. Frequently the concrete expression of maternal concern, food is, in this case, an ironic comment on the absence of this feeling in Memo, which literally eats away Roy's strength, producing hollowness rather than satisfaction, as does Memo herself:

> "Just let Roy head over to the table. He is dying for a bite."
> It was true. Though the thought of having her tonight was on the top of his mind, he could not entirely forget the appetizing food. She led him to the table and he was surprised and slightly trembly at all there was of it—different kinds of delicatessen meat, appetizing fish, shrimp, crab and lobster, also caviar, salads, cheeses of all sorts, breads, rolls and three flavors of ice cream. It made his belly ache, as if it had an existence apart from himself [183].

And the quality of her past reinforces that basic drive for self-preservation that motivates Memo, preventing her from functioning in a supportive capacity, even had she wanted to: "Roy, don't bawl me out for not seeing you for a while. There are some things I just can't take and one of them is being with people who are blue. I had too much of that in my life with my mother and it really makes me desperate" [166]. Nor does she respect or understand his heroic dimensions, minimizing the significance of his genius because it is too predictable, too intense, too grim, unlike Bump Bailey's irresponsible, often harmful, playfulness.

Memo's most damaging action, however, is the willful destruction of Roy's belief in and connections to an idyllic youth. Throughout the novel Roy has been haunted by a vision of a boy and his dog in a deep primitive forest, a symbol of an innocent past before suffering, before failure, a reminder of loss. Returning from a treacherous drive with Memo to a polluted unswimmable beach (a journey to be repeated later with Iris Lemon and with different results), the image not surprisingly recurs, since Memo's malevolent complexity makes him yearn for remembered simplicity:

> The white moonlight shot through a stretch of woods ahead. He found himself wishing he could go back somewhere, go home, wherever that was. As he was thinking this, he looked up and saw in the moonlight a boy coming out of the woods, followed by his dog. Squinting through the windshield, he was unable to tell if the kid was an illusion thrown forth by the trees or someone really alive. After fifteen seconds he was still there. Roy yelled to Memo to slow down in case he wanted to cross the road. Instead, the car shot forward . . . [122-123].

And there can be no chance for apology or redemption because although Roy attempts to find out whether anything real has been hit, he cannot; the swirling fog hides truth. Memo has taken from him the power of his mythic childhood.

But, ultimately, Memo's obsessive desire for revenge is self-defeating. When that single-minded impulse has been satisfied, when there is no further need for punishment because ruin had been accomplished, what has she left, this used doll, whose value, even to herself, is as a sexual toy? Only an anguished recognition of her own emptiness. In a scene parallel to Harriet Bird's violent humiliation of the hero, Memo finds that in spite of her hatred, she cannot kill Roy Hobbs and attempts suicide, to be rescued by the very man she has destroyed. Given the archetypal symbolism that has defined Memo Paris's role in *The Natural*, it is significant that Malamud does not leave us with the iconography of a bloodthirsty goddess gloating over her success, but rather with a distraught, confused woman "sobbing hysterically" [236].

Iris Lemon, bittersweet guardian of the rainbow's promise, as her name suggests, seems at first to be acting out her archetypal role as beneficent mother-goddess in the mythic design of Malamud's novel. Given the attributes assigned to the *magna mater* by such scholars as Joseph Campbell, Sir James Frazer, Jessie Weston, and Mircea Eliade,[6] she can be both virginal young girl and sensual woman, a paradox reinforced by her physical presence: "Her thighs and rump were broad but her waist was narrow and virginal. Her breasts were hard, shapely. From above her hips she looked like a girl, but the lower half of her looked like a woman" [162]. Yet this very substantial body, signifying quality of character as well, produces an oddly mixed reaction in Roy Hobbs who, preferring the flimsy Barbie-doll femininity of Memo Paris, is unable to recognize and embrace with consistency the life-giving power symbolized by Iris Lemon's physiology:

> Despite his good intentions he was disappointed right off, because she was heavier than he had thought. ... He didn't like them hefty, yet on second thought it couldn't be said she really was. Big, yes, but shapely too. Her face and hair were pretty and her body—she knew what to wear on her feet—was well-proportioned. He admitted she was attractive although as a rule he never thought so unless they were slim like Memo [151-152].

She radiates a giving, satisfying sexuality—perhaps it can be said that she *is* sexuality—and provokes erotic responses, in varying degrees, from the men she comes in contact with. Her fertility is unquestioned. In fifteen years she apparently has had intercourse only twice, and in each case, the result has been pregnancy. It is clear too that we are meant to view Iris in mythic terms, virgin as well as mother, for she does say to Roy, "You are really the first" [162], ascribing purity to this new beginning where "suddenly everywhere I looked seemed to be tomorrow" [210]. And her almost magical fecundity has been inherited by her daughter, married and like her mother, "a mother before she was seventeen" [210]. For Malamud, it is this reproductive capacity that is the ultimate source of feminine strength and authority because it makes it possible for women to actually be, in the deepest physical sense, the force of human continuity, binding the past and the future, history and promise. It is significant in this regard that in four of Malamud's seven novels, the female protagonists (Iris Lemon, Pauline Gilley, Raisl Bok, and lastly Maud Dubin) find themselves pregnant by men not their husbands, or mothers with children needing legitimization, as if to underscore the anarchic potency of the woman's generative drive. However, if an orderly, stable society is to endure, biology demands the controls inherent in the creation and structure of the family as socializing unit. Therefore a paternal figure is required. Malamud's conservative vision asserts that if childbearing is the primal feminine act, then the acknowledgment of paternity, actual or psychic, is the crucial masculine decision, insuring not only the perpetuation of the species, or the subtle immortality of the self, but also the survival of civilization. Malamud is under no illusions that the family is a liberating institution, or that rearing children is a fulfilling achievement; it is simply a moral necessity. It is the men in Malamud's fiction who are particularly entrapped by this unavoidable responsibility, losing freedom and denying possibility. For women, biology is still destiny.

But to be just a childbearer without a sense of loving concern is insufficient. Iris Lemon is the nurturing parent for whom "the child meant everything" [162]. Although there is a concerted effort to make this unwed mother give up her child—"They said it would be bad for her to be brought up by an unmarried mother, and that I would have no time to myself or opportunity to take up my normal life" [210]—she cannot, especially after nursing her, the outward physical manifestation of the maternal instinct. And in spite of the difficulties Iris undergoes, her daughter's "loveliness and gaiety and all the tender feelings I had in my heart for her made up for a lot I had suffered" [210]. However, since Iris's capacity for mothering has mythic consequences, her feelings are more generalized and encompassing than biological maternity would dictate, as we can see if we examine her effect on the novel's hero, Roy Hobbs.

She appears in his life during a deep, despairing slump, and initially his response to her is conditioned by sexual curiosity: "she interested him, in that red dress, and he would have liked a close gander at her but he couldn't get out there without arousing attention" [143]. But the sexuality inherent in their relationship becomes increasingly complicated and ambiguous for Roy, until it is reduced to something to be ashamed of. Yet when Iris, motivated by principle and belief, sacrifices her private identity in a public display of confidence in Roy's power, he recognizes the importance of such behavior, and the way in which it creates change and redeems heroes:

> Roy was thinking about Memo. . . . For a while things had looked good between them but no sooner had he gone into a slump when she began to avoid him. Had she been nice to him instead, he'd have got out of his trouble sooner. However, he wasn't bitter, because Memo was remote, even unreal. Strange how quick he forgot what she was like, though he couldn't what she looked like. Yet with that thought even her image went up in smoke. Iris, a stranger, had done what the other wouldn't, in public view what's more. He felt for her a gratitude it was hard to hold in [152].

Her gentle and comforting manner releases Roy, at least momentarily, from the iron prison of his shattering personal history, offering him choices outside his predetermined fate, quite unlike the parallel encounter with Memo that destroys his Edenic time. On a clear, blue night, on a "deserted beach, enclosed in a broken arc of white birches" where "the wind . . . was balmy and the water lit on its surface" [153], Roy confesses his past to the soothing, understanding Iris. In a scene designed to awaken memories of Harriet Bird's catechism of the hero and deliberately reminiscent of his fog-bound drive with Memo, Iris attempts to show him the value of human experience in order to provide a context by which Roy can truly judge and evaluate his anguished life. Suffering, says Iris, educates. She tries to explain:

> "Experience makes good people better. . . . "
> "How does it do that?"
> "Through their suffering."
> "I had enough of that," he said in disgust.
> "We have two lives, Roy, the life we learn with and the life we live with after that. Suffering is what brings us toward happiness" [158].

In Iris's presence, he feels relief and the ability to "see yourself as something more satisfying than you were" [187]; and in the memory of her presence, Memo's dark power diminishes until all that remains is nausea and "an odd disgust" [225].

But Roy is unable to cope with the fact of Iris's age—she is thirty-three—since it indicates an acceptance of responsibilities; nor can he respect her status as a grandmother. Iris becomes threatening because she serves as a reminder of the passage of time, the loss of youth, strength, virility, and his chance at immortality. Roy's belief in reality as the sum of surface appearances results in further difficulties, for it induces perceptual confusion, causing him to ascribe to Memo Iris's roles as wife and mother: "It later struck him that the picture he had drawn of Memo sitting domestically home wasn't exactly the girl she was. The kind he had in mind, though it bothered him to admit it, was more like Iris seemed to be, only she didn't suit him" [180]. He remains quite literally entranced by the superficial veneer of Memo Paris because it is just that brittle attractiveness that Roy has been taught to want by his culture. He sees the truth of Iris Lemon's existence when it is too late, and he has once again been condemned by his own cupidity and naive desires to enter another round of suffering.

But the simple schematics of myth give way to the author's need for human complexity. There has once again been an attempt on Malamud's part to go beyond the archetypal functions assigned to Iris Lemon and to create a character of some depth. Iris, like Memo, is an individual as well as a mythic personification, conditioned to react and respond, behave and judge, in accordance with the events of a given past. She has forged a strong identity out of a difficult choice made not without guilt or pain, and lived responsibly in spite of the consequent limitations on her freedom of action. It is a self fashioned out of denial and isolation, perhaps without sufficient testing among ordinary humanity. Her attitude defining suffering as positive and redemptive has been shaped by her own distress:

> Since Papa wouldn't have her in his house I decided to . . . bring her up myself. That turned out to be a lot harder than I expected, because I earned not very much and had to pay for baby's care all day, her things, the rent of course, and the clothes I had to have for work. At night I had supper to think of, bathing her, laundry, house cleaning, and preparing for the next day, which never changed from any other.
>
> Except for my baby I was nearly always alone, reading . . . although sometimes it was unbearable, especially before I was twenty and just after. It also took quite a while until I got rid of my guilt, or could look upon her as innocent of it, but eventually I did. . . . Yet I was tied to time—not so much to the past—nor to the expectations of the future, which was really too far away—only to here and now, day after day . . . [210].

Iris Lemon would appear to be the only one of the author's major female protagonists who is allowed the usually male prerogative of making the morally right decision that in Malamud's fiction invariably leads to psychic imprisonment or to the frustration of human possibility. Her dangerous innocence, the inevitable by-product of her solitary existence, her extensive but undisciplined reading, and her minimal experience in the world, is the source of misjudgment as well as wisdom. Iris's naive idealism, however admirable given the corrupt society of *The Natural*, permits her to be deceived by the superficial appearances of the actual—reality defined simply as what it presents itself to be; in this she is not unlike Roy Hobbs. The romantic belief in the need for heroes without whom "we're all plain people and don't know how far we can go" [154], whose "function is to be the best and for the rest of us to understand what they represent and guide ourselves accordingly" [154], finally betrays her.

Although Iris has received hints that Roy Hobbs is less than her heroic vision—"He seemed so big and bulky next to her, and close up looked disappointingly different from what she had expected. In street clothes he gained little and lost more, a warrior's quality he showed in his uniform. Now he looked like any big-muscled mechanic or bartender on his night off" [152]—she persists in her conviction that Roy is a true example of the genus. It is such misguided perception that guarantees more unremitting pain to be legitimized and made ennobling by the value she gives to suffering. The dream of promised freedom and a liberated self dies in another pregnancy, an ironic elaboration of Iris's pointed observation that suffering "teaches us to want the right things" [158].

What may have started as straightforward representations of mythic femininity have become, by the novel's end, ambiguous, complicated portraits of two specific women. The clarity of the usual archetypal division into earth mother and death goddess has blurred. Iris Lemon, virgin-mother-mistress (given a name implying hope), womanly woman, symbol of maternal solicitude and tranquility, a Malamudian ideal of sorts, whose knowledge is the book's message, is left to repeat her original sin, if you will—a second pregnancy that gives no sign of being redemptive. She has very likely been deserted by Roy and the author as she is being taken to the hospital. Perhaps she has been cast off as a loose end because the contradictions that arise out of her dual role as individual and archetype cannot be resolved. On the other hand, Memo Paris (named as a reminder of betrayal through sexual license), seductive agent of a debased culture, has ceased to be the presumed embodiment of feminine evil. Instead she is treated as a troubled, suicidal girl whose frightening emptiness reflects prevailing societal attitudes and whose desperate vengeance is rooted in lovelessness.

The forces which have shaped Iris Lemon and Memo Paris find further expression and development in the characterizations of Ida and Helen Bober and Pauline Gilley, women central to the actions of *The Assistant* and *A New Life* respectively. The most important advance over the portrayals in *The Natural* is that the figure of the female is no longer divided into elemental polarities. Such a design is no longer functional; nor is it sufficiently complex to incorporate the multiple contraries that Malamud perceives to be the essence of the feminine personality. Even Iris and Memo escape the structured dichotomy of myth into tangled, intricate humanity. Ida, Helen, and Pauline are unitary embodiments of the bewildering female principle, whose warring . interior demands provide depth and drama. It is also worth repeating at this point that Malamud's vision of woman is basically a conservative one. Whatever her discontents, however real her ambitions or justified her angers, a woman's primary purpose is still centered in the claims of biology. Her patterns of behavior are determined by the maternal instinct and the communal as well as the psychological need for the continuities inherent in the family as fundamental social unit. Malamud's women, in the final analysis, are most often searching for an appropriate, sensitive male with whom to create life and/or a suitable, vitalizing environment in which to establish familial order, stability, and permanence. Those women who choose to deny the importance of these factors—Memo Paris, Helen Bober at the beginning of her education, Annamaria Oliovino, the *pittrice* of "Still Life,"[7] Etta mourning at her husband's grave in "Life Is Better Than Death"[8]—do so at the expense of their symbolic moral significance, and the unavoidable neurotic distortion of personality that follows such negation.

We have already seen in Chapter One the extent to which the clash between the aggressive, open materialism of American society and the humane, old-world ethics of the Jewish immigrant has controlled the identities of Ida Bober and her daughter. But these two feminine temperaments require additional examination.

Ida is not just a nag or a frightened, aging woman in an alien, predatory civilization who is eager for security and safety at any price, whether the cost be her own soul or her daughter's future. She comes out of an orthodoxy that has given the woman virtually unlimited jurisdiction over the home, while assigning her no role of any significance to play in the world at large. The functions she exists to perform are those of wife and mother. These areas are her dominion, for marriage and motherhood form the bases from which the Jewish woman can fulfill her ambitions and exercise her not inconsiderable power. It is she who rears the children—the hoped-for promise of better; it is she who transmits the rituals and customs that create the solidarity necessary for endurance; it is she who preserves the family in the face of persecution and hostility. Most of all, it is she who insures survival.[9] That Ida Bober reacts as she does when her province is threatened by Morris's weakness, or Frank's deceit, or America's lies should not then surprise because what is being attacked, in reality, is selfhood, her very significance as an individual. Nor should her resentment at her dead husband's failure shock. After all, his impotence, his debilitating passivity in this land of opportunity, has made her task all the more difficult, hardening her resolve that her daughter must succeed in America by achieving the shelter of a prosperous marriage, Ida's only definition of accomplishment:

> Ida, holding a wet handkerchief to her eyes, thought, So what if we had to eat? When you eat you don't want to worry whose money you are eating—yours or the wholesalers'. If he had money he had bills; and when he had more money he had more bills. A person doesn't always want to worry if she will be in the street tommorow. She wants sometimes a minute's peace. . . .
> She wept because her judgment of the grocer was harsh although she loved him. Helen, she thought, must marry a professional.[10]

Because it is her responsibility, even duty, to protect and enhance her daughter's possibilities, Ida is willing to use any means, including the dehumanizing materialist's logic of her adopted country, to prevent Helen from repeating her mother's mistakes by marrying defeat and hopelessness. To engineer a substantial marriage, one that assures the requisite status necessary for American acceptance—whether or not such an arrangement is Helen's aim is irrelevant—is also Ida's victory in a life that has had too few triumphs. Her insistent dislike for Frank, gentile, thief, apostle of Morris's futile doctrine of honesty, accountability, and *mentshlekhayt*,[11] and her chronic mistrust of his intentions toward Helen are, therefore, understandable—a prophetic recognition that he represents only more of the same shriveled existence.

In Ida, simple maternal concern has been transformed into

suspicion, worry, and nagging anxiety by two factors: the need to affirm the traditionally sanctioned feminine position, and the concomitant desire to assert a personal sense of self made insecure by a civilization that denies her worth because, assessed in monetary terms, she is to be marked "insufficient funds." To survive with a portion of her identity intact, Ida's moral awareness, an important component of feminine strength for Malamud, has narrowed, and her almost deliberate insensitivity has crippled her humanity. Like Eva Kalish in the author's short story "Take Pity,"[12] or Bessie in "The Loan,"[13] she has had to blunt sympathy and to dull womanly feeling to persevere in the face of ongoing disaster or remembered tragedy.

Helen Bober, however, is confused about what actually constitutes her feminine identity: what she is, what she can be, what she must do in order to become a fulfilled woman, and whether that particular goal conflicts with finding a measure of completeness as a human being. Her mother, at least, had the limited certainty enforced by custom. But to Helen, the Jewish heritage, reinforced by the whole history of Western culture, offers only one prescription for womanly contentment and that is the familial role. However, American society seduces by promising an emancipated self open to opportunity, risk, change, then often closes the door. The present has trapped Helen in dissatisfaction and circumscription with frustrated ambitions and frustrating dreams: "I'd like to be doing something that feels useful—some kind of social work or maybe teaching. I have no sense of accomplishment in what I'm doing now. Five o'clock comes and at last I go home. That's about all I live for, I guess" [99]. And until Frank enters her life, a man suitable for use as a vehicle for her plans, through whom she can vicariously live her hopes, she cannot perceive an altered future.

Her ambivalent behavior, then, is conditioned by a variety of stereotypic demands and the claims for individual autonomy. Although she wants for herself, Helen is giving to the point of unnecessary personal deprivation, perhaps to compensate for the death of her brother, Ephraim. As a good daughter and well-trained woman, she is obsessively sacrificial. By surrendering the primacy of her expectations to her parents, or to Frank, whose own supposed aspirations have been concocted for the purpose of seduction, Helen prolongs dependence, insures protection and minimizes the pain of entering an aggressive, inhospitable, but adventurous society. Yet Helen is equally determined to create that autonomous self through a liberating humanistic education, rejecting the dominant materialism of her surroundings typified by her mother, Nat Pearl, the Karps, translating her father's submissive virtue into utilitarian activism: "she wanted to travel, experience, live" [105].

Helen's hesitancy, her lack of confidence, her doubts about the nature of her femaleness are most clearly revealed in her attitudes toward sex. And it is in this context that the most unsettling instance of Malamud's sexual chauvinism occurs—his subtle justification of Frank Alpine's rape of Helen Bober.

There is no question that Helen resents being considered an object, sexual or otherwise, and is angered by her treatment as a commodity. There is a certain amount of irony, I suppose, in the fact that Helen is a secretary at Levenspiel's Louisville Panties and Bras, bosoms and behinds being the most obvious tokens of feminine identification used by men to signify the woman as erotic product. She wished to love—to give—because to be loved involves a judgment of worth, and Helen is fearful of being undervalued, accepting to a great extent, as she does, the notion that she is merchandise. No doubt one of the reasons for this preoccupation with human accounting is the knowledge that as a female child she *is* worth less than her dead male sibling in whom the real hopes of the family resided. When Ephraim died, the small opening into the world that his birth provided for the Bobers closed: "When Ephraim was alive, when they were kids, her father liked to go bathing Sunday afternoons at Coney Island; and on Jewish holidays they would sometimes see a Yiddish play, or ride on the subway to the Bronx to call on landsleit. But after Ephraim died Morris had for years gone nowhere" [105]. And the actions of Nat Pearl, Louis Karp, and Ida serve to confirm her discomfiting evaluation. To withhold sex then, her solution, is perceived as a means of controlling the price of self, unlike Memo Paris who uses her body as a way of manipulating others.

Frank Alpine, however, is a man who "at least . . . made her dream" [106]. His movement, disguising rootlessness, his ambitions, masking lust, his sensitivity, hiding a deep and bitter guilt, cause Helen, another of Malamud's naive romantics taken in by appearance, to idealize his capacities and radically misjudge his quality. His love warrants consideration because her emotional requirements have transformed him into a mirror reflecting her own possibilities, a future she *wants* to accomplish, but that *her* man *must*. However, while Helen may be willing to yield her dreams to the male (women have been doing that for centuries), she does not, indeed cannot, give him her body simply because Frank asks for it as the one proven sign of her love. To do so would not only mean conceding that fragile identity she has precariously been building, but also it would imply the surrender of the only power Helen has to rule her own destiny. So on a deceptively spring-like February evening, after rescuing her from Ward Minogue's attempted assault, Frank rapes her, quite literally stripping away humanity as well as womanhood; and then he cannot understand why she will not forgive, forget, and absolve.

It is a curious rape that Malamud depicts; it hardly seems a rape at all, although rape it surely is. Described vaguely and briefly, the language used is that of love not terror, of an almost Platonic idealism, not carnality:

> "I love you, Helen," he murmured, attempting clumsily to cover her breast with the torn dress as he drew her deeper into the dark, and from under the trees onto the star-dark field.
> They sank to their knees on the winter earth, Helen urgently whispering, "Please not now, darling," but he spoke of his starved and passionate love, and all the endless heartbreaking waiting. Even as he spoke he thought of her as beyond reach, forever in the bathroom as he spied, so he stopped her pleas with kisses [167-168].

It occurs on the very evening Helen has come to confess her love: "Frank, she thought with tremulous joy. . . . She held him tightly with both arms, weeping, laughing, murmuring she had come to tell him she loved him" [167]. And Frank has just saved her from a much more graphically portrayed attempted rape. Since it is less a violation than an affirmation of love, what could possibly explain Helen's rage against the man whom she calls "uncircumcised dog"? [168]. Indeed, by the end of the novel, it is she who is implicitly condemned for her lack of charity toward Frank, who is, after all, a changed man. Or can one explain or excuse the deed by calling it an acting out of Helen's Oedipal fantasies or sibling incest with her father's assistant, surrogate son, and ultimate heir?

Having explored Helen's responses to Frank at some length here and in Chapter One, perhaps we ought to examine Frank's behavior toward Helen if we are to account for this rather puzzling treatment of rape in *The Assistant*.

Frank both fears and is intrigued by Helen Bober—exotic Jewess—realizing almost immediately that her attraction goes beyond the merely erotic, although the only language he knows to define his feelings are those purely sexual, often degrading terms society has given men to describe the relations between the sexes:

> He had the feeling as he spoke to her ... that he knew more about her than anyone would give him credit for. He got this thought the first time he ever laid eyes on her, that night he saw her through the grocery window. When she looked at him he was at once aware of something starved about her, a hunger in her eyes he couldn't forget because it made him remember his own, so he knew how wide open she must be. But he wouldn't try to push anything, for he had heard that these Jewish babes could be troublemakers and he was not looking for any of that now.... besides, he didn't want to spoil anything before it got started. There were some dames you had to wait for—for them to come to you [61].

As she had idealized Frank, making him into the embodiment of her values and dreams, so Frank comes to idealize Helen, seeing in her a chance for redemption through a selfless and elevating love (in the manner of Frank's Christian ideal, St. Francis of Assisi). But Frank has been trained by the accumulation of history to regard women as instruments for male use, satisfaction, and possession. Therefore, the single proof of love that he knows is the female's ready submission to masculine sexual desire. Helen's continued withdrawal is to be interpreted as rejection, a symbol of the absence of true feeling, the diminution of self:

> "I love you, Helen, you are my girl."
> They kissed breathlessly, then he undid the buttons of her blouse. She sat up to unhook her brassiere but as she was doing it, felt his fingers under her skirt....
> "What are we waiting for, honey?" He tried to move his hand but her legs tightened and she swung her feet off the bed.
> He pulled her back, pressing her shoulders down. She felt his body trembling on hers and for a fleeting minute thought he might hurt her; but he didn't.
> She lay stiff, unresponsive on the bed. When he kissed her again she didn't move....
> "Christ," he muttered.
> "I'm sorry," she said softly. "I told you I wouldn't."
> ... "Are you a virgin, is that what's eating you? ... I thought you were," he said surprised. "You act like one.... why do you act like one? Don't you know what it does to people?"
> "You don't have to be a virgin to have ideals in sex...."
> "I don't get it," said Frank.
> "Loving should come with love."
> "I said I love you, Helen, you heard me say it."
> "I mean I have to love you too.... Don't be hurt, Frank."

"I'm tired of that," he said harshly.

"Frank," said Helen . . . "I suppose I felt I wanted to be free, so I settled for sex. But if you're not in love sex isn't being free, so I made a promise to myself that I never would any more unless I really fell in love with somebody. I don't want to dislike myself. . . ."

"Crap," said Frank . . . [138-140].

Like Helen, Frank is being torn in many directions by conflicting personal impulses and societal demands and expectations.

Prior to the rape, Frank, his thievery discovered, is banished from the sanctuary the store has provided by a hurt and angry father. Gone is the opportunity for expiation, gone the sustaining illusion that "I am a different person now" [162]. His manhood severely damaged, impotent to resolve his failed existence, Frank uses Helen, *his* girl, the way men have used women—as property—for generations, in a confused attempt to prove his love, his power, his masculinity, and in an effort to exorcise his anger against Morris, who has exiled him, and Helen, who has denied his passion. That the act changes Frank there is no doubt. For in abusing love, for being a too violent, a too hungry Paris to a reluctant Helen, he has contracted a debt that requires an altered life as repayment, not just money or confession. In order to be pardoned, he must become the moral man he has so desired to be. By accepting the cleansing, but difficult burden of paternal responsibility for the Bober family, he is made new. Finally, he offers Helen the gift of freedom—her education—at the cost of his own entombment. Such is the price of redemption.

Helen, on the other hand, must bear the weight of what comes to seem increasingly unjustified anger, as the depth of Frank's metamorphosis is revealed. It is she who commits the greater sin by being unforgiving almost to the last. A more serious indictment, however, against this depiction of rape is the way in which Helen comes to preceive the attack as deserved. In a socially determined reaction, not untypical of victims who have suffered this form of male brutality, the assault is somehow her fault, a clear case of the oppressed assuming the justification of the oppressor: "Although she detested the memory of her experience in the park, lately it had come back to her how she had desired that night to give herself to Frank and might have if Ward hadn't touched her. She had wanted him. If there had been no Ward Minogue, there would have been no assault. If he had made his starved leap in bed she would have returned passion. She hated him, she thought, to divert hatred from herself" [239].

This writer hesitates to fall into a conventional response, but to present rape, even obliquely, as punishment is to exhibit, albeit unconsciously in this instance, all the traditional masculine attitudes and fantasies about rape.[14] First, Malamud portrays a rape described in the vocabulary of love thereby diminishing, if not disguising, the fact of rape as outrage. Second, although the rapist does, indeed, undergo a moral transformation as absolution, he is never quite able to grasp the reasons for his victim's hostility and skepticism. Since he acted out of love, he honestly believes that all he need do is apologize in order to obtain her forgiveness. In fact, it is Frank who is angry when he cannot make Helen recognize and accept his metamorphosis. Finally, the victim moves from rage to guilt, reversing what Susan Brownmiller has seen as the usual psychological pattern of rape victims.[15] Instead, Helen's ultimate rationalization, rather than her initial response, is to assume blame for the assault. If she is to prove her humanity, Helen must pardon her attacker, the man who destroyed her sense of worth. When at last Helen acquits Frank, the act of rape as the deepest violation of a woman's essential self is dissolved in the success of his purgation. Perhaps the way in which Malamud subconsciously shapes this particular incident and its aftermath can be attributed to his fundamental conservatism about the roles women are to play in establishing a stable, cohesive, just society. Nevertheless, it does seem, in this case, that Malamud is primarily concerned with the fate of a man's soul.

Loved, if not loving, Helen at the end of the novel, is on her way to school, having acknowledged the continuing value of Frank's gift—"I wanted you to know I'm still using your Shakespeare" [244]—and resolved to create and develop her autonomy. However, there is a further ambiguity to be mentioned concerning Helen's design. Her drive for an independent self is as much contingent on a male presence—in this case the memory of her ethical but ineffectual father—as it is on the urgency of the internal demands of her psyche:

> Standing at the kitchen window, she gazed out at the back yards in flower, feeling sorrow for her father lying in his immovable grave. What had she ever given him, ever done to make his poor life better? She wept for Morris, thinking of his compromises and surrenders. She felt she must do something for herself, accomplish some worthwhile thing or suffer his fate. Only by growing in value as a person could she make Morris's life meaningful, in the sense that she was of him. She must, she thought, in some way eventually earn her degree. It would take years—but it was the only way [234].

Pauline Gilley, however, seems to possess those very things sufficient to content the Malamudian woman, at least if one is to judge by apparent reality: a husband engaged in an occupation of considerable societal importance; two children on whom she can lavish maternal concern; and a home in the best of all possible environments. But the surface lies, and the image of happiness that Levin takes for truth on his first evening in Easchester is false. The husband is sterile in more than just biological ways. The children, adopted, are difficult, subject to frequent illness, used as tools to keep a broken marriage together. And we have seen in Chapter Two what a complicated failure the Edenic paradigm actually is.

In fact, Pauline is another one of Malamud's female mirrors, reflecting in feminine terms the same romantic ideals and discontents that affect his male protagonists. Pauline is in search of an identity that can encompass both her feminine impulses and her personal needs, which in this novel turn out to share an uneasy similarity, unlike Helen Bober's warring consciousness in *The Assistant*. In addition, Pauline's function as an Eve figure, cause of man's eviction from paradise and reason for his loss of primal innocence, increases her ambivalent status within the novel and within the putative Garden she inhabits.

That she is flawed Levin notes early, defining the limits of her womanhood physiologically: "She had pinned a rose to her poor chest. Why not two, he thought, one for each flat side? . . . It did bother a bit, the observer conscious that nature had cheated where it hurt most."[16] This is not simply the response of a male chauvinist aware of the female only as sex object. For Malamud, breasts have a nurturing, comforting, maternal significance as we have seen in the descriptions of Iris, Memo, Helen, and of Avis Fliss, whose large, but shapeless and scarred breasts so disappoint and pain Levin. Pauline's flat chest symbolizes not only her restricted capacity for mothering, but also the lack of fulfillment in a particularly barren marriage.

When Levin discovers that it is circumstance—Gilley's sterility—and her own sense of inadequacy that are the causes for this circumscribed emotional reach, when he recognizes in Pauline that ability to give—"He had not expected wanting so much in so much giving" [198]—which is such an important component in the Malamudian heroine, it ceases to matter. Instead that physical lack becomes a sign which distinguishes her from her complacent social circle: "Now and then he saw her at people's houses, a star, a flower amid the full-breasted faculty wives. What they lacked she had. What she hadn't nobody needed" [236]. Yet Pauline is cognizant of what she is missing, disclosing her pregnancy with references to the emblematic significance of breasts: "Touch my breasts, they're beginning to grow.... They'll shrink after the baby is weaned but at least you'll know how I look with little ones" [365].

As with Helen Bober, a portion of Pauline's dissatisfaction and confusion can be ascribed to the father. Says Gilley with some accuracy and much hostility: "I blame her old man for this, to some extent. I understand he was a fine physician and a nice thoughtful person—I've suffered myself from his virtues—but it's plain to me that he gave her a blown-up idea of herself. She was an only child, too, be that as it may" [352-353]. Pauline's father, a strong figure principled to the point of sacrifice (a physician who lived and died the Hippocratic oath, according to Pauline), a model to whom other men can be compared and found wanting, and easily the dominant parent, endowed his daughter with a self. more suited to an ambitious, competitive male, but without the attendant, socially approved machinery for gratification or accomplishment, rather than the compliant feminine persona esteemed by the culture. That this may, in part, account for her dislocated sense of identity can be seen in the curious androgyny of both of her names before marriage—Pauline Josephson, an odd combination of male-female names and status.

We have already observed how both Gilley and Levin use Pauline in order to support their private illusions and public deceptions. For Gilley, *his* Pauline, by right of the marriage contract, is necessary to sustain the paradisal image. Although he is aware of her faults, her unhappiness, her psychic discomforts, he nonetheless wishes the marriage to continue. This, at least, permits him to assign culpability for any failure to the inappropriate feminine disaffection of an Eve foolish enough to find the Garden inhibiting. Levin wants Pauline because she represents LOVE—the romantic encounter in the Adamic woods, and the hope of renewal in the ideal of family: "In his thoughts he crossed the street and entered his house. She was waiting for him. They ate together, then when the kids were in bed, talked, read, listened to music. They went to bed and made love without ache or fear—was there ever such a life? Anyway, it was love and he had it, until he was standing alone across the street as she lay in bed with a stranger . . ." [243]. However, when Pauline ceases to be the "mistress of a quick lay" [247], when she can no longer achieve immediate sexual satisfaction because the complications of adultery no longer heighten passion but intensify guilt, he gives her up; a decision reinforced by the discovery that Levin-Adam was not her first lover, an affront not only to his masculinity, but to his idealism, which had exalted Pauline and romance in equal measure. What preserves Levin as a moral man, then, is not simply ethical belief. His rejection of Pauline is also based on what he perceives to be an undermining of his male pride. Having made of Pauline an exalted romantic ideal, he is disappointed to find out that she is only human.

Pauline, loving Levin and believing in returned love, wants a divorce in spite of the problems which she knows would ensue. She does not realize that his declaration was made to a fantasy Pauline constructed to meet Levin's subconscious desires. When she re-enters his life, expecting him to honor his pledge, it is at a time when such action would erode his position as the reformer and the man of virtue in the departmental election. His impulse is, not unexpectedly, to avoid, to evade, to run, because the campaign, embodying his future, is more important. Besides, by choosing to follow her own inclinations into a prior involvement with Leo Duffy, Pauline has betrayed him as she has deceived her husband. Only when he recognizes that her affair with Duffy is independent of her feeling for him rather than an attack on his maleness, and that his redemption lies in relearning to love the actual, can he confront and acknowledge his duty.

Another element of Pauline's ambivalent character is the extent to which she accepts Gerald's, and therefore society's, analysis of her failures as a woman. Even though she is uncomfortable with feminine stereotypes, the civilization presents her with no alternatives but to adopt another's definition of her identity. She is not a *good* wife, if *good* means accommodating, obedient, happy. And she feels guilty that she is not because she has been taught by history and culture that female selfhood depends on the cleanliness of the home and the quality of the dinner. When Gerald informs Levin that Pauline is a poor housekeeper, it is meant as a severe condemnation of her lack of true womanliness:

> "If you happen to want someone who is a good housekeeper and will keep the house as neat and orderly as I've seen your office—I'm not talking about those fireballs who do canning, baking, gardening, civic activities, refinishing furniture, bean picking in

summer, and play tennis besides keeping up the usual household chores—I'm talking about a reduced scale of domestic efficiency—well, you'd better forget it. . . . She doesn't care for housework—it bores her, and even on days she is concentrating on getting it done, her resistance to it cuts down on her accomplishment" [354].

Notice how conventional is his list of domestic virtues.

Pauline is also acutely sensitive about her inadequacies as a mother, feelings confirmed by her adultery which entails frequent absences if she is to be with her lover. Since she believes she is not satisfying her primary function, nor are her children the models of perfection that children are supposed to be, guilt begets guilt. Perhaps this is why it is so critical to Pauline that she retain custody of Erik and Mary, not biologically hers. Their presence re-establishes her sense of natural purpose.

Her sexual fatigue is a worse failing because it is the ultimate denial of her femininity: "Sometimes I get so tired of sex. . . . Please don't worry. I go through these periods. I was in a bad period with Gerald just before the first time with you" [249].

Unhappy as she may be, Pauline is allowed no other viable outlet for her discontents than the framework of pre-existing stereotypes, no doubt because Malamud basically trusts the validity of the orthodox female experience that underlies those stereotypes. Pauline does abandon the security of Eden to risk the hazards of the world, but she cannot leave alone, independently, as a wholly autonomous individual. Before she is able to depart even so uncongenial and frustrating an environment as this frontier Arcadia, she must find the right man to join her. More significantly, however, she exits pregnant, the epitome of the fulfilled woman. Whatever the constituents of her new life, it will continue to have at its traditional center the family.

The women of *The Fixer* and *The Tenants*, Raisl Bok and Irene Bell, present interesting variations on the usual pattern followed by the Malamudian woman, revealing as much by their elected absences as by the quality of their fictive presences.

They do, however, share certain similarities with their fictional sisters. Both are intelligent malcontents, unhappy not with roles they are meant to play but with a threatened or disintegrating culture that can no longer sustain the values those roles represent in the face of oncoming chaos. They are consistently, and often angrily, perceived as disappointed or ungrateful by the men in their lives. Yakov Bok says of the wandering Raisl with a resentment unmitigated by his painful confinement, "I was afraid of you. I never met anybody so dissatisfied. I am a limited man. What could I promise you?"[17] Of his white mistress, Irene Bell, Willie Spearmint/Bill Spear says that "she's a dissatisfied chick both with herself and you if you let her, and nothing much you tell her sets her right in her self-confidence...."[18] And Lesser's first impression of the same Irene Bell contains the following observation, "She wore on her face a depleted smile, sour at the edges, and troubled eyes" [42]. And like Pauline, the two women are acutely aware of their shortcomings, attributing their failures to the traditional structure of feminine experience, particularly their familial and maternal functions.

More intensely presented than in the previous novels, Raisl and Irene are treated by their men as extensions of the male will, or as objects to be used for male satisfaction or as property contracted for and owned, behavior justified in one instance (*The Fixer*) by the customs of Orthodox Judaism, in the other (*The Tenants*) by the exigencies of black-white relations. Yet Yakov Bok, Willie Spearmint, and Harry Lesser would employ women, in their life-giving capacity, as agents of personal redemption, leading these men back, however tentatively or briefly, into the complexity and pain of ordinary existence.

In an intriguing development of a technique begun in the earlier work, the explicit moral and esthetic dilemmas to be explored in *The Fixer* and *The Tenants* are illustrated, almost allegorically, by the central female character. The problem of the Jew's connection to his people's history is embodied in the wandering Raisl, a name that is an anagram of *Israel*, as James Mellard has pointed out.[19] Yakov sees this relationship with his deserting wife as an analogue to the experience of the Biblical Hosea, "the man God had commanded to marry a harlot," a story read with fascination during Bok's confinement: "The harlot, he had heard it said, was Israel, but the jealousy and anguish Hosea felt was that of a man whose wife had left his bed and board and gone whoring after strangers" [242].[20] The esthetic meditation defining artistic creation in *The Tenants* has as its nucleus Lazar Kohn's fragmented, unfinished portrait of his former mistress entitled "Woman." And finally the seemingly insoluble riddle of black, white, and Jewish interaction is embodied in Irene Bell, the lover of the black Willie Spearmint and of the white/Jewish Harry Lesser.

The most significant difference involving these two women, however, is the remarkable fact that they choose to abandon their men when they no longer seem capable of fulfilling their responsibilities within the traditional male-female contract. Raisl leaves Bok only after it is clear that she cannot have a child by him, to become pregnant thus satisfying the basic feminine impulse. She returns only when an acknowledgment of paternity is necessary for the child and for Yakov's ethical growth. Irene, also demanding family, children, life—"Does that disappoint you in me, considering how many women are going the opposite way nowadays?" [188]—departs at the point that art absorbs the energy that belongs to her. The goodby note reads "No book is as important as me" [226].

We have been looking rather generally at these "new" women who, certain at last of identities drawn in conventional terms, are determined to live those identities, unconventionally if need be. Let us be more specific.

Raisl Bok is part of the same orthodoxy that has conditioned Ida Bober. Judaism has trained her for wifehood and motherhood and for very little else. It is worth mentioning that Marfa Golov and Zina Lebedev, the two other women in *The Fixer*, are demonic representations of the feminine principle, precisely because they have distorted those traditional roles out of greed and licentiousness: Marta murdered her son in order to prevent him from revealing her thievery; Zina attempts to seduce Yakov while she is menstruating, when she is considered unclean by Jewish law. Raisl's selfhood is dependent on husband and children, so that in marrying Yakov she expects to find a self. Once a wife, secure in a position sanctioned by her society, Raisl urges Bok to leave Russia because it is an unsafe environment in which to attempt to create family. He will not or cannot leave the limited security provided by the shtetl; perhaps this is why, after five years, there are still no children.

Of course, it is Raisl who is sterile; of course, it is Raisl who is to blame for the failure of their lives; of course, it is Raisl's sin—sleeping with Yakov before marriage—that causes the difficulties in this patriarchal world: "What bothered me most were the curses and dirty names. Because I slept with you before we were married you were convinced I was sleeping with the world. . . . I was barren. I ran in every direction. I flung myself against trees. I tore at my dry breasts and cursed my empty womb. Whether I stayed or left I was useless to you . . ." [286]. It is inconceivable for Yakov to consider that the fault might be his. His masculinity, made precarious by the emasculating conditions of ghetto life, would suffer irreparable harm. In fact, it is only when he has been jailed, tortured, and made truly powerless that he can construct a self that will accept another man's child as his own, willingly, as an act asserting his humanity. Indeed when Raisl runs away, Yakov is convinced that it is with a goy, the ultimate desecration of an already failed woman. Raisl's need for maternity drives her away from the religious tradition that has given her that need as a necessary aim for female identity: "so I decided to leave. You wouldn't, so I had to. I left in desperation to change my life. I got out the only way I could. It was either that or death, one sin or worse. I chose the lesser sin" [286]. She indeed bears a child, but is forced to return to the shtetl for survival where "they blame me for your fate. I tried to take up my little dairy business but I might just as well be selling pork. The rabbi calls me to my face, pariah. The child will think his name is bastard" [289]. And as Yakov has shaved his beard as an act of defiance, Raisl no longer wears a wig, revealing the distance she has traveled from the external signs of the tradition.

In prison Raisl haunts him in dreams not so much as the errant wife, for he comes to terms with her desertion and his part in it, but as a victim of pogroms and persecution. She has ceased to be simply Raisl but has become gradually identified with the fate of the ever-suffering Jews. And when Raisl actually appears, it is to offer him a chance for redemption by acknowledging his responsibility for her as an individual woman with an illegitimate son who requires a father, and also as a symbol for the Jewish people. By accepting Raisl he accepts his Jewishness in the deepest sense, and by admitting paternity he re-enters life, for his son is Chaim, a name the root of which is, in fact, the Hebrew word for life. Without Raisl, Bok would be trapped in the solipsistic prison of denial, rejecting not only his Jewish identity, but history as well. In this respect she is not unlike Isabella del Dongo/della Seta, "The Lady of the Lake,"[21] false aristocrat and true Jew, whose function is to force Henry Levin/Freeman to confront his rejected past. In this instance, however, there is failure, and Isabella as well as love disappear, permanently, one supposes, from Levin/Freeman's life.

The Tenants presents a complex triangle of the exploited, where only the woman retains a sense of autonomy and demonstrates the possibility of an integrated self. Irene Bell, an ironic bringer of peace, whose last name further suggests her status as sexual receptacle, seems at first to exist as others see her.

Without a developed ego of her own, she becomes whatever men want her to be. As she says, "I wanted to act mainly so that I could skip being myself" [118].

To Willie she is "my true bitch" [167], a part of the white world he can control and use, as white men have used black women for centuries. Indeed, Willie Spearmint who becomes the phallic Bill Spear, apparently sees all women as exploitable "meat." He must define females sexually because that is the only way he can control and manipulate them, women being the single minority group over whom everyone and anyone can exercise power. To acknowledge them as thinking and feeling creatures is to endow them with an identity capable of challenging Willie's own. That is why the black's rhetoric is filled with so many of those degrading descriptive terms that label women as less than human. It is also why he neglects to introduce Irene by name the first time she and Harry Lesser meet, an insult that Irene recognizes for what it is: by depriving her of a name, he deprives her of a self. He believes that he has shaped Irene, molded her into his ideal of the feminine, a sweet lay who "couldn't even fuck before I taught her" [167]. That she could not do even that without his instruction not only further demeans Irene as a woman, but also reinforces an imagined mastery over the white environment. He claims:

> "She was a fucked-up nigger-struck chick when I took her on. She had nothing she believed in herself. I straightened her out in the main ways because I gave her an example, that I believed in my blackness."
> "What does she believe in now?"
> "Me more than herself, and sometimes she believes in God, which I don't" [99].

Willie utilizes Irene's body at his convenience, and ignores her when he is writing because she drains his vigor. And she is to be dismissed when her white womanhood makes her an awkward possession. But to lose her, especially to the white Jew, the published writer Lesser, means that he has lost a portion of his masculinity. For Willie, Irene's black hair has been dyed blond, the nails bitten to the quick, her eyebrows plucked out, a living stereotype. He permits only a picture of a black Jesus in her apartment. And he is quite capable of beating her, since she belongs to him.

When Harry Lesser first begins his involvement with blacks,

his desire is for a black woman—"He had never slept with a black girl" [37]—because fantasy dictates that she is the essence of sexuality. Instead, with an ironic twist, reality produces the frigid Mary Kettlesmith. Having been raped as a child, she must act her orgasm rather than experience it. With further irony, Mary appears as Lesser's somewhat reluctant, pregnant bride in his climactic hymeneal vision. And when he falls in love with Irene, it is because she is Willie's girl, as he calls her, not Irene Bell, an autonomous individual, a fact she is astute enough to recognize as part of her appeal. Lesser also makes it quite clear that he has no intention of sharing her with his black double. Harry, in fact, is glad to have taken her away from Willie, since it allows him to reassert his manhood. Irene has drawn the isolated, reluctant author back into life, back into feeling. She is almost a therapeutic aid to his writing: ". . . he felt a fluent breadth to his emotions, a sense of open sea beyond, though he didn't kid himself about objective freedom in the world he lived in.... Because of Irene he lived now with a feeling of more variously possible possibilities, an optimism that boiled up imagination. Love's doing. It helped him write freely and well after having had to press for a while. And when you were writing well that was your future" [151].

Like Willie, Harry utilizes Irene's body at his convenience, and ignores her when he is writing, because she saps his vitality. For Harry, Irene alters her physical self. Her beauty becomes more naturally and perhaps more traditionally feminine. Her hair returns to its original color—Lesser's first demand when they began their relationship, as if to distinguish his Irene from Willie's Irene. Her nails grow long. Her eyebrows grow back. Neither Willie nor Lesser can perceive Irene except as an embodiment of their respective fantasies of woman.

Irene, however, is a person of great strength, whatever her neuroses, doubts, and insecurities may be. She knows and understands herself, even if she does not always like what she sees. More to the point, she knows and understands both Willie and Harry, why they want her, and why they need her. Curiously, she is the only character in any of the novels until *Dubin's Lives* to have undergone psychoanalysis, which may account for her sharp self-awareness. Irene knows what she has been:

> "Willie and I met three years ago—that was about a year and a
> half after I'd quit college to try to be an actress. Not that I was

much of one but the idea of it had become an obsession. My God, what a batty girl I was...."

"You look like an actress but you don't playact."

"I used to an awful lot. Anyway, what it amounted to is acting as a means of getting away from myself. I was fucked-up kid, I drew men like flies and slept around till I began to wake up frightened" [117-118].

She is grateful to Willie for what he has done for her, is upset at having hurt him, but is quite capable of leaving him for Lesser when Willie's care and concern begin going into his writing. By the time she enters the relationship with Lesser, she knows what she wants: a family, children, a home. And when Harry becomes imprisoned in rewriting the book that Willie destroyed, she is also able to leave him for San Francisco and a new life. The world of the artist, or perhaps the world of the failed artist has no room in it for living, as the next chapter will attempt to show.

Malamud's women are motivated by a conservative vision of the feminine experience and a conventional definition of their roles in society: a woman's function is to create and preserve the family as primary social unit. Though they are frequently dissatisfied and often unhappy, they do not reject the stereotypes because beneath the stereotypes lie certain truths about female identity, at least as perceived by a male author. That they have not been given suitable alternatives is indisputable, but equally to the point is that Malamud has not felt the need to provide them with such alternatives. In the last analysis, Malamud's claims for women are traditional, but impressive nonetheless—women are for life, even though civilization increasingly seems to deny the value of that life and is reluctant to maintain the societal machinery that is required to encourage its fulfillment.

If Malamud's women affirm the vitality of existence, his portraits of artists, as will be shown in the next chapter, offer more ambiguous solutions to the problems incurred by the need to work creatively and the demand to live joyfully.

THE BROADER CANVAS

Malamud, Art, and the Artist

As we have seen, Bernard Malamud is clearly not a social critic in the traditional sense of the term. He does not present an institutional or societal cross-section for dramatization and analysis, nor would he want to be regarded as an ideologue or propagandist; as the author himself has said, "Artists cannot be ministers. As soon as they attempt it, they destroy their artistry."[1] However, his undoubted concern with the underlying forces that determine the quality of a civilization has led him to portray not only the confrontational psychology controlling American racial encounters and to depict the mythos of the female and the position of women in various communal situations, but also to consider the meaning and function of art in society and the role of the artist in a given culture.

Malamud has endowed art and the creators of art with enormous, perhaps even godlike, power: "The purpose of the writer is to keep civilization from destroying itself."[2] Often his characters echo this exalted notion of the artist as the possessor of necessary truths about the human condition which must be communicated to the public in order to insure their survival as sentient individuals and to guarantee the survival of mankind: "A writer writes so people don't forget that they are human. He shows us the conditions that exist. He organizes for us the meaning of our lives so it is clear to our eyes. That's why he writes it...."[3] Even so early a work as *The Assistant*, with seemingly little to do with art or artists, reflects the elevated status of creative effort, in this case literature, since Helen Bober's love of books subtly modifies the barren environment of the novel, altering her feelings for Frank Alpine and establishing the bases upon which the relationship grows. It is significant that it is the library, representing both security and liberation, that has been chosen for their meeting place: "That they were meeting among books relieved her doubt, as if she believed, what possible wrong can I do among books, what possible harm can come to me here?"[4] For Helen, her novels—*Madame Bovary, The Idiot, Anna Karenina, Crime and Punishment*—embody deeper truths about experience than Frank's biographies, which purport to explain the behavior of *real* people. Frank is aware of Helen's humility in the face of such art, an attitude that may possibly reflect Malamud's own sentiments: "He noticed she handled each yellow-paged volume as though she were holding in her respectful hands the works of God Almighty. As if—according to her—you could read in them everything you couldn't afford not to know—the Truth about Life" [106].

As literature can reveal, so too can it also teach certain kinds of personal psychological truths. It is Frank's reading of *Crime and Punishment*, for example, that provides one source of his growing recognition concerning the quality of his past and the nature of his immediate existence: "He felt, in places in the book, even when it excited him, as if his face had been shoved into dirty water in the gutter; in other places, as if he had been on a drunk for a month. He was glad when he finished the book ..." [107].

Another element present in Malamud's attitudes toward the fictive word and the printed page as they appear in *The Assistant* is the extent to which an open responsiveness to literature becomes the gauge of moral sensitivity. Those characters who disregard or misuse art's power are emotionally limited: Nat Pearl who prefers his fat law books, his father who enjoys his racing form, and Ida Bober who resents Helen's absorption in reading because it diminishes her value on the marriage market. A more important literary indicator of this narrowness is the way in which Malamud discloses Helen's reluctance to absolve Frank. This disturbing lack of forgiveness, perceived by Malamud as a major flaw in her character, is expressed by what Frank sees as her

apparent inability to understand what she has read: "Those books
you once gave me to read . . . did you understand them yourself?"
[234]. And the development of Frank's ethical sensitivity is
emphasized by his choice of reading material: "To keep from
getting nervous he took out a book he was reading. It was the
Bible and he sometimes thought there were parts of it he could
have written himself" [245].

Yet there are several indications of a curiously pervasive
ambivalence inherent in Malamud's delineation of the artist. His
painters and writers are shown to be trapped in an especially
neurotic, often paralyzing, denial of another's needs. In fact, the
only use that human beings have is to provide grist for the
creative mill. The artist, enamored by the desire not simply to
create but to create perfection, is also someone who has difficulty
in distinguishing between the imperatives of art and the demands
of life, with the requirements of the former taking precedence.
Indeed, involvement in artistic effort is frequently a way of
avoiding entry into an active participation in life. Even in *The
Assistant*, Helen's carefully constructed world of books functions
as protection against the claims of humanity as well as an
invitation to experience. And an artist must be willing to sacrifice
economic security if he is to retain his integrity as a creator. True
artists starve; they do not succeed: "What can a starving writer give
her? A decent home? Can he afford to have children? Will he
consider her first when she needs him . . .? I want her to have a
future, not a cold water flat with a poor man."[5] Certainly artists
have no commitments to the bourgeois ideas of continuity and
family so necessary for the coherence and stability of the
Malamudian universe. But more to the point, the spokesmen for
Malamud's extravagant beliefs in the curative and civilizing
effects of art are, as a rule, *failed* artists. If they have known any
kind of artistic success, it has been transient and self-destructive,
or, as with Arthur Fidelman in *Pictures of Fidelman*, in an allied
craft such as the decorative *and* utilitarian glassblowing.

Three distinct forces shape and condition these seemingly
contradictory impulses present in Malamud's viewpoints about
art and artists as illustrated in his work: the preconceptions of the
Jewish heritage toward the various forms of artistic endeavor; the
romantic and post-romantic conceptions of art and its creators;
and the attitudes of American society concerning the value of
imaginative ability, genius, and skill.

Orthodox Jewish tradition and the inheritance of the Yiddish writer reveal the ambiguous position of both art and the artist within the society of the ghetto. In the communities which sheltered Eastern European Jewry, where all energies were devoted to the complicated tasks of survival, the effort expended in creating imaginative literature necessitated justification. The artist would be tolerated only if his work retained a moral premise or exhibited a strong dedication to the humane ethics of Judaism:

> Among the Eastern European Jews the taste for imaginative literature did not come easily or quickly. . . . Literature had to be *justified*, it had to be assigned a moral sanction. . . . There is hardly a Yiddish writer of any significance whose work is not imbued with this fundamental urge to portray Jewish life with the most uncompromising realism and yet to transcend the terms of the portrayal. . . . Simply to survive . . . Yiddish literature had to cling to the theme of historical idealism.[6]

The independence of art does not seem to have been an issue. And the conviction that art could and should exist for its own sake, as form without regard to content, would have been greeted with not a little skepticism. Leslie Fiedler is not far wrong when he asserts that "our writers have learned their function: to read in the dream of the present, the past which is always to come. . . . For though the means of the Jewish-American writers . . . are poetic and fictional, their ends are therapeutic and prophetic."[7]

This quasi-didactic sensibility can easily be discerned in Malamud's assertions about the objectives in his own art: "My premise is that we will not destroy each other. My premise is that we will live on. We will seek a better life. We may not become better, but at least we will seek betterment. My premise is for humanism—and against nihilism. And that is what I put in my writings."[8] However, there is a further complication that might thwart the inventive abilities of the talented, arising out of the heritage of religious orthodoxy which forbids the making of graven images: literature, contingent on verbal agility and the written word, is an acceptable imaginative mode; but the Biblical injunction may evoke in the pictorial artist a not inconsiderable guilt, a significant motif in the surreal fifth section of *Pictures of Fidelman*, where the would-be painter and disciple is transformed into Judas, selling the savior Susskind for the price of paint, brushes, and canvas.

The assumption of the artist's uniqueness, the reinvigorated

idea of the artist as visionary, the belief in the artist as Faustian
creator, are among the first principles of a nineteenth- and
twentieth-century romanticism (reinforced by elements of Freudian psychology and Jungian archetypes) that has been most
influential in producing the contemporary image of the artist-
figure and all its attached symbolic ramifications. To the
Romantics and their present-day literary and aesthetic heirs, the
artist is not just the sensitive one exquisitely attuned to the secrets
of the heart. Nor is he simply the seer able to penetrate the masks
to reach the hidden, vulnerable self. He is Prometheus, as well as
Faust, whose art is the stolen fire of the gods; and Daedalus, that
old artificer, making visible the labyrinthine unconscious; and
also Orpheus, apostle of Dionysos, singer of the life force whose
artistic power is rooted in primal sexual energy.[9] It is worth
noting at this point the frequency with which Malamud links the
vocabulary of artistic creativity and the language of sexual
potency in his fiction about art and artists.

In the romantic pantheon, the artist becomes the heroic rebel.
By his commitment to the truths of the imagination, by his
adherence to the sanctity of the self, by his insistence on placing
the value of creativity above material gain, the artist is inevitably
hostile to a greedy, ruthless, oppressive, and philistine society. As
the most profound of revolutionaries, he is "that curiously
disinterested, almost diabolical human phenomenon, beyond the
normal bounds of social judgment, dedicated to the morals not of
his time but of his art. He is the hero of the way of thought—
single-hearted, courageous, and full of faith that the truth, as he
finds it, shall make us free."[10]

If the past history of Eastern European Judaism and
romantic aesthetic philosophy offer dissimilar yet oddly congruent
pictures of the artist and his endeavors, then his situation in
America emphasizes the confusions of purpose and worth.
America places the artist in a particularly anomalous position. As
a manufacturer, he is suspect because his product cannot be
quantified, measured, priced, and sold by the standard techniques
of a culture dominated by the economic arrangements of the
marketplace. Art as such has no "use" in a civilization that values
the pragmatic and the functional.[11]

It was Van Wyck Brooks who perceived in 1918 that the
community attitudes toward the creative personality which
dominate Edgar Lee Masters's paradigmatic small town were
merely a reflection of national values. Spoon River, he says, is

a community . . . which has for so many generations cherished and cultivated its animosity towards all those non-utilitarian elements in the human heart that retard the successful pursuit of the main chance that it has reduced itself to a spiritual desert. . . . Poets, painters, philosophers, men of science and religion, are all to be found stunted, starved, thwarted, embittered, prevented from taking even the first step in self-development, in this amazing microcosm of our society. . . .[12]

A not unsimilar idea is voiced by M. L. Rosenthal almost half a century later: "Without a nourishing atmosphere of reciprocal influence between practical power and practical human concerns on the one hand, and intellect and sensibility on the other, can we ever control the conditions that have made this the bloodiest century in history when it might have been the most beautiful?"[13]

American culture demands that art be utilitarian in much the same way that the Jewish tradition requires an ethical rationale. In order to be suitable for national consumption, art must somehow be serviceable. As Benjamin Franklin remarked early in the country's history, "Nothing is good or beautiful . . . but in the measure that is useful. . . ."[14] Tocqueville also notes with his usual acuity:

> It would be to waste time . . . if I strove to demonstrate how the general mediocrity of fortunes, the absence of superfluous wealth, the universal desire for comfort, and the constant efforts by which everyone attempts to procure it make the taste for the useful predominate over the love of the beautiful in the heart of man. Democratic nations, among whom all these things exist, will therefore cultivate the arts that serve to render life easy in preference to those whose object is to adorn it. They will habitually prefer the useful to the beautiful, and they will require that the beautiful should be useful.[15]

That men and women may choose to waste their lives engaged in fashioning the impractical is unthinkable, running against the grain of their country's puritan, pragmatic consciousness and its evangelical spirit.[16] In fact, any artist who succeeds according to the terms dictated by a democratic society is to be viewed warily by all thinking and feeling individuals, since such a person considers only two objects in order to achieve that goal:

> He strives to invent methods that may enable him not only to work better, but more quickly and more cheaply; or if he cannot succeed in that, to diminish the intrinsic quality of the thing he makes

without rendering it wholly unfit for the use for which it is intended....

In aristocracies a few great pictures are produced; in democratic countries a vast number of insignificant ones. In the former statues are raised in bronze; in the latter, they are modelled in plaster.[17]

Success obviously entails compromise and the betrayal of true artistic principles, thereby insuring a more important failure. It has been a comforting truism that the artists who prosper either financially or by accumulating the debilitating currency of fame immediately lose control of their talent which cannot possibly flourish in an atmosphere of satisfied plenty.[18]

Nor is the idea of genius particularly comfortable for a democracy to acknowledge because its very existence defeats the theory of egalitarianism. Genius presupposes an isolating difference, the possession of a unique vision, and the power of being outstanding. And if that genius serves the critical eye, as it so often does in the best of American art, rather than smug complacency, it is even more unwelcome. There is an interesting corollary here to the proposition that great art and equality do not easily mix. For the inhabitants of democratic America, the acquisition of fine art or its imitations frequently becomes the means of asserting a special, discriminating self or a distinctive identity, undermining that selfsame egalitarian impulse that would deny genius its place.

But a measure of an artist's effectiveness is inevitably the extent to which he can move an audience. And like it or not, he must at some level respond to the needs of that audience, which in this country makes specific, if unarticulated, demands that do not always insure sensitivity, greatness, or profundity:

They prefer books which may be easily procured, quickly read, and which require no learned researches to be understood. They ask for beauties self-proffered and easily enjoyed; above all, they must have what is unexpected and new. Accustomed to the struggle, the crosses, and the monotony of practical life, they require strong and rapid emotions, startling passages, truths or errors brilliant enough to rouse them up and to plunge them at once, as if by violence, into the midst of the subject.... Style will frequently be fantastic, incorrect, overburdened, and loose, almost always vehement and bold. Authors will aim at rapidity of execution more than at perfection of detail.... There will be more wit than erudition, more imagination than profundity; and literary performances will bear the marks of an untutored and rude vigor of thought, frequently of great variety and singular fecundity. The object of authors will be to astonish rather than to please, and to stir the passions more than to charm the taste.[19]

In order to explain why the dilemmas faced by Malamud's artists, characters molded by complex, often antithetical, forces, invariably produce failure, I would like to examine closely four of the author's works: the short story "Girl of My Dreams," the novels *Pictures of Fidelman* and *The Tenants*, and "Man in the Drawer" from the most recent collection, *Rembrandt's Hat*.

"Girl of My Dreams" is the first story in which a putative artist appears to deal with the conflicting claims of creativity, imagination, and life. In its depiction of Mitka's fantasies, Olga's nurturing activity, and Mrs. Lutz's needs, the tale is an elementary version of the paradigm that recurs in the more complex fables, *Pictures of Fidelman* and *The Tenants*.

The story opens in autumn, that season of dying creativity and an apt natural analogue reinforcing the theme of artistic failure, and with an act of destruction: Mitka's burning of his "heartbroken novel in the blackened bottom of Mrs. Lutz's rusty trash can in her backyard."[20] The seasonal setting, the sexual vocabulary, the thanatotic imagery emphasize the loss of Mitka's inventive capacity and comment on the negation of his will to experience, reflecting the belief that the artist's genius resides in the same generative force that drives human sexuality and controls time's natural cycles:

> In the late fall . . . the novel had returned to stay and he had hurled it into a barrel burning autumn leaves, stirring the mess with a long length of pipe, to get the inner sheets afire. Overhead a few dead apples hung like forgotten Christmas ornaments upon the leafless tree. The sparks, as he stirred, flew to the apples, the withered fruit representing not only creation gone for nothing (three long years), but all his hopes, and the proud ideas he had given his book . . . [27].

Mitka can no longer taste the fruit of the Tree of Knowledge. And his artistic defeat is seen also as the defeat of Eros, as Mitka quite self-consciously points out: "Sterile writer seeking end of sterility through satisfying epistolary intercourse with lady writer" [34]. Nor does he appear to be tempted initially by the sexual morsels proffered by his landlady Mrs. Lutz. In fact, his inability to create is described as a self-induced miscarriage—"and Mitka, although not a sentimentalist, felt as if he had burned . . . an everlasting hollow in himself" [27-28]—while he calls his second novel an abortion. There seems to be a suggestion here (to be repeated in both *Pictures of Fidelman* and *The Tenants*) that art as a male's pursuit functions somehow as compensation for the biological inability to bear children.

If one accepts the equation that the work is the man, as Mitka apparently does, then to reject his novel is not just a judgment on his worth as an individual. It is also a denial of his very existence. That Malamud has mixed feelings about such an equation is clear since the artists in his fiction who express that particular axiom and are obsessed by it usually do not succeed either in their vocation or as human beings. Without his writing to give him identity, Mitka is reduced to a silent nullity who "had lost the belief that anything he said could make significant meaning . . ." [28]. He retreats from even the most elementary encounters with the world, symbolized in this instance by Mrs. Lutz's importunities to eat, into a solipsistic existence behind the locked doors of his writing chamber, the bare room that defines the self. As it turns out, this attempt at withdrawal from humanity is the original sin for any of Malamud's would-be creators, from Mitka to Arthur Fidelman to Harry Lesser and Willie Spearmint. Such willed isolation reveals an egoist who regards society and its inhabitants as mere projections of the artistic imagination, useful only insofar as they provide material for works planned or in progress. Is this not the explanation given for Mitka's letters to Madeleine Thorn?—"Ultimately he admitted that he wrote because he couldn't do the other kind of writing. . . . Mitka sensed that although he had vowed never to go back to it, he hoped the correspondence would return him to his abandoned book. . . . Clearly then, he was trying with these letters to put an end to the hatred of self for not working, for having no ideas, for cutting himself off from them. Ah, Mitka. He sighed at this weakness, to depend on others" [34]. His concern for Madeleine Thorn is as an instrument to reactivate his creative power, the thorn to prick his inspiration. Since she exists as an extension of his fantasies, as the girl of *his dreams*, it is hardly surprising that he is devastated by her reality.

Evidently, one of the more crucial problems faced by the artist in Malamud's fiction is the discovery and choice of the appropriate source of nourishment for both spirit and talent. This, no doubt, accounts for the obvious food motif that seems at times to overwhelm the story. The rationale that underlies the use of this phagic imagery may be stated as follows: If to eat is to live, then the rejection of sustenance amounts to a denial of life, and, therefore, the destruction of art, because it is experience that nourishes imagination, not isolation from life's painful complexity. To feed solely off one's own consciousness leads not to

vision but to self-annihilation. It is plain that Mitka's reluctance
to consume Mrs. Lutz's "steaming soup . . . with soft while rolls,
calf's foot jelly, rice with tomato sauce, celery hearts, delicious
breast of chicken—beef if he preferred—and his choice of
satisfying sweets" [29], in spite of hunger, is the physical
counterpart of his inability to write and his unwillingness to join
the world. When at the story's end Mitka "realized he felt no
pangs of hunger" [41], it implies the satiation born of human
interaction and a recognition of his connection to mankind.
Compulsive Arthur Fidelman, obsessed by canvas and paint,
would later observe a similar phenomenon in "A Pimp's
Revenge"—the momentary calm induced by shopping in a
Florentine market: "Shopping for food's a blessing, he thought,
you get down to brass tacks. It makes a lot in life seem less
important, for instance painting a masterwork. He felt he needn't
paint for the rest of his life and nothing much lost. . . ."[21]

The presence of two maternal figures to feed the deprived,
barren artist—"Set Mitka adrift and he enticed somebody's
Mama" [38]—adds another significant element to the pattern of
right nurture. Even Fidelman tries, without much success, to
recapture as painted icons a mother whom he does not remember
and his mothering sister whom he has not seen in years, in order
to retrieve and renew his waning creativity; this before he meets
Beppo Fassoli, who "looked in his handsome way much like his
mother" [195], to educate him to possibility and to teach him the
immediacy of love, rather than the imposed distance of bad art.[22]
That Harry Lesser and Willie Spearmint spurn the nourishment
offered by Irene Bell illustrates the depth of their failure as writers
and bespeaks their incomplete humanity, which seems capable
only of violence and hatred.

It is Olga's role in "Girl of My Dreams" to prepare Mitka for
his return to the thorny way of the world. Selecting a pseudonym
(Madeleine Thorn) that emphasizes her awareness of life's
anguish, Olga does not merely slake his appetite, that "everlasting
hollow in himself" [28], by the gift of food: "Olga sipped her
whiskey. 'Eat, it's self-expression.' He expressed himself by
finishing off the salami, also half the loaf of bread, cheese, and
herring. His appetite grew. Searching within the bag Olga
brought out a package of sliced corned beef and a ripe pear. He
made a sandwich of the meat. On top of that the cold beer was
tasty" [39]. She reveals a past of pain, survival, and continued
artistic effort to prove to Mitka the worth of experience. And she

feeds him wisdom that will enable him to cope with life and imagination:

> "Be uphearted, not down. Work every day.... That's what I do. I've been writing for over twenty years and sometimes—for one reason or another—it gets so bad that I don't feel like going on. But what I do then is relax for a short while and then change to another story. After my juices start flowing again I go back to the other and usually that starts off once more. Or sometimes I discover that it isn't worth bothering over. After you've been writing so long as I you'll learn a system to keep yourself going. It depends on your view of life. If you're mature you'll find out how to work"[39].

Finally she leaves him with a rather specific prescription for the improvement of his soul and of his work: "Don't worry about your work, and get more fresh air. Build up your body. Good health will help your writing.... Character is what counts in the pinches, of course properly mixed with talent. When you saw me in the library and stayed I thought, there is a man of character" [40-41].

Olga is able to advise because unlike Mitka she understands the nature of reality, having mastered the distinction between life and art. The confusion of the two, and the subsequent elevation of the requirements of art above the claims of life, are the most troublesome difficulties faced by the Malamudian artist. For example, Mitka's novels are unacceptable apparently because he cannot confront experience directly, blurring meaning and intent with vague symbols: "... they were returning the MS of his novel, among other reasons—but this prevailed—because of the symbolism, the fact that it was obscure.... Yet for a year Mitka labored over a new one, up to the time of the return of the old manuscript, when, upon rereading that, then the new work, he discovered the same symbolism, more obscure than ever ..." [28].

But Mitka's inability to distinguish between imagination and existence causes a deeper bewilderment. When he encounters Madeleine Thorn's story in "The Open Globe" about the accidental destruction of a completed manuscript, he is convinced of its authenticity because he reads into it the truth of his own loss. Succumbing to the biographical fallacy, Mitka believes that the events described happened in fact to the author, that the first-person voice assumed by the writer is actual. He seems unwilling to recognize a deliberately constructed fiction until he is told: "He brayed louder the next day: there was another epistle, the story wasn't true—she had invented every word" [34]. Worse yet, he insists upon meeting Madeleine Thorn, having created his own version of her identity as he would shape a character in a novel: "Now Mitka found himself actively wondering what she looked like. Her letters showed her sensible, modest, honest but what of the human body? ... He pictured her as comely yet hefty. But what of it as long as she was womanly, intelligent, brave?" [34-35]. That reality must disappoint goes without saying, "a lone middle-aged female sat at a long table, reading. ... Hefty she was but yes, eyeglassed, and marvelously plain ..." [36]. Her name is not even the romantic Madeleine Thorn ("Mine is Olga really" [37], chosen perhaps for its harsh closeness to "ugly"). His anger, directed at the woman for not being what his imagination fashioned, is expressed in language that ironically echoes the murder of his manuscripts: "He sat sullenly, harboring murderous thoughts: to hack her to pieces and incinerate the remains in Mrs. Lutz's barrel" [37]. Olga is to blame for her human imperfections, and it is she who is responsible for his disillusionment rather than his fantasy for establishing false expectations. Mitka cannot admit that once again he has created bad art based not on experience but the solipsistic images of his enclosed consciousness.

However, by listening to Olga's recital of the narrative of her survival, Mitka is moved to acknowledge a kinship with all those who suffer and are lonely: "he pitied her, her daughter, the world. Who not?"[41]. And he learns as any artist has to that the making of images must not obscure the real, should not deny life. "Girl of My Dreams" ends in spring, season of rebirth and resurrection, closing with a vision of the hymeneal dance,[23] comedy's traditional homage to continuity: "He thought of the old girl [Mrs. Lutz]. He'd go home now and drape her from head to foot in flowing white. They would jounce together up the stairs, then (strictly a one-marriage man) he would swing her across the threshold, holding her where the fat overflowed her corset as they waltzed around his writing chamber" [41]. We do not know whether Mitka will write again, but we can suppose with some assurance that he will live.

Certain premises about art and artists embedded in "Girl of My Dreams" are clearly important to Malamud since they appear with some modification in the later work. To write or paint requires discipline and dedication but never to the point of egocentric isolation. Such withdrawal inevitably attenuates the creative impulse. The artist who views people as a reflection of his own imagination, to be used as characters, will fail because he reduces, if not eliminates, his own capacity to feel, just as he also reduces the humanity of others. The true artist must live *and* write, must experience *and* create, or else there is no art to speak of. But Mitka is a failed artist (as are Fidelman, Lesser, and Spearmint); therefore if he is foolish enough to select bad art over living in the world, he will necessarily betray his own humanity because the imperatives of existence take precedence over the demands of aesthetic invention.

Pictures of Fidelman: An Exhibition depicts in six panels the picaresque adventures of Arthur Fidelman, quixotic knight-errant (with the emphasis on the multiple significances of the word *errant*) of art, and a more complex person than Mitka. The novel is more than the portrayal of an obsessive-compulsive whose neuroses prevent the production of meaningful art.[24] Tony Tanner describes the book as an archetypal comedy of the innocent American who journeys to corrupt, decadent, and historic Europe to become an artist whose many and near-total defeats symbolically recapitulate "in quick succession...the varied experiences of a hundred years of American artistic aspirants in Europe," a man who "shows most powers of invention when it comes to finding different ways of failing in his chosen thing."[25] Fidelman travels through Rome, Milan, Florence, and Venice, cities significant in the history of art, with subtle connections to the works of Giotto, Titian, Rembrandt, Tintoretto, and Modigliani which are admired and copied by the would-be painter from America. As he experiments with criticism, imitation, forgery, reproduction, even originality, as he moves deeper into the subconscious until the surreal disintegration of "Pictures of the Artist" and the reintegration of personality that occurs in the final episode, we watch the unmaking of an artist in an inverted parody of the *Künstlerroman*. Each chapter, representing Fidelman's encounters with various facets of the creative experience, functions as indirect proof of his inability to live up to those impressive injunctions about the meaning of art stenciled on the walls of his studio in "A Pimp's Revenge":

Constable: "Painting is for me another word for feeling."

Whistler: "A masterpiece is finished from the beginning."

Pollock: "What is it that escapes me? The human? That humanity is greater than art?"

Nietzsche: "Art is not an imitation of nature but its metaphysical supplement, raised up beside it in order to overcome it."

Picasso: "People seize on painting in order to cover up their nakedness" [97].

In each written canvas, Malamud attempts to mirror in a verbal mode what Fidelman vainly tries to accomplish in his use of so many pictorial styles. It also is important that Malamud has chosen to make Fidelman a painter rather than a novelist, and the book an embodiment of the values and strategies of pictorial art, because he considers painting a general artistic paradigm, particularly useful in educating the author: "Remember what Hemingway has said, how painting teaches us to write. Painters, of necessity, have to abstract, they have to highlight, they have to compress."[26]

Fidelman begins his journey with the greedy, easy arrogance of the American who believes he need not choose between "perfection of the life, or of the work," as the book's epigraph by Yeats insists. He is to realize that to have both requires pain, sacrifice, imprisonment, and a significant lowering of ambition, experiences that our congenitally optimistic culture derides, ignores, or wants no part of.

In "Last Mohican," Arthur Fidelman appears in Rome to write a critical study of Giotto, painter of St. Francis. As "a self-confessed failure as a painter" [3], Fidelman's inventive capacities are, perforce, limited; therefore his access to creativity must be associational, coming at the secondary level as criticism or in the analysis of another's genius. Perhaps if he can uncover the secrets of Giotto's brilliance and master his techniques he may be able to reinvigorate his lost talent. In any case, to be able to organize and define Giotto's imagination at all indicates skill, intelligence, and percipience on Fidelman's part. His completed first chapter, that tangible sign of ego and identity, even has the power to resurrect the painter himself, "the precious thing he had created...the long diligent labor, how painstakingly he had built each idea, how cleverly mastered problems of order, form, how impressive the finished product, Giotto reborn!" [31].

But Fidelman, in "his gum-soled oxblood shoes, a tweed suit he had on despite the late-September sun slanting hot in the Roman sky" [3], is alien to the spirit of the city and its art. He perceives his task as regulating the flow of history, domesticating the patterns of genius, and controlling the movement of life through a rigid work schedule that drains joy, spontaneity, and true comprehension from his study of Giotto and his stay in Rome, and acts as a protection against and an evasion of human encounters:

He got himself quickly and tightly organized. He was always concerned with not wasting time, as if it were his only wealth... and he soon arranged a schedule that made the most of his working hours. Mornings he usually visited the Italian libraries, searching their catalogues and archives, read in poor light, and made profuse notes. He napped for an hour after lunch, then at four, when the churches and museums were re-opening, hurried off to them with lists of frescoes and paintings he must see [11].

The appreciation of history as "mysterious, the remembrance of things unknown... in a way a sensuous experience" [12] that is part of Rome's ambience, belongs to the creative artist's sensibility, not the critic's. And the demands of another, in this case the *luftmensch* Susskind, are perceived as distracting intrusions, diverting his attention from the urgencies of his research.

Susskind, perennial exile, refugee even from Israel, living testimony to the ongoing Diaspora, exists to test Fidelman's capacity for involvement, to renew his diminished emotional vitality, and to enlarge his limited humanity. As the traditional figure of the *schnorrer* (or beggar),[27] Susskind's importuning presence requires that the American choose between his responsibilities as a man and his profession as a critic. When this student of Giotto makes the wrong moral choice, refusing the beggar his suit, Susskind steals the manuscript. How can an individual who is incapable of giving possibly understand the compassionate painter of "The Life of St. Francis"? To know methodology is not necessarily to apprehend essence.

Deprived of the ego that the stolen chapter confirmed, Fidelman's tightly controlled personality disintegrates because it lacks a focusing center. Without an internalized sense of identity and robbed of the external proof of his existence and worth, Fidelman can no longer write:

> Time went without work, without accomplishment. To put an end to this appalling waste Fidelman tried to force himself back into his routine research and picture viewing.... He kept his eyes glued to paper, sitting steadfastly at his desk in an attempt to re-create his initial chapter, because he was lost without a beginning. He tried writing the second chapter from notes in his possession but it had come to nothing. Always Fidelman needed something solid behind him before he could advance, some worthwhile accomplishment upon which to build another. He worked late but his mood, or inspiration, or whatever it was, had deserted him, leaving him with growing anxiety, almost disorientation; of not knowing—it seemed to him for the first time in months—what he must do next, a feeling that was torture [24-25].

Because he has defined being exclusively, solely as the single-minded commitment to create a masterwork, to shape perfection somehow, when the terms of the definition are radically altered by circumstances outside the dominion of his ordering principle, Fidelman cannot easily adapt. In his own eyes he has become a purposeless cipher.

As he begins to search through the Roman ghetto and the Jewish cemetery for the vanished Susskind in order to retrieve the stolen chapter that creates Fidelman, the bereft critic enters the human world of pain and recovers the anguish of history:

> In the cemetery, deserted on the Sabbath...Fidelman went among the graves, reading legends on tombstones....Many were burial places, he read on the stained stones, of those who, for one reason or another, had died in the late large war. Among them was an empty place, it said on a marble slab lying on the ground, for "My beloved father/ Betrayed by the damned Fascists/ Murdered at Auschwitz by the barbarous Nazis/ *O Crimine Orribile*" [29-30].

Confronted by such a devastating historical catastrophe, the still unenlightened Fidelman responds, "But no Susskind" [30]. He has not yet escaped the tyranny of his own circumscribed view of experience contingent on the superiority of art over life.

After entering Susskind's hovel, "pitch-black, freezing cave" [35] whose location Fidelman discovers by following the refugee as Susskind once followed him, he manages to step outside the confines of his own restricted consciousness to acknowledge the environment of another individual. As a consequence of this visit, from which Fidelman "never fully recovered" [35], he has a final, absolving vision:

> The fresco...revealed this saint in fading blue, the sky flowing from his head, handing an old knight in a thin red robe his gold cloak. Nearby stood a humble horse and two stone hills.
> Giotto. San Francesco dona le vesti al cavaliere povero.
> Fidelman awoke running [36].

He recognizes, at last, that in order to know the soul of the painter, one must experience the spirit of the subject; he will give Susskind his blue gabardine suit, regain his manuscript, and begin again with wisdom. But his revelation may have come too late to transform Fidelman's perceptions, as the equivocal ending would indicate. Susskind, having burned the chapter—"I did you a favor....The words were there but the spirit was missing" [37]—escapes Fidelman's temporary rage. The critic is left without his manuscript, still holding Susskind's gift in an unfinished act of charity, shouting and half sobbing, "Susskind, come back.... The suit is yours. All is forgiven" [37]. Given the incompleteness of Fidelman's redemptive exercise, the permanence of his generous impulse and the durability of his new knowledge may be questioned.

Fidelman (like Mitka and the other artists in Malamud's fiction) must continue to learn how to separate the I of the self and the eye of art. And in the remaining pictures of Fidelman, this educational process eventually leads to the abandonment of the world of art for the risks, chances, and surprises of experience.

In "Still Life," the next canvas in Malamud's gallery, Arthur Fidelman has resumed painting, "having recalled dreams he had dreamed were dead" [39], perhaps as a result of the partial discovery made with Susskind's help in "Last Mohican" about the nature of community and human responsibility. He works in a studio he rents from and shares with the neurotic *pittrice* Annamaria Oliovino. That his re-entry into the world of art may have been a mistake based on the imperfect understanding of his earlier Roman adventure and simply another occasion for Fidelman's ambiguous failure is indicated by the story's title: "Still Life," a representation chiefly of inanimate objects, suggesting not only the promise of survival but also implying death-in-life, a factor strongly emphasized by the repeated use throughout of the Italian equivalent, *natura morta*.

Because of Fidelman's limitations and Annamaria's hysteria, the shared studio becomes a battleground, an arena for the exercise of power, rather than a suitable home for the making of art. Debasing himself to obtain the frigid Annamaria, lending money, being manipulated, giving in order to possess, he unlearns Susskind's lesson—"He was by now giving her presents —tubes of paints, the best brushes, a few yards of Belgian linen, which she accepted without comment; she also borrowed small sums, nothing startling—a hundred lire today, five hundred tomorrow.... Fidelman, though always worried about money, assented. He would give his last lire to lie on her soft belly, but she offered niente, not so much as a caress—" [50-51]. Fidelman loses his essential maleness, his sexual potency, and his creative identity.

On the other hand, Annamaria, mediocre at best ("But she's a fake" [62], says a fellow-artist), turns out canvases with speed, gimmickry, and lack of talent:

She went on with her lyric abstractions based on the theme of a hidden cross.... Having mixed coffee grounds, sparkling bits of crushed mirror, and ground sea shells, she blew the dust on mucilaged paper.... She composed collages of rags and toilet paper. After a dozen linear studies... she experimented with gold leaf sprayed with umber, the whole while wet drawn in long undulations with a fine comb... when she had temporarily run out of new ideas she did a mythological bull in red clay . . . afterwards returning to natura morta with bunches of bananas; then self-portraits [48-49].

Art becomes merely a search for the novel, with little need for explanation; after all "who can explain art" [43], she says impatiently. The *pittrice* uses this fertility, rooted in her repressed sexuality, to humiliate Fidelman who works with difficulty and few ideas. She expresses her contempt for his imagination by freely editing his compositions: "She changed lines and altered figures, or swabbed over whole compositions that didn't appeal to her. There was not much that did, but Fidelman was grateful for any attention she gave his work, and even kept at it to incite her criticism" [49]. All her angers and hostility are directed toward the grovelling Fidelman, whom she treats as less than a man and less than an artist, especially after his failure to consummate intercourse. Note again the insistent connection between Eros and the inventive impulse.

Under such conditions, art is employed as a means of seduction and as an agent of flattery: "Thinking it might please her . . . the art student experimented with some of the things Annamaria had done—spontaneous holes, for instance, several studies of 'Lines Ascending,' and two lyrical abstract expressionistic pieces based on, interwoven with, and ultimately concealing a Star of David, although for these attempts he soon discovered he had earned, instead of her good will, an increased measure of scorn" [50]. Or it is a way of controlling private demons and stealing souls: "What more intimate possession of a woman! He would paint her, whether permitted or not, posed or not—she was his to paint.... Maybe something will come, after all, of my love for her" [54]. Finally, it is a tool of mocking laughter: "But Annamaria's drawing was representational, not Fidelman although of course inspired by him: A gigantic funereal phallus that resembled a broken-backed snake" [63]. In "Still Life," art is meant to satisfy neurotic compulsion; it rarely arises out of true imaginative need.

This story also introduces a discussion of what constitutes

originality, a theme which takes on an increasing resonance and
added complexity in the later episodes of Fidelman's creative
biography. Arthur Fidelman proves to be a derivative painter
with an imitative vision, whose imagination is a storehouse of the
previously done:

> Every time he looked at unpainted canvas he saw harlequins,
> whores, tragic kings, fragmented musicians, the sick and the dread.
> Still, tradition was tradition.... Since he had always loved art
> history he considered embarking on a "Mother and Child".... Or
> maybe a moving "Pietà," the dead son's body held like a broken
> wave in mama's frail arms? A curse on art history.... Sometimes
> I'd like to forget every picture I've seen, Fidelman thought [47-48].

In "Naked Nude" so that he may properly copy Titian's "Venus
of Urbino," he undertakes a study of the history of the female
form "from the Esquiline goddess to 'Les Demoiselles d'Avig-
non'" [82] until he prefers the duplicate to the genius of Titian.
The motif is further elaborated in "A Pimp's Revenge" where the
disillusioned painter says, "That's my trouble, everything's been
done or is otherwise out of style—cubism, surrealism, action
painting. If I could only guess what's next" [96]. The fifth
section, "Pictures of the Artist," leads immediately into the
accumulated detritus of the artist's unconscious, inhabited by
Rembrandt, Modigliani, Courbet, Murillo, Van Leyden, Renoir,
Soutine, Bonnard—an endless list of Fidelman's sources. And in
the final story, he attempts in glass to re-create, to re-produce.[28]
And whenever Fidelman talks about art, he either lapses into
meaningless professional jargon, or sounds like an encyclopedia
—as if he were too frightened to confront his own lack of vision,
his own emptiness:

> "This is a spray job, an undercoating of apple-green acrylic
> resin, then a haphazard haze of indigo, creating a mood and a half
> before I applied a reconciling rose in varying values and
> intensities. Note how the base colors, invading without being
> totally visible, infect the rose so that it's both present and you
> might say evanescing.... We're dealing with certain kinds of
> essences.... Frankly the inspiration is Rothko but I learned a trick
> or two from some of the things I've seen in *Art News* done by my
> contemporaries" [195-196].

Among such a welter of styles and talents, perhaps originality
is no longer possible. Or perhaps, as Angelo, the fat *padrone* of
"Naked Nude," claims, there is no such thing as originality if it is
defined simply as doing something new: "Didn't he [Titian] steal

the figure of the Urbino from Georgione? Didn't Rubens steal the
Andrian nude from Tiziano? Art steals and so does everybody
else" [77-78]. It is more likely, however, that Fidelman is
incapable of fashioning a work of lasting value because he has
lost touch with the roots of humanity and the basis of creativity in
the inchoate energy of the unconscious.

Fidelman manages to create works of art that are total
integrations of experience and perception on only two occasions;
and in each of these cases, the painting is a felt response to his
immediate psychic condition, not an intellectual exercise.[29] These
works are destroyed because Fidelman has not absorbed Whistler's
advice that "A masterpiece is finished from the beginning" [97]
and foolishly seeks to make his painting "perfect." Then in "The
Glass Blower of Venice," Fidelman, finally having learned love,
is at last able to shape a simple glass bowl, "severe and
graceful.... It held the clear light and even seemed to listen"
[208], the ideal of form. This time, however, it is not ruined by
Fidelman's compulsiveness, it is stolen (echoing Susskind's theft
of the failed manuscript). But by the end of the novel, Fidelman's
identity is not damaged by the disappearance of the bowl (as it
was when his chapter was taken at the beginning of the novel), for
he no longer requires tangible proof of his worth as a man. Art no
longer exercises its perverse tyranny over the restored Fidelman.

As a story about art forgery, "Naked Nude" confronts more
directly various aspects of the dilemmas faced by Fidelman in
earlier episodes: the notion that all art, even great art, is
unoriginal and to some degree fraudulent, the copy of a copy; the
question of what constitutes a masterpiece; the nature of the
artist's ego, even though the artist is mediocre and the ego second-
rate; and finally, the problem of discriminating between the self
and the work, if, in fact, such distinctions can or should be made.
Arthur Fidelman, in a further decline from indifferent painter to
apprentice forger, must copy Titian's "Venus of Urbino" in order
to win release from imprisonment, psychological as well as
actual.

Fidelman's initial reaction to Angelo's proposition is
singularly inappropriate, given his own situation as a prisoner in
a Milanese brothel, and the fact that his survival is at stake; but it
does reflect his elevated, romantic, quasi-religious attitude
towards art, as well as the state of his self-involved ego: "Am I
worthy? Can I do it? Do I dare?" [76]. He is hesitant because he
considers the theft of another painter's ideas and work as "sort of

desecration" [78]. However, he is quickly disabused of the idea that he was selected because it required any genius, or even much talent to fake a masterpiece:

> "All I might do is just about copy the picture."
> "That's all we ask. Leave the technical business to us. First do a decent drawing. When you're ready to paint I'll get you a piece of sixteenth-century Belgian linen that's been scraped clean of a former picture. You prime it with white lead and when it's dry you sketch. Once you finish the nude, Scarpio and I will bake it, put in the cracks, and age them with soot. We'll even stipple in fly spots before we varnish and glue [77].

And as the forger works, he must be cautioned that what is wanted is not an original Fidelman but a competent copy of the "Venus of Urbino." He needs frequent reminders of his position, function, and identity: that he is not Titian and can only approximate the Renaissance artist's vision—"Remember you are painting the appearance of a picture. The original has already been done. Give us a decent copy and we'll do the rest with chemistry" [87]. But Fidelman is not only attempting to recreate Titian's "Venus"; he is also engaged in a more complicated but related construction—the rebuilding of an individual that can escape his physical jail, and, perhaps, his emotional cage as well, a joint process that occurs in four steps.

First he must view the original, called by Fidelman a miracle, which provokes in him a storm of feeling. The painting, in his opinion, is an icon to be adored and worshipped: "The golden brown-haired Venus, a woman of the real world, lies on her couch in serene beauty, her hand lightly touching her intimate mystery, the other holding red flowers, her nude body her truest accomplishment" [79]. He perceives the essence of the artist's genius in his ability to ennoble flesh, turning body into spirit, an idea that is Fidelman's perverse reading of Nietzsche's definition of art inked on the wall of Fidelman's studio in "A Pimp's Revenge"—"Art is not an imitation of nature but its metaphysical supplement, raised up beside it in order to overcome it" [97]—and an achievement ever beyond Fidelman's mediocre ability. It is conceivable, then, that by copying the Titian he might possess some of its soul.

Struck by passion (described in phallic terms—"he has swallowed lightning and hopes it will strike whatever it touches") [80], Fidelman assumes that intense emotion is sufficient to enable him to reproduce the "Venus," that fervor alone can generate art. He is, of course, wrong: "He tries at once to paint Titian directly on canvas but hurriedly scrapes it clean when he sees what a garish mess he has made. The Venus is insanely disproportionate and the maids in the background foreshortened into dwarfs" [80]. He recognizes that he must learn discipline and technique in order to shape and control aroused sensibility, if he is to succeed. This recognition, which is both artistic and personal, is step two.

Step three in Fidelman's double education consists of the acquisition of method and direction through the examination of history (the nude form from ancient to modern times), the testing of experience (the use of Teresa as a live model, whom he paints "with flat chest, distended belly, then hips and hairy legs, unable to alter a single detail" [83], and as a potential sex partner), and the probing of his unconscious through dreams ("That night he dreams of Bessie about to bathe. He is peeking at her through the bathroom keyhole as she prepares her bath.... Her hefty, well-proportioned body then is young and full in the right places; and in the dream Fidelman, then fourteen, looks at her with longing that amounts to anguish . . ." [86]). But his dream turns out to be one of taking—"when Bessie begins to soap herself with Ivory soap, the boy slips into her . . . poor purse, filches fifty cents for the movies, and goes on tiptoes down the stairs" [87]—and remembering Angelo's cynical belief that everybody steals, Fidelman determines to steal the Titian himself. Through abduction and theft (and a possible emblematic rape), he will not only retain the loved object, but also assert his humanity and establish an ambivalent link to the world. While this is the first independent choice Fidelman has made in "Naked Nude," it hardly signifies the birth of a compassionate man, although it does release the creative impulse, allowing him to paint at last.

The fragments of perception coalesce and fuse in the fourth step, and the forgery is completed because Fidelman finally paints with what is left of his heart:

> As he paints he seems to remember every nude that has ever been done, Fidelman satyr . . . piping and peeking at backside, frontside, or both, at the "Rokeby Venus," "Bathsheba," "Suzanna," "Venus Anadyomene," "Olympia"; at picnickers in dress or undress, bathers ditto, Vanitas or Truth, Niobe or Leda, in chase or embrace, hausfrau or whore.... He is at the same time choked by remembered lust for all the women he had ever desired, from Bessie to Annamaria Oliovino, and for their garters, underpants, slips or halfslips, brassieres and stockings [88].

But it is at this point that the educational process falters. Fidelman, pressured by memory and desire, falls in love with his own creation, and we have returned to the claims of the parasitic consciousness. The forger has once more lost the ability to distinguish between self and work: "'The Venus of Urbino, c'est moi'" [89]. Fidelman, enamoured of the product of his own ego, steals not the masterpiece but his own handiwork. Solipsism triumphant! Again, the ending is weighted with considerable ambiguity. For while Fidelman is free in the physical sense, he is still imprisoned in a closed psychic structure, isolated by self-love, trapped by the notion of art as a form of autoeroticism.

The remaining three stories—"A Pimp's Revenge," "Pictures of the Artist," and "Glass Blower of Venice"—form a triptych portraying not only the decomposition and reconstruction of Fidelman's identity, but also the final rejection of the despotism of art for the anarchy and unpredictability of life.

In "A Pimp's Revenge," Malamud is preoccupied with dramatizing the enigma of means and ends, especially as it affects the making of art. He is concerned with illustrating the degradation willingly undergone for what are assumed to be lofty ideals—in this case, the fashioning of a masterwork—only to discover that dubious and questionable proceedings distort any noble goal. Fidelman's *chef-d'oeuvre* created at great human expense—the return of Esmeralda to prostitution with the artist as pimp—is destroyed by the painter's compulsive need to achieve an ideal, to impose some standard of perfect order on the imaginative embodiment of a relationship that symbolizes disorder and corruption.

Fidelman (known throughout as F, no doubt indicating his partial humanity), has settled in Florence to create a masterpiece, a Kaddish for a mother he never knew "trying to bring them together in the tightly woven paint so they would be eternally mother and son as well as unique forms on canvas. So beautifully complete the idea of them together that the viewer couldn't help but think no one has to do it again because it's been done by F and can't be done better; in truth a masterwork" [114]. However, in order to achieve his dream of transmuting his mother's photograph from the immobilized reality of a woman whose truth he cannot invent because he never mourned her death into an artistic vision of mother and son, Fidelman has withdrawn from the flow of experience and seceded from a life of feeling. He is warned by the local fortune teller that he will never achieve greatness through retreat:

"Tell me, signora, will I ever make it? Will I finish my five years' painting of Mother and Son? my sure masterpiece—I know it in my bones—if I ever get it done."
Her shrill sibylic reply made sense. "A good cook doesn't throw out yesterday's soup."
"But will it be as good, I mean? Very good, signora, maybe a masterwork?"
"Masters make masterworks."
"And what about my luck, when will it change from the usual?"
"When you do. Art is long, inspiration short. Luck is fine, but don't stop breathing" [98].

Yet he is unable to complete the painting because "The truth is I am afraid to paint, like I might find out something about myself" [116].[30] It is easy, then, to understand why Fidelman has no difficulty turning out well-carved Madonnas for the tourist trade: only distance and objectivity are necessary for that task, not emotional involvement or commitment. Like Harry Lesser in *The Tenants*, Fidelman cannot finish because it means coming to terms with time, memory, old age, and death, which as a non-mourner, he is incapable of doing.

That Fidelman has deliberately chosen to reduce his capacity for affection, concern, and love can be seen in his treatment of Esmeralda (aptly named—if she can redeem Hugo's Hunchback of Notre Dame, can Fidelman be much of a problem?); he accepts her as a convenience, simply to be used, warning that her presence can not "interfere with my painting. I mean I'm devoted to that" [106]. His callous egotism is emphasized by the fact that the culture he has adopted functions by establishing dependencies and survives through familial and communal responsibility. As Ludovico reminds Fidelman, "Italy is a poor country. Here each of us is responsible for the welfare of four or five others or we all go under" [108]. The extent to which Fidelman's values have been crippled by his pursuit of the elusive masterpiece is further exposed when he sends Esmeralda back to the streets so that he may continue his creative effort. Under the circumstances, the havoc wrought on the finished work by Fidelman's obsessive drive for perfection becomes more than simply the ruin of a fine painting, but the murder of Esmeralda's soul. If art is to be fashioned at the price of human dignity, how valid is Fidelman's belief in the truth and morality of the artist's role?

Appropriately enough, it is just such a romantic attitude, accepted with special intensity by Fidelman, that is openly challenged for the first time in an ironic interview between Fidelman and Ludovico, critic and Esmeralda's former pimp.

This diaglogue serves as a commentary on Fidelman's own behavior, on his exalted definition of the worth of the artistic endeavor, and on his unconscious hypocrisy:

> F: Well, art is my means for understanding life. . . .I make art, it makes me. . . .
> LUD: Are you saying the canvas is the alter ego of the artist's miserable self. . . . Maestro, once you spoke to me of your art as moral. What did you mean by that?
> F: . . . I suppose I mean that maybe a painting sort of gives value to a human being as he responds to it. . . . it enlarges his consciousness. If he feels beauty it makes him more than he was, it adds . . . to his humanity. . . .
> LUD: An emotion is an emotion. . . . In itself it is not moral or immoral. Suppose someone responds to the sunset on the Arno? Is that better or more moral than the response to the smell of a drowned corpse? What about bad art? suppose the response is with more feeling than to a great painting—does that prove that bad art is moral . . . ?
> F: I guess not. . . . Maybe the painting itself doesn't have it, . . . but maybe the artist does when he's painting—creating form, order. Order protects us all, doesn't it?
> LUD: Yes, the way a prison does. Remember, some of the biggest pricks . . . have been great painters. Does that necessarily make them moral men? Of course not. What if a painter kills his father, and then paints a beautiful Ascension?
> F: . . . Maybe what I'm trying to say is that I feel most moral when I'm painting, like being engaged with truth [128-129].

But the sharp distinctions and clear choices presented by this traditional, no doubt insoluble, argument between the aesthetic and moral functions of art are blurred by the identities of the participants. The sympathy that might instinctively be offered Fidelman's viewpoint because of the attractiveness of such ideas as truth, morality, emotional responsiveness, humanity, and the creation of order is diluted by two factors. First, there is his inability to articulate his position without qualification. It appears that Fidelman has never considered the ramifications of his philosophy, and the language used reflects this lack of assurance. When probed by the questioning Ludovico, Fidelman must retract and alter his perceptions in response to the connotative imprecision of words like "truth," "morality," "emotional responsiveness," "humanity," and "the creation of order." This linguistic insecurity reveals a deeper psychological problem that is the second reason for skepticism. Considering Fidelman's own weaknesses, his selfish lack of compassion, his limited capacity for feeling and responsibility, much of what he says smacks of cant or pretense. Of course, it is no easier to acknowledge the authenticity of Ludovico's criticisms, since his eagerness to humiliate his successor as Esmeralda's protector is all too apparent. It would also seem that this consistent elevation of the significance of art is an unconscious effort on Fidelman's part to insure his own sense of uniqueness, to ennoble what is, in fact, a repressed, enclosed, and manipulative personality. However, in "A Pimp's Revenge," the reader begins to re-evaluate the artist's character, a process made necessary by Esmeralda's astute observation about the essential Fidelman: "The reason I stayed here is I thought you'd be kind to me. Besides, if a man is an artist I figured he must know about life. If he does maybe he can teach me something. So far all I've learned is that you're like everybody else, shivering in your drawers. That's how it goes, when you think you have nothing there's somebody with less" [121].

As for the painting itself, the marvel that Fidelman is, for one moment, able to create—it is his most honest piece of work because it is not an act of intellectual rationalization. Nor is it a copy, or a reproduction of an unremembered past. It is, instead, a spontaneous, felt perception shaped by a profound psychic recognition of his own role in the human comedy—the image of the artist as user, the reality of Fidelman as exploiter:

> Esmeralda was now the nineteen-year-old prostitute; and he with a stroke here and there aging himself a bit, a fifteen-year-old procurer. This was the surprise that made the painting. And what it means, I suppose, is I am what I became from a young age. . . .
>
> The picture completed itself. F was afraid to finish it. . . . But the picture was, one day, done. It assumed a completion: This woman and man toegether, prostitute and procurer. She was a girl with fear in both black eyes, a vulnerable if stately neck, and a steely small mouth; he was a boy with tight insides on the verge of crying. The presence of each protected the other. A Holy Sacrament. The form leaped to the eye. He had tormented, ecstatic, yet confused feelings, but at last felt triumphant—it was done! Though deeply drained, moved, he was satisfied, completed—ah, art! [142-143].

But Fidelman is not satisfied, although he has been warned by Esmeralda, "Don't touch it. . . . You'll never make it better" [145]. Perhaps he is frightened by completion, for it just means he must begin again. Perhaps the painting does not match the preconceptions of five year's work on his "Mother and Son." Perhaps he fears the vision of self he has seen and made concrete. We do know that Fidelman is compelled to perfect in order to achieve the control in art that he lacks in life. In any case, he answers Ludovico's objections (a pimp's revenge)—"my only criticism is that maybe the painting suffers from an excess of darkness. It needs more light. I'd say a soupçon of lemon and a little red, not more than a trace " [145]—by trying to realize an unattainable idea. Instead, he destroys the effectiveness of what is. It should not surprise that the story concludes with a fantasy of violent annihilation. And it is this vision of destruction that Ludovico calls a moral act. With his masterpiece obliterated, what has Fidelman left of self?

The artist's subconscious is the subject of "Pictures of the Artist." If Fidelman is to rebuild his fragmented identity, shattered in the symbolic suicide concluding "A Pimp's Revenge," he must plunge into the disorder of the subconscious and attempt to reach the neurotic dreams that have conditioned his failed life. This chaotic underground is the Sargasso Sea of Western culture, an anarchic recapitulation of names and allusions to the creative geniuses of civilization whose definitions of the imaginative experience have served as inappropriate models for Fidelman's commonplace talent, his exaggerated visions, and his defeated existence:

> Collage. The Flayed Ox. Rembrandt. Hanging Fowl. Soutine. Young Man with Death's Head. Van Leyden. Funeral at Ornans. Courbet. Bishop Eaten by Worms. Murillo. Last Supper, Last Judgment, Last Inning....
> Painting is nothing more than the art of expressing the invisible through the visible. Fromentin. Indefinite Divisibility. Tanguy. Definite Invisibility. Fidelman.
> I'm making the last paintings anyone can make. Reinhardt. I've made them. I like my paintings because anyone can do them. Warhol. Me too.
> Erased de Kooning Drawing. Rauschenberg. Erased Rauschenberg. de Kooning. Lithograph. Eraser. Fidelman. [160-161].

What is of major importance is that Fidelman's unconscious associations are not with fulfilled ability, but rather with loss, disappointment, frustration, impotence, dissolution, and death, those very forces he has been evading in his conscious life: "Everybody says you're dead, otherwise why do you never write.... Lives of the Saints. S. Sebastian, arrow collector, swimming in bloody sewer. Pictured transfixed with arrows. S. Denis, decapitated. Pictured holding his head.... S. Stephen, crowned with rocks. Shown stoned.... S. Catherine, broken apart on spiked wheel. Pictured married to wheel.... S. Bartholomew, flayed alive. Standing with skin draped over skinned arm" [150].

At the center of "Pictures of the Artist" are three complete fantasies. The first two illustrate Malamud's proposition that a commitment to art may demand the betrayal of one's humanity, of one's personal history, of one's heritage. The third offers promise of redemption, but only on the condition that art be abandoned.

In the first dream, Fidelman has turned his talents to the creation of absolute emptiness—the digging of the perfect hole, the fashioning of the perfect form. Interested only in maintaining the purity of his vision, Fidelman rejects any responsbility for his audience—leaving them to confusion and doubt, or insisting on a dishonest response as proof of their sensitivity or gullibility:

> They viewed the sculptures . . . in amazement and disbelief, whether at the perfect constructions or at their own stupidity. . . . Some of the viewers . . . were like sheep in their expression, as if wondering whether they had been deceived; some were stony faced, as if they knew they had been. But few complained aloud, being ashamed to admit their folly, if indeed it were folly. To the one or two who rudely questioned him, saying, Why do you pass off on us as sculpture an empty hole or two? the artist . . . replied, It were well if you relaxed before my sculptures, if you mean to enjoy them, and yield yourself to the pleasure they evoke in the surprise of their forms. At these words he who had complained fell silent, not certain he had truly understood the significance of the work of Art he had seen [154].

Fidelman's irresponsibility, his callous disregard for another's opinion and another's need, especially of one who sees through the sham of form without content—"Holes are of no use to me, my life being full of them, so I beg you to return the lire that I may hasten to the baker's shop to buy the bread I was sent for" [156]— asserted in the tone and jargon of an artistic confidence man drives a person to suicide. It is clear at this point that Malamud is concerned with exploring the relationship between the artist's appetite to create and the viewer's equally strong hunger to respond, especially when the definition of art pursued denies value to and mocks the perception of that viewer.

The problem to be confronted is that if Art exalts the idiosyncratic and the private above the responsibility to communicate truthfully to those who wish to understand and learn and be moved, does not Art then become a fraud? Malamud answers the question by having the spirit of the drowned young man return as the devil to exact the price of his revenge. In a colloquy with this

demon, Fidelman reveals the depths of his own emptiness as well
as that of his creations:

> If you'll excuse me, said the stranger at last, please explain to me
> what means these two holes that they have in them nothing but the
> dark inside?
>   The meaning lies in what they are as they seem to be, and the
> dark you note within, although I did not plan it so or put it there,
> may be thought of as an attribute of the aesthetic....
>   All I saw was nothing. To me, if you'll pardon me, is a hole
> nothing.... If you look in the small hole there is now an apple
> core. If not for this would be empty the hole. If empty would there be
> nothing.
>   Emptiness is not nothing if it has form.
>   Form, if you will excuse my expression, is not what is the whole
> of Art.
>   One might argue that, but neither is content.... This I will tell
> you. You have not yet learned what is the difference between
> something and nothing [159-160].

To elevate form and diminish content permits the exploitation of
an audience's responsiveness and the manipulation of a viewer's
desire for beauty. Such behavior not only abuses Art, but it also
demeans the soul. The price is death: "Bending for the shovel, the
stranger smote the horrified Fidelman with its blade...the
sculptor toppling as though dead into the larger of the two holes
he himself had dug.... So it's a grave, the stranger is said to have
muttered. So now we got form but we also got content" [160].

The second dream within the surrealistic dream of "Pictures
of the Artist" represents another, more complex form of disloyalty
and betrayal, based once again on a romantically exaggerated
conception of the force of art—the image of the artist as Judas.
Fidelman, in this instance, is not simply engaged in discarding
the notion of personal accountability as a function of the creative
process; he is turning his back on the humanism and compassion
of the Judaeo-Christian tradition in order to pursue his forbidden
profession. Given his role in "Last Mohican," it is hardly
surprising that Susskind is the new Christ preaching the old
message: "Tell the truth. Dont cheat. If its easy it dont mean its
good. Be kind, specially to those that they got less than you. I
want for everybody justice. Must also be charity. If you feel good
give charity. If you feel bad give charity. Must also be mercy. Be
nice, dont fight. Children, how can we live without mercy? If you
have no mercy for me I shall not live. Love, mercy, charity. Its not
so easy believe me" [162].

Because loyalty cannot be divided nor allegiance conditional, Susskind insists on one taboo: "no paints or paintings. Remember the Law, what it says. No graven images, which is profanation and idolatry. Nobody can paint Who I Am.... Dont try, its a sin" [162-163]. It is clear that Susskind/Christ recognizes that he who creates art follows another master whose injunctions are often antagonistic to Susskind's gentle, humane creed, and whose obsessive authority is no less demanding, or, perhaps, no less necessary: "This talent it is death to hide lodged in me useless. How am I ever going to make a living or win my spurs? How can I compete in this world if both my hands are tied and my eyes blindfolded? Whats so moral about that? How is a man meant to fulfill himself if he isn't allowed to paint? Its graven images versus grave damages to myself and talent. Which harms the most there is no doubt" [165]. Knowing that his selfish egocentricity means inevitable death to the putative Messiah, Fidelman, with considerable self-justifying cynicism, betrays anyway; and in so doing he brings into being the Crucifixion he is so determined to paint, just as Willie Spearmint in *The Tenants* creates the revolution he so determinedly writes about. However, the canvas for the Resurrection is left blank—waiting. Indeed, it seems that in this vision treachery, disobedience, and rebellion become the main sources of art, which may indeed be the case.

The last fantasy begins like the others, depicting a commitment to artistic creativity that overwhelms Fidelman's obligations to family and subverts his responsibility to the values that derive from an accommodation to one's personal past. Fidelman, the primitive Adam clad in loincloth, has taken up painting in Plato's cave of deception; or possibly it is the unconscious, etched in memory and pain, or maybe even the womb/tomb, safe and protected until he is capable of rebirth. This space is located, significantly, beneath his sister Bessie's house, she who had served as mother, as object of his adolescent lust, as financer of his European stay:

> The walls and part of the roof of the huge cave that he had been decorating for years and years and estimated at least two more to go before his labors were ended, were painted in an extraordinary tapestry of simple figures in black, salmon, gold-yellow, sea-green and apricot...a rich design of circles and triangles, discrete or interlocking, of salmon triangles encompassed within apricot circles, and sea-green circles within pale gold-yellow triangles, blown like masses of autumn leaves over the firmament of the cave [170].

He believes that he is attempting to complete his work so that he might show it to Bessie, ill and alone now, his massive accomplishment a tribute to her: "Bessie, he would say, ı did this for you and you know why" [171]. But in fact his endeavors are another example of Fidelman's evasion of responsibility. He keeps extending and complicating his elaborate designs, visual analogues to the complex system of rationalizations and defenses that have controlled and limited his existence, just so that he might avoid confronting his sister with his flawed, failed life.

At this point Fidelman receives a series of illuminations aided by a comic-book light bulb, with a Yiddish accent no less, that leads him out of art's prison into a feeling world, redeemed by the possibilities of love. Fidelman is made to face the fears, neuroses, and egotism that have driven him to art at the expense of human relationships:

> I hate the past.
> So why do you blame her for this?
> I don't blame anybody at all. I just don't want to see her. At least not just yet.
> If she dies she's dead. You can talk all you want then but she won't answer you.
> It's no fault of mine if people die. There's nothing I can do about it.
> Nobody is talking about fault or not fault. All we are talking about is to go upstairs.
> I can't I told you, it's too complicated. I hate the past, it caught me unawares. If there's anything to blame I don't blame her. I just don't want to see her is all, at least not just yet until my work here is done.
> Don't be so proud my friend. Pride ain't spinach. You can't eat it, so it won't make you grow. Remember what happened to the Greeks.... Watch out for hubris. It's poison ivy. Trouble you got enough, you want also blisters? [173].

Although this is fantasy, with the assistance of his mystic light bulb, Fidelman is at last able to choose Bessie and the connections established by human relationships, emerging from the decorated cave of his walled consciousness. "Pictures of the Artist" concludes with a final question which must be raised if Fidelman's regeneration is to begin: "If you're dead how do you go on living?" [175].

Fidelman's rebirth is completed in "Glass Blower of Venice" (Malamud's pornographic pun), according to Barbara Lefcowitz a comic inversion of Thomas Mann's *Death in Venice*, where bisexuality becomes a sign of life's possibilities rather than an emblem of decay and mortality.[31]

Having abandoned his art, Fidelman, the ex-painter, has not yet found an appropriate substitute to fill the emptiness. He begins a quite conventional affair with Margherita Fassoli, a married Venetian matron, whom he has pursued with the same compulsive idealism that had once been a major component in his attitude toward painting, only to be disillusioned, as usual, by her matron's body. Perhaps his disenchantment with Margherita's feminine physicality has made him susceptible; possibly he senses the need for another kind of sexuality rooted in comfortable fraternity; maybe he has become aware of the restrictive limits of his own experience. Whatever the reason, Fidelman gradually becomes involved with Beppo, her husband, a man who "loved to breathe" [199], who is open, who is generous with gifts and with self. Beppo becomes Fidelman's teacher in art, life, and love. He begins with a metaphoric assault on Fidelman's identity by wrecking what is left of his work, telling him the painful truth about the destructiveness of his commitment when he lacked the talent to re-create his vision, when the vision itself belongs to others:

> Your work lacks authority and originality. It lacks more than that, but I won't say what now. If you want my advice there's one thing I'd do with this stuff.... Burn them all.... Show who's master of your fate—bad art or you.... Don't waste your life doing what you can't do.... After twenty years if the rooster hasn't crowed she should know she's a hen. Your painting will never pay back the part of your life you've given up for it [197-198].

It is interesting under the circumstances that Beppo should select an analogy predicated on the confusion of sexual identification, for he next assaults Fidelman quite literally: "'Think of love,' the glass blower murmured. 'You've run from it all your life'" [199]. Through the physical and psychological penetration of another into Fidelman's constricted awareness, which strips away the rigidity of accepted roles, Fidelman is taught to care, to respond, to transcend the imposed limits of the obsessive ego-centered self that sought expression in the tyranny of art. With newly acquired knowledge, Fidelman realizes that he "had never in his life said 'I love you' without reservations to anyone. He said it to Beppo. If that's the way it works, that's the way it works. Better love than no love. If you sneeze at life it backs off and instead of fruit you're holding a bone. If I'm a late bloomer at least I've bloomed in love" [199].

More than that, Fidelman learns that he can create. However, before he can return to shaping and fashioning the images of his imagination, he must experience all the manifestations of that libidinal energy which is the prime constituent of the creative impulse. Following Beppo's prescription—"If you can't invent art, invent life" [199]—Fidelman connects once again with his revitalized sexuality, stimulated by love rather than the neurotic need to control, becoming an apprentice glass blower, willing at last to be instructed in a craft that is explicitly erotic in its exploration of human possibility and artistic form. It is ironic that the most fragile of materials—glass—proves to be the most suitable for teaching Fidelman about the variety and malleability of life's promises as well as the flexibility of visionary power:

> Working with hot molten glass excited Fidelman sexually. He felt creative, his heart in his pants. . . . Fidelman . . . loved dipping the tapered blowpipe into the flaming opening of the noisy furnace—like poking into the living substance of the sun for a puddle of flowing fire—Prometheus Fidelman—a viscous gob of sunflesh hanging from the pipe like a human organ: breast, kidney, stomach or phallus, cooling as it gaseously flamed, out of which if one were skilled enough . . . he would create glass objects of expected yet unexpected forms. He blew gently into the red-hot glowing mass a single soft bubble of breath . . . a small inside hole . . . a teardrop, gut, uterus, which itself became its object of birth: a sculptured womb; shaped, elongated by pendulum swing of pipe. . . . Every move they made was in essence sexual, a marvelous interaction because, among other things, it saved time and trouble: you worked and loved at once [201-202].

But the seemingly godlike potential of the glass blower's craft drives Fidelman back into the obsessions of the past—the impatience to master all skills immediately, the urgent requirement that he dominate the material and order the form, the exploitation of Beppo's willingness to teach, the fanatic desire to be an artist at any price, to create the masterpiece that gives worth to self and work—until Beppo warns, "You're doing the same things you did in your paintings. . . . It's easy to see, half a talent is worse than none" [206]. This time, however, Fidelman has learned enough about what is to be truly valued in existence so that he smashes his experiments, deciding "that he had no true distinction as an artist and this time would try not to forget it" [206].

Fidelman's re-education is finished when he can return Beppo, the loved object, to his proper role within the Fassoli family unit, recognizing that the pain of responsibility and sacrifice are as necessary to the integrated personality as love. And he can finally fashion that perfect object because he is no longer under any compulsion to do so; the isolating, selfish drive is no longer the imperative of his existence. That he can accept the theft of the bowl, stolen perhaps so that it cannot be kept and adored as a reminder of what could have been, means that he is free to return home. It would appear that to become a craftsman in glass and to love men and women is far more important to Malamud than to create a masterpiece. Life, after all, is better than art.

The Tenants recapitulates the major themes and minor premises about art and artists that have already been discussed at length in "Girl of My Dreams" and *Pictures of Fidelman*. However, there is an added dimension: the creation of art in this novel has become a profoundly political act; and art itself has become a political statement, even when some who call themselves artists choose to deny its social force.

The environment of *The Tenants*, the tenement inhabited by Harry Lesser and Willie Spearmint, offers an image of cultural disintegration that is the modern world, emphasized by the anarchic version of literary history that dominates the book, filled with obscure inferences, obvious puns, and esoteric allusions to the makers of literature. It is this heritage, however disordered it has become in the chaos of contemporary society, that Harry wishes to preserve and that Willie wishes to obliterate.

Harry Lesser is the typical Malamudian artist. White, Jewish, with two published novels to his credit, he has withdrawn from experience and rejected active participation in life in order to work on his third, nine long years aborning, and surely a minor masterpiece if only he can finish it. Lesser has isolated himself on the top floor of a decaying New York City apartment, symbol of civilization's dissolution, viewing himself, his books, and his records as the sole remaining voice of humanistic liberalism to stave off the oncoming apocalypse. Art, for Harry, possesses enormous power not only to rescue a society in decline, but also to ennoble both creator and audience. Therefore he defines his own task in quasi-religious terms: "This isn't just any novel we're talking about.... It exemplifies my best ideas as an artist as well as what life has gradually taught me. When you read it, Levenspiel, even you will love me. It will help you understand and endure your life as the writing of it has helped me sustain mine."[32] As Willie later observes, "You talk and you act like some priest or fuckn rabbi" [88]. As we have seen, this elevated conception of art's importance is often an unconscious mechanism to enhance the ego of the artist who has given up his humanity to create. Given such a sacrifice, how worthy is Harry Lesser, if art is perceived as anything less than civilization's saviour? To acknowledge the limitations of art is to demean, perhaps even to negate the artist's identity.

Like Fidelman and Mitka, Lesser has denied or controlled his capacity to feel in order to devote all his emotional energy to his writing. All concern is self-concern, as witness his hostility to the very real, Job-like problems that Levenspiel, his landlord, must face in the world from which Lesser has seceded. And Levenspiel is quite right when he says, "Art my ass, in this world it's heart that counts" [22]. That Lesser does not get the message is apparent in his attitude toward Willie Spearmint and his treatment of Irene Bell. He bitterly rejects Willie's demands on his time and on his sensibilities, especially when the result is a debilitating anger and hostility. Lesser's liberalism, if such be it, is based not on commitment but on a desire to avoid the intensity that should be part of his book. Irene, who initially attempts to lead Harry back into the complex and painful world, is useful only insofar as she releases in him the ability to continue writing. His needs invariably take precedence over her claims on his time and affection. Nor is he able to understand or maintain the connection between love and creativity. So he drives her away, which is hardly surprising. Why should a woman of sympathy and concern and perception take second place to a forever unfinished book?

For Lesser, writing has become a substitute for living. He writes, in fact, to teach himself to feel. And when he describes his novel about love, it is clear that he is describing himself:

> Anyway, this writer sets out to write a novel about someone he conceives to be not yet himself. He thinks he can teach himself to love in a manner befitting an old ideal.... Still, if during the course of three books he had written himself into more courage, why not love? He will learn through some miracle of transforma-tion as he writes...perhaps a kind of suffering. What it may come to in the end, despite the writer's doubts, is that he invents this character in his book who will in a sense love for him; and in a sense love him; which is perhaps to say...that Lesser's writer in

this book, in creating love as best he can, if he brings it off in imagination will extend self and spirit; and so with good fortune may love his real girl as he would like to love her, and whoever else in a mad world is human [192-193].

It is equally apparent that the incomplete book is an extension of the incomplete Lesser, illustrating the old confusion between self and work. The extent to which the novel is Lesser's identity can be ascertained by his response to its destruction: "Now they were ashes. He saw himself buried in ashes" [179]. When the manuscript is burned, Lesser is forced to re-examine his own history only to find he cannot reconstruct the perfection of what was, because he is no longer the same Lesser; he cannot return to the experiences that shaped the earlier version: "How can one write the same thing twice? It's like trying to force your way back into yesterday" [226]. He will forever be incapable of ending the novel because to end is to confront the failures of his own life, the passage of time, the reminders of mortality. To stop writing is to invite death: "One thing about writing a book you keep death in place; the idea is to keep on writing" [198].

To Lesser, then, creation is a matter of imposing order, design, and discipline on the forces of chaos at large or within. Without form, art, self, and even civilization die. When the achievement is no longer possible, all that remains is Lesser's exposed unconscious, no longer controlled by the shaping power of art, filled with rage, violence, and destruction.[33]

For Willie Spearmint, later Bill Spear (emblem of phallic energy) making his literary identity the real man, art is the assertion of self, the embodiment of disorder. He is engaged in writing what appears to be an archetypal black autobiography indebted to the patterns of Richard Wright, Eldridge Cleaver, and Malcolm X: "The book, although for various reasons not a finished piece of work, was absorbing to read, Willie's human history: from 'Downsouth Boy' to 'Black Writer'; via progression 'Upsouth,' 'Harlem Nights,' 'Prison Education.' The short last chapter was entitled, 'I Write for Black Freedom.' The book was mainly naturalistic confessional, Willie's adventures simply narrated, the style varying from Standard English to black lingo, both the writing and psychology more sophisticated than Lesser would have guessed" [60].

Willie deeply resents the fact that he must come to Lesser for help in effectively forging his black fictive identity. The notion of apprenticeship, particularly to a white Jew is anathema. In this instance, the rejection of the role of assistant, usually an honorific moral position in Malamud's work, can be attributed to a social reality that makes the acceptance of secondary status an impossibility. And Willie comes to find Lesser's advice unpalatable. He resists the demands of form—"Art can kiss my juicy ass. You want to know what's really art? *I* am art. Willie Spearmint, *black man.* My form is *myself.*" [75]—because it imposes on the black imagination the structures that determine white inventive success, an act of creative emasculation (an image that haunts *The Tenants*). Indeed, the more his blackness is jeopardized by Lesser's criticisms and his theft of Irene, the less Willie is concerned with conventions of form and the more he is compelled to assert his violent and destructive fantasies unmediated by structure. If Willie's art is to be dedicated to freeing black identity from white control, it must of necessity deny white concepts of order, design, and the value of rationality. Anatole Broyard has perceptively attempted to explain Willie's responses:

> Apparently, the black sees the Jew—who thinks of himself as the black's best friend—as an infiltrator, someone who tries to soften his heart and subvert his revolution with sympathy, who wishes to convert him to rational action. This is not the Jew slum lord, the pawnbroker or loanshark: it is far more complicated than that. The Jew might well be hated as an unattainable ideal: rich or cultivated, versed in the arts and sciences, powerful—the pinnacle of American personality.[34]

If art is religion to Lesser, to Willie it is power, the ability to reach masses of people with his angry, hostile vision of blood, creating the apocalypse by writing it, as Fidelman created the Crucifixion by his need to paint it. It is through art, more than through sexuality, perhaps, that Willie can manipulate white society as he has been exploited. And when Lesser becomes a betrayer, he becomes a symbolic figure in Willie's annihilative fictions. In fact, Willie's inability to be published is perceived as a function of powerlessness rather than as a lack of talent:

> "Why don't you send your manuscript to a publisher and get somebody else's opinion if you're not satisfied with mine?"
> "Because I tried ten of those rat-brained Jews and they all turned it down for a lot of horseshit reasons, because they are *afraid* of what the book says" [75].

Clearly, however, Willie's ego is defined by his work, just as Lesser's is. When Lesser steals Irene, Willie strikes back in the most effective way possible: he murders Lesser by destroying his manuscript.[35] But Willie carries his rage further, obliterating white culture by ravaging Lesser's books and records. All that remains for Willie, when writing his hatred solves nothing, is the possibility of an authentic homicide.

When art can no longer universalize experience, when it becomes an arena for the fantasies of violence, when it isolates and separates rather than draws men together, when art fails, even as therapy, only death is possible.

It is true that in Malamud's fiction art has become increasingly politicized. And one particular idea bears repetition: the limits of art as a civilizing force. This is not a new idea in Malamud's work. In "The German Refugee,"[36] neither intelligence, nor sensitivity, nor Whitman's belief in *Brudermensch* can save Oscar Gassner from suicide, or the world from the effects of the Holocaust. But in *The Tenants*, the sense of pessimism is deeper, for it is the present and the future that seem hopeless. Art cannot protect, or elevate, or save, if it ever could. It has ceased reminding men and women of their humanity. Art, once civilization's agent, has itself become a battleground, hastening the apocalypse.

The title story in Malamud's most recent collection, *Rembrandt's Hat*,[37] continutes the author's exploration of the idea that a commitment to art makes human relationships difficult at best, especially if the artist possesses a limited and insecure talent and his antagonist, an art historian, is all too convinced of his intellectual superiority. "Man in a Drawer," about a writer trapped in a totalitarian system, offers other possibilities. This story does not evince Malamud's usual ambivalence concerning art and artists, nor does it continue the vein of pessimism begun in *The Tenants*; instead, it seems to be a tale of nobility and heroism.

Feliks Levitansky is the man in the drawer, a Russian-Jewish writer whose work cannot be published because it seems to embody ideas hostile to the regime. While Howard Harvitz (a name perhaps parodying the notion of "Harvard liberals"), the narrator, and Malamud, and Levitansky himself are dubious about his continued freedom in a society that has made art a tool of the totalitarian system, we are not permitted to question his artistry or his commitment.[38] His wife, reluctant to remain with a man who takes such chances, attests to the strength of his fiction as does the narrator who has been asked to smuggle Levitansky's manuscript out of the country, although we are permitted only synopses of the short stories.

Levitansky's courage is admirable: "If they take him away in prison he will write on toilet paper. When he comes out, he will write on newspaper margins. He sits this minute at his table. He is a magnificent writer. I cannot ask him not to write ..." [75]. It is even contagious, forcing Harvitz, himself a free-lance writer in a society where that is not an ironic profession, to re-evalute his own concepts of personal and artistic responsibility:

> My own problem is not that I can't express myself but that I don't. In my own mind Vietnam is a horrifying and demoralizing mistake, yet I never really opposed it except to sign a couple of petitions and vote for congressmen who say they're against the war. My first wife used to criticize me. She said I wrote the wrong things and was involved in everything but useful action.... In a curious way, I'm just waking up to the fact that the United States government has for years been mucking up my soul [70].

Not only does the self-doubting narrator finally agree "to give the book its liberty" [80], but he also decides he will ask his first wife to re-marry, a decision equally important to his equivocal manhood. Nor can Levitansky's wisdom be doubted:

> I do not believe in bolshevization of literature. I do not think revolution is fulfilled in a country of unpublished novelists, poets, playwriters, who hide in drawers whole libraries of literature.... I think now the State will never be secure—never! It is not in the nature of politics, or human condition, to be finished with revolution.... I have learned from writing my stories...that imagination is enemy of the State. I have learned from my writing that I am not a free man [71-72].

Perhaps the artist's ambivalent situation is lacking in this story because the state is so patently wrong, so clearly evil, unlike the paradoxes that tear at the American consciousness. There are no ambiguities in this authoritarian world. And while survival is difficult for an artist, even tormenting, heroism is more simply defined than in a democracy: to continue to create in an environment that imprisons or silences those who would speak the truth is heroic. Art is politics in the most profound way.

But irony is not absent from "Man in a Drawer" because it is not a certainty that Levitansky's work will reach publication. The narrative, as such, stops before Harvitz reaches Moscow airport. Indeed, the final image, from a summary of the last of the

Russian's short stories, is one of art, talent, and heritage destroyed. And if the important action is Harvitz's transformation into a man of principle and courage, Malamud does not guarantee the success of the American's mission. Perhaps, then, the equivocating narrator's heroism consists of choosing to act at last, independent of the success of the gesture or the permanence of the metamorphosis.

As we have seen, the relationship between the races, the position of women in a given culture, the nature and importance of art have all been subject to the forces of historical change. But what is Malamud's attitude toward history? How does it act upon the behavior of the single isolated individual? Upon society? Chapter Six will attempt to answer these questions.

THE GOOD MAN'S DILEMMA

The Fixer, The Tenants, and the Historical Perspective

From the mythic transliteration of baseball history in *The Natural* to the adaptation of the Beiliss case that forms the basis of *The Fixer* to the angry eschatology of *The Tenants,* Bernard Malamud has been concerned, either obliquely or overtly, with the ways in which history shapes the individual, defining the nature of inward perception and controlling the relationships with the institutions and personnel of the external environment. Indeed, the ambivalence and growing pessimism of the later fiction might be attributed to the anomic tendencies, the nihilistic futility, and the overpowering violence of contemporary history. To be sure, most critics are quite correct when they find as the predominant theme in Malamud's work a continuing affirmation of man's capacity to mature, to accept responsibility, and to create through experience a moral structure within which to function. Yet it cannot be denied, it seems to me, that the ethical system so prized by Malamud, called *mentshlekhayt* by Josephine Zadovsky Knopp,[1] becomes increasingly ineffective as a force to insure order or stability and increasingly ambiguous as a determinant of personal emancipation when confronted with events occurring in historical time. No longer does the development of a principled sensibility liberate in the presence of the anarchic disorder that seems so much a condition of modernity. Rather, such a sensibility would appear to imprison and isolate,[2] producing only internal psychic changes. Granted that to Malamud it is precisely this altered consciousness that is of the utmost significance; nonetheless, there seems to be a radical disjuncture between the transfigured self and the world in which the transformed individual ultimately must act.

Malamud has illustrated in the course of his novels and short stories that history has proven the American dream to be corrupt and the possession of Eden illusory, that race and sex lead to war rather than harmony, that the artist's power to discipline chaos is negligible, while the attempt to do so is often self-destructive. What then is man to do in the face of history's power? The prophetic chronicle of Yakov Bok, the fixer (1966), and the chiliastic tale of Harry Lesser and Willie Spearmint (1971), tenants in the crumbling house of history, offer two different responses to the question of man's involvement in history and his ability to utilize the multiple perspectives of history in order to fashion an identity that might be applicable in society at large. It is interesting to observe too that the implications of these variant responses have themselves been conditioned by dissimilar historical times. It should not be particularly surprising that this subject absorbs Malamud's imagination given not only the sacralization of history that is a major component of Jewish theology,[3] but also the evangelical impulse that seeks to explain and justify the events of the American past.

Judaism, as a religious force, exalts history. As a social and cultural phenomenon, its fate has been frequently determined by interaction with the historical moment. In fact, for Judaism history is theophany: the Jews confirm and reconfirm their sacred identity as the Chosen People through God's active intervention in the historical process.

> For the first time, we find affirmed, and increasingly accepted, the idea that historical events have a value in themselves, insofar as they are determined by the will of God. This God of the Jewish people is no longer an Oriental divinity, creator of archetypal gestures, but a personality who ceaselessly intervenes in history.... Historical facts thus become "situations" of man in respect to God, and as such they acquire a religious value that nothing had

previously been able to confer on them. It may, then, be said with truth that the Hebrews were the first to discover the meaning of history as the epiphany of God.... In the Israel of the Messianic prophets, historical events could be tolerated because, on the one hand, they were willed by Yahweh, and on the other hand, because they were necessary to the final salvation of the chosen people.[4]

This strategy of sanctification effectively transmutes both personal suffering and historical catastrophe from negative conditions to experiences with positive spiritual content, and may, perhaps, provide a partial explanation to account for the continued existence of the Jews as an identifiable, coherent group in spite of the Diaspora, the absence of geographical nationhood, the lack of similar racial characteristics, almost endless persecution and pain, and the constant pressures from within and without calling for assimilation:

> Among the Hebrews, every new historical calamity was regarded as punishment inflicted by Yahweh.... No military disaster seemed absurd, no suffering was vain, for beyond the "event," it was always possible to perceive the will of Yahweh. Even more: these catastrophes were... necessary, they were foreseen by God so that the Jewish people should not contravene its true destiny by alienating the religious heritage left by Moses.... Only historical catastrophes brought them back to the right road by forcing them to look toward the true God.... [5]

More to the point, as Will Herberg asserts, "the Jew becomes a 'true Jew' and makes available to himself the resources of divine grace under the covenant by making Israel's past his own, its sacred history the 'background' of his own life."[6] This requisite identification of the individual Jew with the destiny of Israel is a particularly significant symbolic motif in *The Fixer* and will be explored further.

The irony inherent in Judaism, reflected in the self-deprecation of Jewish humor and pervasive not only in Yiddish literature but also in the fiction of the Jewish-American writers, is clear: affliction and disaster are necessary to prove uniqueness and to reinforce the idea of chosenness. Theology and experience compel the Jew to deal with the disparity between the ideal and the actual and the contradictions arising from the union of God's Promise with the reality of the ghetto, in a world where the possibilities of redemption are everywhere and fulfillment nowhere.[7] It would appear to be the paradox of Jewish identity that in order to endure as a people and to sustain their position as moral exemplars, the Jews must continue to be civilization's scapegoats. No wonder, then, that the Jew seems to have become a paradigm for modern man trapped in the inexplicable forces of the twentieth century.

For the American, as for the Jew, history is exemplary, a moral process, rather than a compendium of irrational acts. Beginning with the Puritans, whose Old Testament philo-semitism molded, in part, their historical awareness, Americans have attempted to read their past as a series of redemptive gestures and occasions coupled with an intense messianic nationalism and a fervent missionary zeal to stand as the model for right societal development, a pattern traced by such historians as Hans Kohn, Ernest Tuveson, and Cushing Strout.[8] But unlike the calamitous archives of Jewish existence, the American experience, mingling religion and politics as it does, seems to be an unending chronology of successes, conquests, and consummated oppor-tunities. The effects of this millenarian attitude have been briefly described by John Schaar:

> The close interrelation between religion and politics has been, on the whole, of such a sort as to support uncritical patriotism and the powers that be, and to encourage Americans to think of themselves as superior in virtue and mission to other peoples. Ever since the Puritan founding, many of our prominent statesmen and religious leaders have spoken and acted as though God had once again entered history as the Lord of Hosts, and had concluded a covenant of nations with this people, choosing it to fight His battles.[9]

But there is an equally strong countervailing tendency within the national consciousness that legitimizes the denial of history's permanence. It has been a cornerstone of this country's regenerative image that individuals could deny an unsatisfactory past and an inadequate identity for a new life independent of all that has gone before in personal terms as well as in an historical context. If the Jew is imprisoned in history, the American can reject its demands because that very history has shown that negation is not only permissible, it is even necessary if one is to conform to the Edenic ideals of this society. The results of two such disparate, warring views of man's place in historical time can be seen in Malamud's short story, "The Lady of the Lake."[10] Settling in Italy, Henry Levin, following the resurrective American design, believes he can assume a new persona, becoming a Freeman without any consequences, only to discover that in spurning his Jewish birth and sacrificing the heritage of the Holocaust, he loses love's redeeming grace. In this cautionary tale, it becomes obvious that the American predisposition to forever reshape the self breeds an unprincipled irresponsibility, while adherence to an inheritance that insures inevitable persecution is a sign of ethical strength. If *The Fixer* is a novel controlled by this concept of Jewish historicism, then *The Tenants* is the work of a disillusioned American idealist driven to apocalyptic rage by disappointment.

The Fixer is informed by the spirit of Old Testament historiography. It is prophetic fiction as defined by the critic Robert Alter: "... a courageous engagement in even the most threatening history.... The prophets of the Hebrew Bible ... were not oracles; they evoked the future as vividly as possible because they believed that human actions could determine what the future would be, and they wanted desperately to affect their auditors' actions."[11] In fact, *The Fixer* can be seen as an extended meditation on history: the various and often antagonistic kinds of historical perception that operate to determine the course of events in the world; the relationship between man and the historical forces that act upon him; and the ways in which an individual can manipulate the engine of history, if he so chooses.

For the Russian and the Jew who exist within the confines of Malamud's novel, as well as for the present reader, who translates the horrors attendant on their fictional encounter in Kiev during the pre-Revolutionary years, 1911-1913, into the facts of actual historical circumstance, the past is so awash in violence and hatred "there's no getting rid of the blood any more."[12] Indeed, the imagery of blood runs through the novel like a red thread, from the accusation of ritual murder to the hemophilia of the young Tsarevitch, from the menstrual flow of Zina Lebedev to Yakov's visions of bloody pogroms, as a constant reminder of history's poisoned inhumanity to men.

The majority of the Russian characters appearing in *The Fixer*, regardless of occupation, social position, and education, perceive history to be a succession of demonic acts perpetrated against Christian civilization by the satanic Jews. They are dominated, to the point of paranoid obsession, by the traditional, grotesque anti-semitic fantasies rooted deeply in Western culture in which the Jew is viewed as the wicked son denying the saving power of Jesus, the terrifying father re-enacting the crucifixion by murdering innocent children, and finally, as the Devil's agent corrupting the world and the Word:[13]

> When the old eschatological prophecies were taken up by the
> masses of the later Middle ages all these phantasies were treated
> with deadly seriousness and elaborated into a weird mythology....
> The Jews tended to be seen as demons attendant on Satan.... They
> were often shown as devils with the beard and horns of a goat
> while in real life ecclesiastical and secular authorities alike tried to
> make them wear horns on their hats. Like other demons, they were
> imagined and portrayed in close association with creatures which
> symbolize dirt and lust.... Conversely Satan himself was commonly
> given Jewish features and was referred to as "the father of the
> Jews." The populace was convinced that in the synagogue Jews
> worshipped Satan in the form of a cat or a toad, invoking his aid in
> making black magic. Like their supposed master, Jews were
> thought of as demons of destruction whose one object was the ruin
> of Christians and Christianity.[14]

The Charon who ferries Yakov to the hellish city of Kiev is a
peasant whose poverty and ignorance are necessary to maintain
the Tsarist autocracy: his limitations, his prejudices, his discontents
can be directed and exploited by the regime for its own
preservation. This nameless representative of Russia's poor
knows for a fact that "a Jew's a devil ... and if you ever watch one
peel off his stinking boot you'll see a split hoof, it's true. I know,
for as the Lord is my witness, I saw one with my own eyes. He
thought nobody was looking, but I saw his hoof as plain as day"
[27]. And as the personifications of diabolic maleficence, the Jews
deserve anything that the past has inflicted upon them, or that the
future might provide as damnation.

> And the only way to save ourselves is to wipe them out.... Wipe
> them all out....
> "And then when we've slaughtered the whole cursed tribe of
> them—and the same is done in every province throughout Russia,
> wherever we can smoke them out ... we'll pile up the corpses and
> soak them with benzine and light fires that people will enjoy all
> over the world. Then when that's done we'll hose the stinking
> ashes away and divide the rubles and jewels and silver and furs and
> all other loot they stole, or give it back to the poor who it rightfully
> belongs to anyway. You can take my word—the time's not far off
> when everything I say, we will do, because our Lord, who they
> crucified, wants his rightful revenge" [27-28].

It takes little for the reader to extend the ferryman's monstrous
vision into the reality of Nazi slaughter; the imagery demands an
identification be made between the deliberately shaped fictive
environment of Tsarist Russia and the actual history that is to
come. And it is this insistent, purposeful fusion of imagined

events and the reader's presumed knowledge of authentic history
that is used by Malamud to help establish the truth of the fixer's
experience.

To Marfa Golov, herself a thief and murderess, the Jews are
arch-criminals and sexual perverts, while to Father Anastasy, in a
mad theological analysis, they are Christ-killers and destroyers of
the only true faith whose most profound rituals, as Bok notes,
with no small irony, depend on devouring the body and blood of
the dying god. For Grubeshov, the prosecuting attorney, the Jews
represent a political threat, a vast conspiracy which he must
expose and overcome if he is to fulfill his ambitions: "The Jews
dominate the world and we feel ourselves under their yoke. I
personally consider myself under the power of the Jews; under the
power of Jewish thought, under the power of the Jewish press. To
speak against the crimes of the Jews means to evoke the charge
that one is either a Black Hundred, an obscurantist, or a
reactionary. I am none of these things. I am a Russian patriot! I
love the Tsar!" [226].

Even Tsar Nicholas II, whose absolute authority should
guarantee protection, cannot escape the touch of the omnipotent
Jews: "It isn't only that the Jews are freemasons and revolutionaries
who make a shambles of our laws and demoralize our police by
systematic bribery for social exemptions—I can forgive that a bit
but not the other things, in particular the terrible crime you are
accused of, which is so repellent to me personally. I refer to the
draining of his lifeblood out of Zhenia Golov's body" [331-332]. It
is noteworthy that not only does each character effectively project
his or her own particular weakness onto the all-powerful, mythic
Jew, but in subduing a figure of such potency, he or she proves
capable of controlling his or her psychic fate, as well as
fabricating the essential illusion that the individual can determine
his or her political and social future. That the fantasy of pervasive
Jewish domination is an imaginative construct created to meet
personal and societal needs, rather than a validation by history,
goes without saying; that the Russians in the novel (and anti-
semites, in general) choose to respond to the demonic mythology
rather than learn to perceive the truth of actual events is equally
obvious. But the Jew, in this instance Yakov Bok, is entrapped by
this diabolic historiography. Because Bok has been transformed
into an all-powerful symbol of evil by the requirements of the
collective imagination and the needs of the individual psyche

rather than by a confrontation with the facts of Jewish existence, there is little he can do or say that will contravene that assumption or prove that he is simply human. Impotent, in fact, by custom and law, Yakov can be freely punished for his supposed misuse and perversion of power. In the conflict between history and demonology, the reality of the historical situation has become irrelevant in the face of the multiple satisfactions derived from the myth. Thus Yakov Bok and, by extension, the Jews become history's losers.

Prior to the murder of Zhenia Golov and the confinement that would alter forever his life, Yakov Bok wished only to avoid history, to escape its dominion (symbolized by his rejection of Judaism and its agonized past): "I am in history . . . yet not in it. In a way of speaking I'm far out, it passes me by. Is this good or is something lacking in my character? What a question! Of course lacking but what can I do about it? And besides is this really such a great worry?" [60]. However, once accused, jailed, and tortured, in order to make his experience comprehensible Yakov must counterpoise to the view of history as collective madness a system that endows his suffering with both means and limits. Several factors assist the fixer in his attempt to order, explain, and utilize the history that has imprisoned him metaphorically and quite literally: the Russians—Bibikov, Julius Ostrovsky, Suslov-Smirnov, even the guard Kogin—who teach that truth, not demons or scapegoats, can be discovered if one examines the facts of history, that men can be changed by such an examination, and that those men can, in turn, affect history; Spinoza, whose un-Orthodox ideas about man's relation to God and society liberate Yakov's intellectual curiosity, forcing him to confront, with ambivalent results, the world beyond the Pale; Christianity, which provides an alternative archetypal framework in which Yakov's particular existence can be universalized to conform to the pattern of Jesus's life; and, most important, the gradual recovery of his own Jewish identity.

Bibikov, the Investigating Magistrate, is the first sympathetic and humane Russian whom Yakov meets. He does not believe in the accusation of ritual murder, and uses history as a lawyer might, to uncover the requisite evidence to refute so patently false a charge. Above all he believes in the law, itself a product of historical development, telling Bok: "Mercy is for God, I depend on the law. The law will protect you" [80]. If the law fails, all,

Jew and Russian alike, become subject to the nightmare of history that has entombed Bok: "If the law does not protect you, it will not in the end, protect me. Therefore I dare not fail you" [176]. In his allegiance to the Law, Bibikov seems a secular counterpart to those Jews in Malamud's fiction—Morris Bober and Shmuel, Yakov's father-in-law—who have made their commitment to the Law as it is embodied in the Torah. However, because the society of Imperial Russia suffers a corruption more profound than that found in *The Assistant*, Bibikov's adherence to his principles does not merely imprison him, it kills him.

Bibikov is also concerned with the fixer's education, attempting to convince the fixer that Spinoza does not countenance men's withdrawal from the historical process:

> Spinoza conceded a certain freedom of political choice.... He perhaps felt that the purpose of the state—the government—was the security and comparative freedom of rational man. This was to permit man to think as best he could. He also thought man was freer when he participated in the life of society than when he lived in solitude as he himself did. He thought that a free man in society had a positive interest in promoting the happiness and intellectual emancipation of his neighbors [78].

In addition, Bibikov is the earliest of Bok's teachers to point out that his incarceration, based as it is on a thoroughly distorted awareness of human worth, is symptomatic of Russia's profound corruption: "There's something cursed, it seems to me, about a country where men have owned men as property. The stink of that corruption never escapes the soul, and it is the stink of future evil" [172]. Once again, Malamud's literary device permits the American reader to recognize and acknowledge a legitimate but devastating value judgment assessed against one aspect of his own national history through the agency of a fictional Jew in a Russian prison.

As Yakov's father-in-law Shmuel supplies the theological premises, as Ostrovsky the political explanation, as Bok the experiental corroboration, Bibikov, not surprisingly, given his admiration for and knowledge of Spinoza, offers the philosophical substructure for Yakov's developing theories about man's obligations as a participant in history. For the Investigating Magistrate, the individual loses a portion of his humanity when he denies his responsibility to act within the confusions of history, even though he may be darkly pessimistic concerning the future of civilization:

"I respect man for what he has to go through in life, and sometimes for how he does it, but he has changed little since he began to pretend he was civilized.... That is how I feel, but having made that confession let me say...that I am somewhat of a meliorist. That is to say, I act as an optimist because I find I cannot act at all, as a pessimist. One often feels helpless in the face of the confusion of these times, such a mass of apparently uncontrollable events and experiences to live through, attempt to understand, and if at all possible, give order to; but one must not withdraw from the task if he has some small thing to offer—he does so at the risk of diminishing his humanity" [173].

However, in a society as obdurate and pernicious as Imperial Russia prior to the Revolution, such sensitivity can be dangerous and self-destructive. That is certainly the case with Bibikov, whose humanism, belief in the law, and commitment to the pursuit of truth leads only to jail and suicide, where his ghost haunts Yakov's growing consciousness and his awakening historical accountability.

It is Julius Ostrovsky, Jewish member of the Kiev bar, who enlightens Yakov about the politics of his case as it is woven into the fabric of recent Russian history: the nature of Kiev, a medieval city that "has always been the heart of Russian reaction" [305]; the disastrous and unpopular Russo-Japanese War; the Revolution of 1905, erupting out of defeat and frustration; the reluctant liberalization, followed by increased repression—"In a sick country every step to health is an insult to those who live on its sickness" [308]; and the need for a scapegoat to justify the return to absolutism and tyranny—"Popular discontent they divert into anti-semitic outbreaks. It's a simple solution to their problems" [309]. But history is not inflexible, nor is it an unchanging monolithic process. The outcome of a particular set of historic circumstances is not always predictable or certain. Even within a managed autocracy, the honesty and the integrity of the people may prevail, as the democratic Ostrovsky points out:

"Freedom exists in the cracks of the state. Even in Russia a little justice can be found.... On the one hand we have the strictest autocracy; on the other we are approaching anarchy; in between, courts exist and justice is possible. The law lives in the minds of men. If a judge is honest the law is protected. If that's the case, so are you. Also a jury is a jury—human beings—they could free you in five minutes.... In our favor is that although they may be ignorant peasants and shopkeepers, simple folk, as a rule they have little love for state officials, and when it comes to facts they can smell when they stink" [311].

Ostrovsky, like Bibikov, also reminds Yakov that the extreme vulnerability of the Jews is an accurate measurement of the threat to the freedoms of all men subject to an oppressive and arbitrary system.

And Suslov-Smirnov, Bok's Ukranian lawyer, former anti-semite, "now ... a vigorous defender of the rights of the Jews" [312], as well as the prison guard Kogin, who sacrifices his life to insure Yakov's safety, illustrate at two different levels the extent to which a man might be changed by an intellectual or personal encounter with a specific historic phenomenon. So much, then, for the Russians who influence and educate the fixer's sensibilities.

Spinoza is another perhaps more equivocal presence in Yakov's attempt to understand and deal with the historical machinery that has imprisoned him. In his philosophy and his life, Spinoza represents liberation, the escape from stultifying tradition and a fixed destiny. As Bok explains, "I read through a few pages and kept on going as though there were a whirlwind at my back.... When you're dealing with such ideas you feel as though you were taking a witch's ride. After that I wasn't the same man" [75-76]. What initially attracts Bok to the philosopher is his apparent reduction of God from a demanding, unreasonable, unforgiving Jewish patriarch to an idea, to a thought, defined in part, as man's capacity for reason. For Yakov, as a most reluctant Jew, this dimension of God's power allows, even encourages, the wished-for escape from the ineluctability of Jewish history. But this leap into freedom proves ironic, as Tony Tanner carefully explains,[15] since it is precisely this curiosity for the varieties of experience and the deracination contingent upon experimentation that puts Yakov in jail. And it is in prison that Yakov not only recognizes the limits of attempting to live a philosophy but also perceives the disjunction between theories constructed in the serene isolation of one's own choosing and the accomplished reality of his cage and the actual circumstances that brought him there. Spinoza was

> free in his thoughts, his understanding of Necessity, and in the construction of his philosophy. The fixer's thoughts added nothing to his freedom; it was nil. He was imprisoned in a cell, and even in memory because so much that had happened to him during a life that had perhaps, at times, seemed free, now seemed designed to lead him to this imprisonment. Necessity freed Spinoza and imprisoned Yakov. Spinoza thought himself into the universe but Yakov's poor thoughts were inclosed in a cell [207].

However, although there is considerable sardonic ambiguity in the use to which Spinozan concepts are put, he is not abandoned as one of Yakov's teachers for two reasons. His life—an apostate Jew persecuted by his brethren for his heresies, the determination to continue studying, writing, thinking, elaborating intellectual and ethical systems, in spite of illness and poverty—serves an exemplary purpose, a lesson in survival. And his political beliefs, as explained by Bibikov and perceived by Bok, provide the philosophic justification for Yakov's final, impassioned re-entry into history: "What is it Spinoza says? If the state acts in ways that are abhorrent to human nature it's the lesser evil to destroy it. Death to the anti-Semites! Long live revolution! Long live liberty!" [335].

Christianity, especially in its archetypal connections with the myth of the suffering and dying god whose sacrifice redeems the world, the scapegoat who shoulders the sins of men that they may experience salvation, furnishes Yakov with another sanctioned version of history into which he can fit the seemingly inexplicable occurrences of his life. That Bok, whose name in German means "goat," is such a figure needs no further explanation. We have already noted the ways in which he, or the mythic Jew into which he has been transformed, has absorbed precisely those doubts and inadequacies that most trouble each character, the most significant in this context being the guilt that may inhere in the rite of Communion where the body and blood of Jesus is ritually eaten. That Bok's existence is drawn to resemble Christ's is equally obvious: a fixer, a carpenter who abandons the traditional community in his thirtieth year, in order to begin a new ministry among the godless; arrested in April during the Passover season; imprisoned with thieves and murderers; figuratively lost to the world; and even resurrected.[16] However, what is read and remembered from the New Testament, given to Yakov by Zhitnyak's wife, are only those incidents that conform to and reinforce the peculiarly Jewish pattern of historical suffering:

> Yet the story of Jesus fascinated him and he read it in the four gospels. He was a strange Jew, humorless and fanatic, but the fixer liked the teachings. . . . He was deeply moved when he read how they spat on him and beat him with sticks; and how he hung on the cross at night. Jesus cried out help to God but God gave no help. There was a man crying out in anguish in the dark, but God was on the other side of the mountain. . . . Christ died and they took him down. The fixer wiped his eyes. Afterwards he thought if

that's how it happened and it's part of the Christian religion, and they believe it, how can they keep me in prison, knowing I am innocent? [232].

But the Christian strategy has qualified usefulness as a comfort for the confined Jew. Bok recognized immediately the discrepancy between the Word and the behavior he has witnessed and has been subjected to. Unlike the Old Testament which chronicles the continuing encounter between man and Yahweh in historical time, the New Testament delineates what appears to be a single powerful hierophany. The words of Jesus that haunt Bok because they function as a moral commentary on his travails carry little ethical authority in the Christian world as he has known it. The injunctions he memorizes

> "Which of you convicts me of sin? . . . If I tell the truth, why do you not believe me?"
> "But it is easier for heaven and earth to pass away, than for one dot of the law to become void."
> "Judge not, that you be not judged. For with the judgment you pronounce you will be judged and the measure you give will be the measure you get" [234].

make no impact on Christian action. To Kogin they seem unfamiliar and strange, "When you say the words they sound different than I remember them" [234]. Yet, as with Spinoza, some of the wisdom remains:

> "What about the sayings you used to say by memory? Why don't you say any of them any more?"
> "I've forgotten them."
> "This is one I remember," says the guard. "'But he who endures to the end will be saved.' It's either from Matthew or Luke. . . ."
> Yakov is moved so deeply he laughs [272].

The most critical determinant of Yakov's changing responses to the historical process is his re-emergent sense of his Jewish identity and how that consciousness of self affects his awareness and interpretation of the events he experiences. His initial rejection of Jewishness, symbolized by a multitude of specific gestures such as the absence of a beard, the deliberate loss of his prayer shawl and phylacteries as an answer to the ferryman's anti-semitic diatribe, the taking of an obviously non-Jewish name, the abandonment of Kiev's Jewish quarter, is linked to a heightened feeling of emancipation and material opportunity.

This denial is also coupled with, and perhaps accounts for, Yakov's antagonism toward history and toward politics, through which the individual can to a greater or lesser degree, control, alter, or manipulate the forces unleashed by history. He repeats often to Schmuel, to Lebedev, to Bibikov, to Grubeshov that he is not a political man. After all, if one no longer is a Jew, one ceases to be obsessed by history's exactions and demands. But it is not so easy to lose so major a component of one's personality. Indeed, it is the residual legacy of that unwanted Judaism as it unconsciously appears in his behavior that ultimately makes him suspect: his acts of charity toward Lebedev and the Hasid whom he shelters (ironically it is precisely that charitable impulse that Shmuel claims his son-in-law is without); his tense, watchful honesty; his reaction to Zina Lebedev's seduction while she is menstruating.

In prison, Yakov can neither evade nor escape his essential Jewishness. He must confront it directly, continuously, even compulsively, since it is the single cause of his torment and suffering that is accessible to him. And should he desire a respite from the enforced contemplation of the problem, his jailors make that impossible not only through agonizing physical torture, but by attempting, in very concrete ways, to shape Bok into their fantasy of the conspiratorial, threatening, demonic Jew, imposing the outward signs of a religion and a heritage he has surrendered. As the encounter unfolds and Yakov comes to terms with the self he has disdained, his attitudes toward authority, toward history, toward the nature of his political responsibilities given history's madness, undergo a radical but not particularly surprising metamorphosis.

At first Yakov is overpowered by his own impotence, his powerlessness in the face of inevitable destiny. He did nothing to warrant such punishment, to endure such a personal catastrophe. The reason is external, its source in an identity he has chosen to will away in order to obtain possibility:

> During Yakov's first days in the courthouse jail the accusation had seemed to him almost an irrelevancy, nothing much to do with his life or deeds. But after the visit to the cave he had stopped thinking of relevancy, truth, or even proof. There was no "reason," there was only their plot against a Jew, any Jew; he was the accidental choice for the sacrifice. He would be tried because the accusation had been made, there didn't have to be another reason. Being born a Jew meant being vulnerable to history, including its

worst errors. Accident and history had involved Yakov Bok as he
had never dreamed he could be involved. The involvement was, in a
way of speaking, impersonal, but the effect, his misery and
suffering, were not [155].

Because he has impersonalized his Jewishness, placing it outside
the psyche, contingent upon his persecutors' definition, Yakov is
simply a victim. There is no anger or true understanding; there is
only an uncomprehending, albeit painful, endurance. Yakov's
awe of authority, at this early point in the novel's development, is
concomitant to this sense of helplessness. Since he is not yet
capable of sustaining an independent self, perhaps those in power
can assist, if he pleases them.

  After Bibikov's death and Yakov's further isolation in
solitary confinement, after an attempted poisoning and Grubeshov's fanatic irrationality, anger begins, and there is hostility
directed at an unpitying God's history: "They say God appeared
in history and used it for his purposes, but if that was so he had
no pity for men. God cried mercy and smote his chest, but there
was no mercy because there was no pity. Pity in lightning? You
could not pity anything if you weren't a man; pity was a surprise
to God. It was not his invention" [207]. After an exposure to
Grubeshov's governmentally sanctioned, politicized hatred, this
generalized rage against a pitiless God removed from the cares of
men is soon particularized and focused as it is turned against his
Jewish fate: "His fate nauseated him. Escaping from the Pale he
had at once been entrapped in prison. From birth a black horse
had followed him, a Jewish nightmare. What was being a Jew but
an everlasting curse? He was sick of their history, destiny, blood
guilt" [227]. The process of introjecting not simply an externalized
identity, but a mode of perception, an explanation of the historical
why, has started.

  Discovering the New Testament, given him after he had
broken the phylacteries to read of the rewards for loving and
serving God and the punishments for denial, Bok recognizes the
divergence between the actual words and experience of Jesus
Christ and the deeds committed by believing Christians in his
name. This awareness leads to his first assertion of participation
in and identification with Jewish destiny. When a priest is
permitted to enter Bok's cell in order to convert and absolve the
Hebrew of his sins, he states, "I forgive no one" [236]. And, in a
major gesture of defiance, Yakov dons prayer shawl and
phylactery. The fixer's wrath has at last found the appropriate

objects to use in order to express his rage against those representatives of imperial Russian orthodoxy and oppression that have imprisoned him. No longer is that fury directed at himself and/or the Jews.

The next step in the fixer's transformation into a political man, inhabiting rather than avoiding history, is a reconsideration of the facts of Jewish sacred experience. Bok learns that it is based on an actively sought personal as well as tribal covenant, noting with a new appreciation that the deity is not distant or remote but immediately present, interfering, overbearing, a God who appears to need the Jews as much as the Jews need Him, a God in search of man:[17]

> He read longer and faster, gripped by the narrative of the joyous and frenzied Hebrews ... whatever they were doing always engaged in talk with the huffing-puffing God who tried to sound, maybe out of envy, like a human being.
> God talks. He has chosen, he says, the Hebrews to preserve him. He covenants, therefore he is. He offers and Israel accepts, or when will history begin? Abraham, Moses, Noah, Jeremiah, Hosea, Ezra, even Job, make their personal covenant with the talking God. But Israel accepts the covenant in order to break it. That's the mysterious purpose: they need the experience. So they worship false Gods; and this brings Yahweh up out of his golden throne with a flaming sword in both hands. When he talks loud history boils.... Having betrayed the covenant with God they have to pay: war, destruction, death, exile—and they take what goes with it. Suffering, they say, awakens repentance, at least in those who can repent. Thus the people of the covenant wear out their sins against the Lord. He then forgives them and offers a new covenant. Why not? This is his nature, everything must begin again, don't ask him why. Israel, changed yet unchanged, accepts the new covenant in order to break it by worshipping false gods so that they will ultimately suffer and repent, which they do endlessly [239-240].

What is crucial in this mytho-historical analysis is the meaning Yakov assigns to the covenant: "The purpose of the covenant ... is to create human experience, although human experience baffles God" [240]. To reject the contract is to deny not only one's Jewishness but one's humanity as well.

Bok's metamorphosis is complete when he recognizes that self-knowledge and historical consciousness are insufficient unless the wisdom they offer is accompanied by the willingness to step outside the limitations of a necessarily ego-centered life to identify personal suffering with the community's historical pain and anguish. Indeed, it is precisely this awareness of the

individual's relation to the community of others and the actions
taken in the name of such a vital connection that define
Malamud's concept of the political person, according to Terrence
Des Pres.[18] For Bok, it is imperative that he acknowledge debts
owed: first to Shmuel, his father-in-law, the rejected model of the
righteous man whose existence revealed the spirit of the Law; and
second to the Jewish people, of whom he is the visible and
tortured embodiment:

> To the goyim what one Jew is is what they all are. If the fixer
> stands accused of murdering one of their children, so does the rest
> of the tribe. Since the crucifixion the crime of the Christ-killer is
> the crime of all Jews....
>   He pities their fate in history. After a short time of sunlight you
> awake in a black and bloody world. Overnight a madman is born
> who thinks Jewish blood is water. Overnight life becomes
> worthless. The innocent are born without innocence. The human
> body is worth less than its substance.... All he can do is not make
> things worse. He's half a Jew himself, yet enough of one to protect
> them. After all, he knows the people; and he believes in their right
> to be Jews and live in the world like men. He is against those who
> are against them. He will protect them to the extent that he can.
> This is his covenant with himself. If God's not a man he has to be.
> Therefore he must endure to the trial. And let them confirm his
> innocence by their lies [273-274].

With this covenant, Yakov Bok deliberately and actively
chooses to enter the events that shape human society. It is
important to mention here another symbolic device that Malamud
uses to emphasize man's responsibilities in meeting the pressing
demands of the world of deeds and circumstances: the conflation
of Yakov Bok's individual history with that of the Jews in a
generalized pattern that Malamud perceives to be "First the
Prophets' 'way of gentleness'; the sins of the people, Punishment,
Exile and return."[19] Indeed, Yakov Bok does not merely find a
self; or having found that self, possess the capacity to redefine his
relationship to history. Bok's life *is* the life of the Jewish people.
It is neither allegory nor analogue but equivalency, a profound
illustration of Will Herberg's contention that "Jewish faith is the
affirmation of the sacred history as one's own particular history
or as one's own 'true past.'"[20]

But in order to join the community of men as he has become
part of the community of Jews, Bok must extend his vision:

> All night the cell was crowded with prisoners who had lived and

died there. They were broken-faced, greenish-gray men, with
haunted eyes, scarred shaved heads and ragged bodies crowding the
cell. Many stared wordlessly at the fixer and he at them, their eyes
lit with longing for life. If one disappeared two appeared in his
place. So many prisoners, thought the prisoner, it's a country of
prisoners. They've freed the serfs . . . but not the innocent prisoners.
He beheld long lines of them, gaunt-eyed men with starved
mouths, lines stretching through the thick walls to impoverished
cities, the vast empty steppe, great snowy virgin forests, to the
shabby wooden work camps in Siberia [317].

The persecution of the Jews, the most visible, available, and
acceptable victims in Western culture, is an indication of deep
corruption and far-reaching decay. No man is free, least of all the
persecutors, when the innocent are, as a matter of course, of
politics, of history, destroyed. This is the final lesson learned in
Yakov's hallucinatory encounter with the Tsar, when Bok in the
ultimate act of rebellion assassinates the Little Father, in spite of
Bibikov's humane protestations: "What the Tsar deserves is a
bullet in the gut. Better him than us. . . . One thing I've learned, he
thought, there's no such thing as an unpolitical man, especially a
Jew. . . . You can't sit still and see yourself destroyed. Afterwards
he thought, Where there's no fight for it there's no freedom"
[334-335]. History is not irreversible, and the principled individual
might be able to alter the future. It is only the unpolitical man
who is at Clio's mercy. There is, however, the usual ambivalence
in Malamud's ending. Granted that Yakov has changed both as a
man and as a Jew; granted also that his new knowledge has
brought him into history. Nevertheless, the force of Yakov's
apparently liberating violence is contained, diminished, and
perhaps even negated because it has occurred in a fantasy. There
is only imagined regicide, not actual revolution. Yet once again
the ambiguities created by real events are present. For when the
actual revolution did occur, how improved was the state of
human freedom? Yakov's final imagined gesture of rebellion,
however, is unlike the process by which the accumulating
hostilities and racial fantasies of *The Tenants* take over, then
explode that novel's form.[21]

There is still another way to manipulate history, to control its
force and direct its energy, that ought to be noted, however
briefly, in connection with *The Fixer*, and that is through art.
The artist is able to rearrange, distort, and omit the actual facts of
a real situation, in this instance the Beiliss case,[22] in order to make
events intelligible or arrive at an emotional verisimilitude

impossible to achieve using historical data. It seems either absurd or self-evident to say that the writer or painter is not a liar, at least in the common use of the term. But given the commentary that inevitably appears upon the publication of such a book as *Ragtime* or the attempts to prove that Picasso was less than honest when he painted the monumental "Guernica," it is worth repeating that the artist is revealing, perhaps, another side of truth, that imagination needs to be faithful only to its own vision, that the artist's arrangement of information is his attempt to order a universe. The artist as historian is a valid concept so long as we do not equate honesty with fictive reality.

The Tenants, as we have noted, is eschatology, a book concerned with despair, violence, and the fall of civilization in these worst of times, an echo of the Biblical days of wrath in the time before the end of time. It is apocalyptic fiction, as defined and explained by Robert Alter:

> Apocalyptic writers, ancient and modern, are not really interested in the facts of history or human nature because they scarcely believe anymore in either—or, to put it another way, because what they assume to be essential facts of human existence are wholly known.... Apocalypse which means "uncovering" in Greek is a perfectly appropriate name for this kind of literature because there are no genuine, human surprises in it, only a breaking open of seals, tearing away of masks, lifting of veils—nothing but "revelation" of what is already known.[23]

In *The Tenants*, history rides man because it has deprived men of the opportunity to develop an autonomous sense of self, a possibility lost in the welter of historically conditioned misperceptions, roles played, masks worn, and identities assumed. Harry and Willie respond not to each other directly but to the multiplicity of projected images that builds walls and insures frustration, anger, and hate. In a society that encourages transience, geographically and emotionally, and destroys with relative ease the sources of stability, security, and continuity, it is difficult to confront and master the complexities of history because all value systems seem to be constructed of quicksand. Where ethics, morality, and conscience can no longer operate, there can be no inner strength—Willie and Harry are isolates whose connections with others are exploitative rather than caring. Without that inner strength, all behavior becomes reactive, determined by others. There is safety only in prisons, such as Harry Lesser's apartment barricaded against the barbarians at the gate. And surcease, if it can be called that, is to be found either in Lesser's fantasies of an island Eden, eventually invaded by the black destroyers, or in the hallucinatory violence of Willie Spearmint's fiction. *The Tenants* ends in despair, in a cry for mercy that will go unanswered, because history is neither the dispenser of mercy nor the guarantor of certainty.

By examining the social forces that condition Malamud's world, we have attempted to show in this study that affirmation is ambiguous and hope equivocal. The American dream is corrosive, prizing just those skills that guarantee moral failure, while honesty, duty, responsibility, and integrity assure material ruin and circumscribe experience. Eden, if it is to be possessed at all, is bought at the price of complexity and feeling, and those who are exiled from such a simplistic environment are trapped by the obligations of being human. Race, sex, and art offer warfare, rather than brotherhood, love, or beauty. History imprisons at best, destroys at worst with violence as the mediator. Perhaps it is Malamud's recognition of the ways in which paradox shapes our lives—to be truly free is to be imprisoned in obligation and accountability—that is the source of his moral as well as artistic strength. After all, growing up is a matter of compromise and accomodation; and maturity is a matter of discovering acceptable limits. When man exceeds those critical determinants that shape his humanity in an effort to pursue a quixotic ideal, he fails and loses what he is. Malamud wants the individual to inhabit the world and to function in society; no matter that the world and society, as portrayed in the fiction, fight the desire for integration every step of the way. It is precisely in such confrontations that man defines his humanity.

Some Notes on *Dubin's Lives*: Biography and the Art of Possibilities

According to at least one critic,[1] *Dubin's Lives*, Bernard Malamud's most recent novel, would appear to be a departure from those earlier works of archetypal victimization such as *The Assistant*, *The Fixer*, and *The Tenants*. As Robert Towers notes, "Dubin is a successful freelance biographer who lives comfortably in a small town.... Keeping fit, he strides and sometimes runs through a landscape of fields, woods, barns, covered bridges and mountains . . . he is in no sense a victim. . . . The bearer of a superior moral insight ... he is, in short, a man not a *mensch*." But Towers writes only with seeming acuity about Malamud's fiction, assuming that the author's rich complexity of themes can be reduced to the single belief in the precise, ennobling morality of suffering. Rather, *Dubin's Lives*, like *The Natural*, *A New Life*, and *Pictures of Fidelman*, is yet another tragicomic attempt to define the frequently contradictory choices offered an individual if he or she is to live responsibly within the boundaries of the essential human condition. Malamud himself regards *Dubin's Lives* as a novel of summary, a statement of "what he has learned over the long haul,"[2] a presentation of "what my experience

174

totaled up to," hardly separate from issues raised in his previous fiction.

Just as every other one of Malamud's protagonists from Roy Hobbs to Harry Lesser has had to discover painfully what constitutes a worthy, ethically satisfying life, so too must the characters in *Dubin's Lives* test the self in the tangle of the world in order to find the appropriate modes of conduct necessary to create a poised, responsible existence. The novel's chosen battleground is an old one and the conflict a critical one for all the characters: the biographer Dubin, approaching sixty, fighting the truth of his own mortality, declaiming "It's mad to die;"[3] for Kitty, in her early fifties, "mourning [her] losses" [157]; and for the young Fanny Bick who has "ideas about what I ought to be doing but am afraid of the next move" [135]. The men and women of *Dubin's Lives* must learn to negotiate with care the claims on perception and behavior of two fierce antagonists: the regenerative anarchy of the sexual impulse exploding communal rules and institutions and the productive discipline of the mind's work isolating the self, denying passion, and inhibiting human connection. This ongoing struggle between instinct and intellect which controls both the structure and metaphysics of the novel as well as the fate of its actors is a confrontation between two equally powerful, equally demanding forces, each embodying the dualities of possibility and limitation: a renewal and dissolution of imagination and analysis.

Biography—the study and re-creation of lives—has been used as a controlling motif to contain these problems not only because the material of biography can be exploited for thematic emphasis, but also because it provides a suitable framework for the novel's questioning of ego and experience. Nor is it particularly surprising, then, that Dubin should be engaged in writing *The Passion of D. H. Lawrence* whose similarly divided consciousness is the presiding spirit of *Dubin's Lives*. For Dubin, a fragmented sensibility, Lawrence is "the essential broken self" [28]: an intellectual anti-intellectual theorist, trusting the redemptive potential of the blood's wisdom; who, on the one hand, "wants man to risk himself for a plenitude of life through love" [303], while vehemently denouncing "women whose evil power over blood males emasculated them" [303], who "called the public 'stinking humanity' and equated socialism with syphilis" [303].

Clearly, the biographical obsession accounts for the overwhelming amount of information about so many well-known figures—Thoreau, Twain, Frost, Carlyle, Johnson, Hardy, Fitzgerald are only a small sample of those whose lives appear in the novel—who function as analogues and reflections of Dubin's own divided nature. By organizing the facts of these lives, by attempting to locate "where the dominant action of the life starts, the moment of insight, cohesion, decision" [24], the biographer can anneal "the pieces of his own poor life... into a unity" [98]. Indeed, *Dubin's Lives* is a work of fiction in which all lives are grist for the analytical mill, compulsively examined and re-examined from all perspectives by acutely self-aware and self-conscious individuals: Kitty Dubin, with her *Handbook of Psychiatry* trying to master her disintegrating universe; Fanny Bick, Dubin's much younger mistress who needs to know what to do with her unfocused life; Maud, who like her father, seeks to find in life both discipline and spontaneity; even the absent, lost Gerald who writes in a painful effort to understand and to make others understand the reasons for his own ruined existence; and, of course, Dubin himself who devours the lives of others so that he might not regret, beyond bearability, his own. But the biographical impulse goes yet further, for the novel often seems to be Malamud's own literary history, echoing Roy Hobbs's eating binges, Frank Alpine's voyeurism, Levin's Thoreavian love of nature as well as his choice of a difficult wife, Fidelman's lost manuscript, and Harry Lesser's inability to finish a novel. Even the reader is asked to participate in the biographical act as he or she must order the fragments, the misperceptions, the accuracies and inaccuracies, the provisional successes and qualified failures of the characters' behavior, in order to create a coherent vision of the characters' lives.

The biographer William B. Dubin—and it is significant that the name and the profession are interchangeable throughout the text—must, perforce, be concerned with lives, his own as well as others. He seems to regard his work as a religious vocation, frequently performing his duties with the destructive and isolating fanaticism of a zealot. Kitty says with increasing anger as Dubin drifts into depression and impotence, "Maybe you oughtn't to have gotten married, so you could give your life to your biographies.... I doubt you really enjoy being with people.... You're either reading or writing biographies, or thinking your biographical thoughts" [105]. And while this is no doubt true, it is equally the case for Dubin that the contemplation of other lives not only serves as a moral and ethical palimpsest, but also that such knowledge that is gained finally permits an individual to assess the worth of his own existence:

"Biography—literary or otherwise—teaches you the conduct of life. Those who write about life reflect about life. The unconscious is mirrored in a man's acts and words. If he watches and listens to himself, sooner or later he begins to see the contours of the unconscious self. If you know your defenses you pretty much understand what it's about. In my work I've discovered how to discover. You see in others who you are" [130].

The writing of lives becomes an effective way of rationalizing Dubin's peculiar self-absorption and utilizing this complex subjectivity in a sufficiently controlled fashion so that he might recompose the essential spirit of a life, as seems to be the case with D. H. Lawrence:

You assimilated another man's experience and tried to arrange it into "thoughtful centrality"—Samuel Johnson's expression. In order to do that honestly well, you had to anchor yourself in a place of perspective; you had as a strategy to imagine you were the one you were writing about, even though it meant laying illusion on illusion. . . . And though the evidence pertains to Lawrence, the miner's son, how can it escape the taint, subjectivity, the existence of Willie Dubin, Charlie-the-waiter's son, via the contaminated language he chooses to put down as he eases his boy ever so gently into an imagined life? My life joining his with reservations [20].

But the work of the biographer is not only to be defined as taming or directing the subjective impulse. More important for Dubin, who is frightened of risk, chance surprise, the inexplicable, or the unexpected, forces that are inevitable components of living, it is an intellectual discipline imposing a willed pattern on the disparate events of human experience. However, Dubin seems to have forgotten that biography is not life as lived. And it is when he seeks to impose this will-to-order on his immediate existence that the limitations of his biographical philosophy become increasingly evident. For when the unstudied response, the spontaneous emotion, the unconstrained sensuality represented by his erratic affair with Fanny Bick intrudes into the planned design of his marriage, his structured life dissolves into sexual and professional impotence. The ironic structure of the novel further emphasizes this discrepancy as Dubin misjudges the events of his own past, misperceives his parental role, and misinterprets the facts of his own marriage even as he asserts the power of the will to control life's natural disorder. Finally, it is Freud who reminds Dubin with telling impact that "anyone turning biographer has committed himself to lies, to concealment, to hypocrisy, to flattery, and even to hiding his own lack of understanding: for biographical truth is not to be had, and even if it were it couldn't be useful" [299].

The basic dichotomy developed in the novel between mind and nature is reflected in the emblematic way in which Malamud uses marriage. In his earlier fiction, marriage most frequently is presented as a positive moral condition, the inevitable culmination of the ideals of continuity, responsible love, and discipline that the author so values. In *Dubin's Lives*, however, marriage has become an equivocal institution: necessary, even indispensable perhaps, but more often than not an experience of constraint, restricting freedom, inhibiting desire, betraying even its familial function as Gerald chooses exile and Maud an elderly black lover, an illegitimate child, and much pain and anger. Throughout the work, in fact, marriage is identified with intellect, order, and mortality, seemingly unmodified by spontaneity.

Dubin and Kitty begin their relationship not in love but in the need for love and stability, a contemporary version of an arranged marriage, a fact resented by both partners because their life together has been drained of wonder and surprise. Kitty Dubin is consistently associated with the ability to classify and define, "she kept herself informed, judged public events well. She defined things accurately.... She was analytic, skeptical— questioned what Dubin too easily accepted or inaccurately explicated. She hated obfuscation, hypocrisy, ignorance. She praised clear thinking . . ." [96]. To Kitty, a complex literalist, image and imagination are discomfiting illusions, not carriers of a superior truth, "She . . . seemed at times the undying foe of metaphor.... For her Dubin learned to count accurately, tell the time right, recall a number nearly correctly. If he slipped—if he said, Today I saw an eight-foot sailor, she nervously countered: *I never saw one*—as though her statement eliminated a threat to existence" [102]. She is uncomfortable with the physical—"there were areas of sensual experience she made no attempt to know" [348]. She fears escaping gas, cancer, and death.

For Dubin, marriage establishes a controlled and controllable environment in which to work, where he can will into shape the form of a life. He loves, but that too is willed rather than felt, as he has willed so much of his experience: "'I will waking up, for Christ's sake. I will my goddamned work. There are times I will living'" [334]. Indeed, Dubin punning on his own name ("Will i am") creates the impression of the self as the embodiment of an isolating volition. Marriage, then, is not simply a situation which contains and disarms the explosion of disruptive emotion. Dubin, the solitary, perceives the institution as enclosure, as protection, diminishing the need for elaborate networks of personal connection. Because the biographer views marriage as a methodology of seclusion, it is hardly surprising that Dubin should so obsessively fear age, death, and impotence, terrors intensified by the denial of human interaction. Because the marriage does not possess a passional context, it is only a qualified success. And both participants are acutely aware that their partnership has been constructed out of lacks and absences:

> "A long marriage gets hard to take. You must feel it yourself."
> He was thinking of her sameness, dissatisfactions, eccentricities. He was bored with her fears, her unforgotten unforgettable past....
> Kitty criticized his nature—Dubin's sobriety, sameness, inability to enjoy life. She said she enjoyed life. "Until we met, you lived on romantic dreams, on nothing really. Now your devotion is work. Your work is all you think of and then you complain you aren't free" [255].

By the time Fanny Bick appears on the scene, the marriage has hardened into the edgy but nonetheless determined predictability initially demanded by these two anxious, troubled individuals.

Fanny Bick comes to the biographer, as did his impulse to write on D. H. Lawrence, because "There's something he wants me to know" [171], to remind him, no doubt, of the whole realm of sensual experience that Dubin has dismissed, discounted, or devalued. She enters his universe with the immediate and devastating impact of a natural phenomenon. Her radical sexuality claims his consciousness from the start (albeit not always in a convincing manner for the reader):

> It annoyed him a bit that he felt her sexuality so keenly. It rose from her bare feet. She thus projects herself?—the feminine body— beautifully formed hefty hips, full bosom, nipples visible—can one see less with two eyes? ... She was gifted in femininity, Dubin had decided....
> Intermission, he called his viewing of her.... When she bent it was a gracious act. A beautifully formed female figure suggested ideal form.... Ah, my dear, if I could paint you nude, if I could paint.... Too bad she can't feel my admiration—as admiration.... He went back to his study, dejected. Old billy goat—these feelings at fifty-six, disjunctions of an ordered life [23, 26-27].

She is gifted in life, as Dubin often observes, making "life seem larger" [59]. Identified with Persephone/Ceres and the natural cycles of return and revival, Fanny is the earth goddess that Kitty has refused to become. She brings to Dubin the hope of possibilities, the restoration of beginnings in spite of his sharpened knowledge of mortality, or, perhaps, because of that recognition: "Was what he felt for Fanny love? It wasn't the way he had felt toward women in his youth. Do men of more than fifty love less keenly than young men? He thought the opposite was true: the years deepened the need, the force, the channel of love. At fifty there had to be more at stake: love as a breakwater against age, loss of vital energy, the approach of death" [260]. But Fanny also lacks (as does Dubin, as does Kitty). Profligate in her sexuality, Fanny (ironically named after Fanny Price the upholder of traditional moral values and sexual standards in Austen's *Mansfield Park*) often uses sex irresponsibly and without judgment—"I think we're entitled to have sexual pleasure any way we want" [33]—as a weapon and as an indication of self-worth. The exploitation of that essential sexuality acts to disguise Fanny's fear of her unfocused existence and her blurred, insecure identity. She, too, is frightened of death and loss, asking Dubin for his discipline, his belief in the strength of an informed, responsible will in order that she might create a good and worthy life, just as Dubin asks to share her spontaneity, her joy, and her warmth in order that he might recover vitality and promise. It is only through this vivifying exchange that Dubin, man and biographer, finally understands Lawrence's message:

> His experiences with Fanny, in variety, intensity, excitement heightened by her watchful curious knowing, sureness of her sexual self, willingness to give, couldn't have come at a better moment. He understood Lawrence more fully, his religion of sexuality: a belief in the blood, the flesh, as wiser than the intellect [219].

And we watch Fanny grow, crisis by crisis, into an independent, confident, capable woman, Dubin's apprentice, his assistant, his heir. It is important to note here that it is the first time in Malamud's fiction that the role of inheritor, so critical a moral function in his work, has been assumed by a woman. Clearly, Fanny is the author's attempt to come to terms with women's changing consciousness. "Mr. Malamud said he had been influenced by the women's movement through his daughter, Janna, 'who raised my consciousness.'"[4] However, the portrait of the "liberated" Fanny (surely a salacious pun) is not entirely successful, for her value to Dubin ultimately lies not in her capacity for growth and maturation, but rather as the continuing embodiment of the life-renewing, profoundly sexual archetype of the Great Goddess. What really counts, it seems, is not her potential legal career, but that "she seemed always to have energy for sex. 'Or what's it all about?'" [356]. Kitty, rejecting such a role, is increasingly diminished in her husband's eyes, notwithstanding Dubin's ambiguous, equivocal return to marriage at the novel's end.

There is yet one more issue raised by Dubin's complex biographical metaphysics: how can lives be lived as if new beginnings were possibilities, given the human awareness "'that life is forever fleeting, our fates juggled heartbreakingly by events we can't foresee or control and we are always pitifully vulnerable to what happens next'" [34]. Malamud offers his characters (as well as his readers) two prescriptions to combat the despair "of one's essential aloneness: the self's separate closed self-conscious subjectivity ... death's insistence of its presence in life, history, being" [40]. The first is based on three factors: renewal through the expression of human sexuality; through the reintroduction of spontaneity, joy, and ecstatic sensuality into the passional lives of men and women; and finally, through the acceptance of the notion of recurrence as it occurs in the cosmic cycles of nature. This is Lawrence's solution. It is, in part, Fanny's. And, within certain biological constraints, it is Dubin's response.

The other alternative which seeks to challenge death's inevitable dominion is the active play of the mind and all that is necessary for productive work—discipline, responsibility, duty: "In middle age some degree of accomplishment kept me young, aware of youth in me" [299], Dubin asserts as he attempts to deal with his sexual and professional impotence. Indeed, the ongoing efforts of the biographer do more than insure the continuity of tradition; Dubin writes to keep death at bay, "Dubin, you can't relight lives but you can re-create them. In biographies the dead become alive, or seem to" [98]. As if to illustrate the power of the mind's work to counter and diminish death's authority, Dubin's first book, *Short Lives*, concerns figures such as Keats and Schubert who died young, yet achieved much because "these short lives show how intensely and creatively life can be lived even when it is early aborted. In terms of years lived, they missed little ..." [207]. This belief in the efficacy of imaginative work is Dubin's choice as well.

As Dubin recognizes the simple truth that life "includes the life of the mind, and that on its own the life of the mind is no life at all,"[5] he attempts to strike a balance between the contradictions of his personality and the dualities of the human condition. Often this attempted equilibrium is expressed geographically: Dubin, shuttling between the United States, Venice, and Stockholm, between Center Campobello and New York City, between house and renovated study in the barn, between home and Myra Wilson's farm which Fanny has purchased. The need to achieve a poised existence is also expressed structurally, as Dubin experiences two analogous periods of progressively deepening depression contingent upon the loss of Fanny, alternating with parallel bursts of creativity dependent upon Fanny's return. Whether the balance is ever accomplished, as Dubin wavers between Fanny's world and Kitty's domain, we do not know. The plot is incomplete, reminding the reader of the difficulties in resolving so intricate a dilemma, and we are left with a conditionally optimistic ending at best (as is to be expected in Malamud's fiction): the image of Dubin returning "holding his half-stiffened phallus in his hand, for his wife with love" [362]; and a list of the writings of William B. Dubin.

What the reader knows for certain, then, is that the biographer continues to produce, that Dubin has chosen a commitment to the ideal of disciplined work (and all that such a commitment has come to mean both as redemptive and as imprisoning objectives), that he has elected the ambiguity of duty: he finishes *The Passion of D. H. Lawrence*; he writes *The Art of Biography*; and he completes *Anna Freud* with the assistance of Maud D. Perrera, whom I take to be Dubin's daughter, implying at least a partial reconciliation to the notion of family. But these final assumptions are uncertain, perhaps forced on the reader by a wily Malamud who wishes to emphasize that it is not only Dubin, but his audience as well, who are driven to complete unfinished lives, who seek to will a definitive completeness to the process of being.

Notes

CHAPTER 1

The Good Man's Dilemma: *The Natural,*
The Assistant, and American Materialism

1. "The Blossoming Epoch of Jewish-American Creativity," trans. Sylvia Protter and Iska Alter, *The Forward,* 16 January 1977, 6.
2. An excellent, if somewhat dramatized, account of the significance of Chasidism is the subject of Elie Wiesel's *Souls on Fire* (New York: Random House, 1972).
3. Saul Bellow in his Nobel Prize acceptance speech asks for a *return* to precisely the kind of fiction Bernard Malamud has always written. *The New York Times,* 13 December 1976, 9.
4. "Writing American Fiction," *Commentary* (March, 1961), 228-231.
5. *City of Words* (New York: Harper and Row, 1971).
6. "Fantasist of the Ordinary," *Commentary* (July, 1957), 89-92, and *Bright Book of Life* (New York: Delta Books, 1973), pp. 138-144.
7. *After Alienation* (Cleveland and New York: Meridian Books, 1964), pp. 251, 253.
8. "In the Interest of Surprise and Delight," *Folio 20* (Summer, 1955), 17-20, and *Love and Death in the American Novel* (New York: Dell Books, 1969), 499-500.
9. *Standards* (New York: Horizon Press, 1966).
10. Wasserman has written the complete archetypical analysis of *The*

Natural in the brilliant essay, *"The Natural*: Malamud's World Ceres," (*The Centennial Review of Arts and Science*, 9 [1965], 438-460).

11. James Mellard writes such an analysis in "Malamud's Novels: Four Versions of the Pastoral," (*Critique*, 9 [1967], ii, 5-19) as does Edwin Eigner in "Malamud's Use of the Quest Romance," (*Genre*, 1[1968], 55-75).

12. "The Blossoming Epoch of Jewish-American Creativity," 6.

13. *After the Tradition* (New York: E. P. Dutton, 1969).

14. *The Trial of Judaism in Contemporary Jewish Writing* (Urbana: University of Illinois Press, 1975).

15. There are exceptions to this observation, but they are few: Max Schulz, *Radical Sophistication* (Athens, Ohio: Ohio University Press, 1969); John Barsness, *"A New Life*: The Frontier Myth in Perspective," *Western American Literature*, 3(Winter, 1969), 297-302; Walter Shear, "Culture Conflict in *The Assistant*," *Midwest Quarterly*, 7 (1966), 367-380.

16. Bernard Malamud, *The Natural* (New York: Farrar, Straus and Giroux, 1952), p. 179. All citations are from this edition, and further page references will appear in brackets in the text.

17. "Say it ain't true, Roy" does indeed echo "Say it ain't so, Joe," reportedly asked of Shoeless Joe Jackson after the 1919 Black Sox Scandal exploded. For additional information, see Harold Seymour, *Baseball: The Golden Age* (New York: Oxford University Press, 1971), 294-310, and Eliot Asinof, *Eight Men Out* (New York: Holt, Rinehart and Winston, 1963). As Asinof's book indicates, a number of parallels can be drawn between the events of *The Natural* and the actual scandal: the character of Shoeless Joe Jackson who was himself considered the greatest *natural* hitter of his day; the epic cheapness of Charles Comiskey, owner of the White Sox which echoes that quality in Judge Goodwill Banner; the phenomenal luck of the gambler Arnold Rothstein which resembles Gus Sands's good luck.

18. Italics mine.

19. For an accurate, poignant, and complete account of the various phases of Eastern European Jewish immigration to New York City, see Irving Howe's *World of Our Fathers* (New York: Harcourt, Brace, Jovanovich, 1976).

20. "Culture Conflict in *The Assistant*."

21. Robert Alter considers this version of Judaism both sentimental and a falsification of religious traditionalism in his essay "Sentimentalizing the Jews," in *After the Tradition*, pp. 35-45.

22. Bernard Malamud, *The Assistant* (New York: Farrar, Straus and Giroux, 1957), p. 8. All citations are from this edition, and further page references will appear in brackets in the text.

23. *The Trial of Judaism in Contemporary Jewish Writing*, pp. 6-7.

24. Daniel Bell, "Crime as an American Way of Life: A Queer Ladder of Social Mobility," in *An End to Ideology: On the Exhaustion of the Political Ideas of the Fifties* (New York: Collier Books, 1961), pp.

127-150. Bell clearly perceives that crime is the underside of the American dream, and that criminals represent a dark, violent version of the Horatio Alger myth.

25. This ambiguous imprisonment, at once a sign of moral stature and societal failure, is symbolized by an equally ambiguous gesture, that of circumcision which is both an entry into the community of suffering and a castration, the loss of manhood, as observed by Ihab Hassan in *Radical Innocence* (Princeton: Princeton University Press, 1961), p. 168.

26. This sense of community responsibility is very much a part of the heroic paradigm, according to Joseph Campbell in *The Hero with a Thousand Faces* (Cleveland and New York: Meridian Books, 1970).

CHAPTER 2

The Good Man's Dilemma: *A New Life* and the Failure of the West as Eden

1. Ben Siegel, "Victims in Motion: Bernard Malamud's Sad and Bitter Clowns," *Northwest Review*, 5(Spring, 1962), 77.

2. Bernard Malamud, *A New Life* (New York: Farrar, Straus and Cudahy, 1961), p. 229. All citations are from this edition, and further references will appear in brackets in the text.

3. Delmore Schwartz, "The True-Blue American," in *Summer Knowledge: New and Selected Poems, 1938-1958* (Garden City, New York: Doubleday & Co., Inc., 1959). This poem about the expansive appetite of the young Jeremiah Dickson who, when offered a choice between a chocolate sundae and a banana split, wants "Both," is very much concerned with not only the inability, but also the lack of necessity for Americans to make painful, sacrificial choices in a society that seems to provide anything. "The True-Blue American" is a particularly astute presentation of the uniquely American dilemma faced by S. Levin as he explores his westward paradise. As we will see in Chapter Five, it is equally significant as an explanation of Arthur Fidelman's predicament in *Pictures of Fidelman*. His epigrammatic "Both" clearly echoes the greedy, omnivorous innocence of Jeremiah Dickson, and for many of the same reasons.

4. His definition and analysis of the comic mode appears in *The Anatomy of Criticism: Four Essays* (Princeton: Princeton University Press, 1957), pp. 163-186. See also Leo Marx's *The Machine in the Garden* (New York: Oxford University Press, 1969), an excellent study about the relation of technology to the pastoral ideal as it has taken shape in American thought.

5. Numerous literary critics as well as social and intellectual historians

have attempted to analyze various aspects of this symbolic landscape as a significant factor in shaping the national consciousness and to investigate the function of such an iconography for the American character. For the purposes of this study, the most important have been: D. H. Lawrence, *Studies in Classical American Literature* (New York: Doubleday Anchor Books, 1951), in which Lawrence attempts to trace the failures of the American imagination to capture the powerful Edenic vitality of life and landscape in the new world; Leo Marx, *The Machine in the Garden*; R. W. B. Lewis, *The American Adam* (Chicago: Phoenix Books, 1959), whose concern is with analyzing the images of the new Adam who is to inhabit the American Eden; Henry Nash Smith, *The Virgin Land: The American West as Symbol and Myth* (New York: Vintage Books, 1961), which is a thorough examination of the frontier as national symbol; Kevin Starr, *Americans and the California Dream, 1850-1915* (New York: Oxford University Press, 1973), where the ambivalence of California as a paradisal emblem is traced; and Hugh Honour, *The New Golden Land* (New York: Pantheon Books, 1975), which explores the European images of the American continent.

6. John Locke, "An Essay Concerning... Civil Government," in *The English Philosophers from Bacon to Mill*, ed. E. A. Burtt, (New York: Modern Library, 1939), p. 422. In a pamphlet entitled *The American Revolution and the American Landscape* (Washington, D.C.: American Enterprise Institute for Public Policy Research, 1974), Leo Marx comments specifically on the meaning of this statement by Locke:

> "In the beginning," he [Locke] said, speaking of the willingness of men in a state of nature to be satisfied with the conveniences of life, "all the world was America." When Englishmen migrated, they in effect were approximating a return to the natural state in which men are best able to perceive self-evident truths. The Lockean doctrine of natural rights thus provided a philosophical confirmation of a viewpoint that seemed to arise, almost spontaneously, from the American soil [17].

7. "To Find the Westward Path," *Partisan Review*, 29(Winter, 1962), 137-139.

8. *Western American Literature*, 3(Winter, 1969), 297-302.

9. John Lyons, *The College Novel in America* (Carbondale: Southern Illinois University Press, 1962).

10. Leo Marx, *The Machine in the Garden*, p. 9.

11. Tony Tanner notes the comic irony which Malamud employs when he refers to the European and Thoreauvian creed which dominates S. Levin's philosophy and the tone of *A New Life* [336], in one of the more astute commentaries on Malamud, in *City of Words*, pp. 322-343.

12. Richard Hofstadter chronicles the development of this hostility in *Anti-Intellectualism in American Life* (New York: Knopf, 1963). Merle Curti in *The Growth of American Thought*, 2nd. edn., (New

York: Harper and Brothers, 1951) ascribes this condition both to American economic expansion and democratization. And John Lyons (*The College Novel in America*) views anti-intellectualism as a strain in the college novel.

13. *Nixon Agonistes* (New York: New American Library, 1971), p. 81. This description occurs in the context of a psychological analysis of those Western Americans who had been attracted to Richard Nixon's message and politics. It also echoes Nathanael West's portrayal of the California ambience in *The Day of the Locust*. And this curious ambivalence, a mixture of deep hostility, fear, and hope, is one of the major characteristics that Kevin Starr discerns in the American attitude to the California experience, in a fine book, *Americans and the California Dream, 1850-1915*.

14. Tony Tanner says of S. Levin's last name: "The name Levin also means, of course, east, the light, and I have it direct from Mr. Malamud that by a pun on 'leaven' he is suggesting 'what the marginal Jew may bring in attitude to the American scene.'" (*City of Words*, p. 330).

15. Levin's revelation follows much the same psychological pattern as does Frank Alpine's in *The Assistant* (pp. 91-92). Levin, however, does not think of crime as a way *to take* back what is his; rather, perhaps because Levin is already a Jew, he thinks of *giving* service, as the immediate redemptive prescription.

16. *Democracy in America* (New York: Vintage Books, 1959), Vol. II, p. 12.

17. *The College Novel in America*, p. 112.

18. *The College Novel in America*, pp. 161-162.

19. This single-minded categorization leads Lyons into actual mistakes. For example, he accepts Levin's contention that Levin was about to be politically victorious when his sexual peccadilloes are revealed. This is simply untrue. Levin had made himself unwelcome and unpopular in the departmental election long before his affair with Pauline is made public (*A New Life*, pp. 290-293).

CHAPTER 3

The Broader Canvas: Malamud, the Blacks, and the Jews

1. Lenora E. Berson, *The Negroes and the Jews* (New York: Random House, 1971), p. 171.

2. *The Negroes and the Jews,* p. 183.

3. See Chapters Twelve and Thirteen in Berson's *The Negroes and the Jews* for a more thorough account of the economic difficulties that

have arisen between the black inhabitants of the ghettos and the Jewish businessmen who work there.

4. *Notes of a Native Son* (Boston: Beacon Press, 1957), p. 68.

5. Leslie Fiedler, *Waiting for the End* (New York: Delta Books, 1965), p. 88.

6. "Angel Levine" originally appeared in *Commentary*, 20 (December, 1955), 534-540.

7. Bernard Malamud, "Angel Levine," in *The Magic Barrel* (New York: Farrar, Straus and Cudahy, 1958), p. 43. All citations are from this edition, and further page references will appear in brackets in the text.

8. "Bernard Malamud: Jewishness as Metaphor," in *After the Tradition*, p. 130.

9. "Sentimentalizing the Jews," in *After the Tradition*, pp. 35-45.

10. "Black Is My Favorite Color" first appeared in *The Reporter*, 29(18 July 1963), 43-44.

11. Bernard Malamud, "Black Is My Favorite Color," in *Idiots First* (New York: Farrar, Straus and Cudahy, 1963), p. 19. All citations are from this edition, and further page references will appear in brackets in the text.

12. *The Negroes and the Jews*, p. 257.

13. Norman Mailer, "The White Negro," in *Advertisements for Myself* (New York: Signet Books, 1960), pp. 306-313.

14. "The Black Boy Looks at the White Boy," in *Nobody Knows My Name* (New York: Delta Books, 1961), pp. 216-241.

15. See the documents of the black power movement which have been published by August Meier, *et al.*, *Black Protest Thought in the Twentieth Century*, second edition (Indianapolis and New York: The Bobbs-Merrill Company, Inc., 1971), pp. 469-583.

16. *Soul on Ice* (New York: Delta Books, 1968), p. 13.

17. *Doings and Undoings* (New York: Farrar, Straus and Giroux, 1964), pp. 363-364. Podhoretz even uses a young black boy named Quentin the way in which Nat Lime uses Buster.

18. An interesting contrast to Nat's perception of Buster's black environment occurs in Ralph Ellison's "That Same Pain, That Same Pleasure: An Interview," in *Shadow and Act* (New York: Signet Books, 1966), pp. 23-26. Ellison finds his encounter with the white boy Hoolie a liberating experience rather than an imprisoning one.

19. For an account of complex sexual attitudes and myths that are disturbing but important components of black-white relationships, see Eugene Genovese, *Roll, Jordan, Roll* (New York: Pantheon Books, 1974), pp. 413-431 and Susan Brownmiller, *Against Our Will* (New York: Bantam Books, 1976), pp. 133-140, 165-188.

20. Bernard Malamud, *The Tenants* (New York: Farrar, Straus and Giroux, 1971), p. 32. All citations are from this edition, and further page references will appear in brackets in the text.

21. Lenora E. Berson in *The Negroes and the Jews* examines the reality and the myths that have shaped the image of the landlord and his role in the black ghetto, pp. 214-241.

22. An analysis of the black's views concerning white sexual exploitation can be found in Calvin C. Hernton, *Coming Together: Black Power, White Hatred and Sexual Hang-Ups* (New York: Random House, 1971), and Earl Thorpe, *Eros and Freedom in Southern Life and Thought* (Durham, North Carolina: Seeman Printery, 1967).

23. James Baldwin also notes that anti-semitism is, in part, a way that blacks can prove their citizenship in American society (*Notes of a Native Son*, p. 70).

24. This development in the quality of Willie Spearmint's rage parallels the growth of violence and the acceptance of criminality as a political act within the black movement of the late sixties and early seventies as seen by Lenora Berson, *The Blacks and the Jews*, pp. 343-362.

CHAPTER 4

The Broader Canvas: Malamud and the Woman Question

1. How popular this reductive view of women is can be seen in a recent article entitled "Why Do These Men Hate Women? American Writers and Misogyny" by Vivian Gornick, appearing in *The Village Voice*, 21:49(6 December 1976), 12-15. In the article, Gornick attempts to examine the problem of a simplistic view of women, motivated by what she perceives as hostility, that conditions such writers as Philip Roth, Norman Mailer, and Saul Bellow, as well as Henry Miller. Of course, this misogyny, more complex than Vivian Gornick would indicate, is not limited to the Jewish-American writers on her brief list. It is very much a theme to be considered in American literature, as does Leslie Fiedler in his impressive *Love and Death in the American Novel*.

2. Joseph Campbell, *The Hero with a Thousand Faces*, pp. 113-116.

3. "*The Natural*: Malamud's World Ceres," *The Centennial Review of Arts and Sciences*, 9(1965), 438-460. This is certainly the most thoroughgoing analysis of the archetypal design in a single Malamud novel. It exhibits not only a knowledge of Jungian mythology, but also of baseball legends.

4. Bernard Malamud, *The Natural* (New York: Farrar, Straus and Cudahy), pp. 185-186. All citations are from this edition, and further page references will appear in brackets in the text.

5. Much of my discussion of the role of women in *The Natural* is dependent on Carl Jung's *Four Archetypes: Mother/Rebirth/ Spirit/Trickster*, trans. R. S. C. Hall, *Collected Works of C. G. Jung*, Bollingen Series XX (Princeton: Princeton University Press, 1971), and *Man and His Symbols* (New York: Doubleday, 1964), for which Jung served as editor.

6. Joseph Campbell, *The Hero with a Thousand Faces*; *The Masks of God: Occidental Mythology* (New York: Viking Press, 1964); Sir James Frazer, *The Golden Bough* (New York: Macmillan, 1969); Jessie Weston, *From Ritual to Romance* (New York: Doubleday Anchor, 1957); Mircea Eliade, *The Myth of the Eternal Return*, trans. Willard Trask (New York: Pantheon Books, 1954); and not to be omitted is Robert Graves's dazzling, bewildering, sometimes impenetrable but nonetheless influential *The White Goddess* (New York: Noonday Press, 1966). These works, some of whose arguments have been buttressed by the Jungian notion of the archetype, view the *magna mater*, the great mother, as not only the significant feminine force in much of religious history, but also as the major generative power. Indeed, Robert Graves and Joseph Campbell, in particular, lament the diminution and passing of her authority.

7. This story appears in Malamud's second collection of short stories, *Idiots First* (New York: Farrar, Straus and Giroux, 1963), pp. 31-56.

8. This story also appears in *Idiots First*, pp. 89-100.

9. Irving Howe in *World of Our Fathers*, pp. 259-260, 265-271, 295-300, delineates not only the traditional heritage of the Jewish woman, but also the conflicts she had to face (as does Ida Bober) and the choices she had to make in the New America. For considerable additional information on the Jewish woman in American society, see also Charlotte Baum, *et al.*, *Jewish Women in America* (New York: Dial Press, 1976).

10. Bernard Malamud, *The Assistant* (New York: Farrar, Straus and Cudahy, 1957), p. 230. All citations are from this edition, and further page references will appear in brackets in the text.

11. This concept forms the basis of Josephine Zadovsky Knopp's analysis of contemporary Jewish fiction in *The Trial of Judaism in Contemporary Jewish Writing*; see pp. 19-20 in Chapter One of this study.

12. *The Magic Barrel*, pp. 85-95.

13. *The Magic Barrel*, pp. 183-191.

14. There is much to quarrel with in Susan Brownmiller's *Against Our Will*, especially in her use of unverifiable hypotheses as she tries to prove her contention that rape is the source of the prehistoric relations between the sexes. But the book does examine with considerable thoroughness the history and the justification of rape, and the fantasies evoked by the act. Her discussion may explain some of the difficulties that are felt in Malamud's depiction of rape.

15. *Against Our Will*, pp. 387-420. What is also interesting is her portrait of the typical rapist, pp. 189-203, who resembles Frank Alpine in personal and social history.

16. Bernard Malamud, *A New Life* (New York: Farrar, Straus and Cudahy, 1961), p. 17. All citations are from this edition, and further page references will appear in brackets in the text.

17. Bernard Malamud, *The Fixer* (New York: Farrar, Straus and Giroux, 1966), p. 285. All citations are from this edition, and further references will appear in brackets in the text.

18. Bernard Malamud, *The Tenants* (New York: Farrar, Straus and Giroux, 1971), p. 160. All citations are from this edition, and further references will appear in brackets in the text.
19. "Malamud's Novels: Four Versions of the Pastoral," *Critique*, 9(1967), 7.
20. Martin Buber in *The Prophetic Faith* (New York: Macmillan Co., 1949) further explores and elaborates the theological significance of Hosea's marriage to a whore as the symbol of the Jew's relation to his religious commitment:

> His marriage with a "woman of whorishness," that is to say whose heart inclines to whoredom, represents the marriage between YHVH and this land, his love which his wife has betrayed represents YHVH's love which Israel has betrayed. His separation from the faithless one the divine separation, his mercy on her God's mercy.... In his own feeling the divine feeling is figured so strongly that in every stage he can read from his own lot the course of the relations between YHVH and Israel . . . [111-112].

It is clear that to assign such an analogue to the marriage of Raisl and Yakov is to add a major historical dimension to the relationship between men and women in *The Fixer*.
21. *The Magic Barrel*, pp. 105-133.

Chapter 5

The Broader Canvas: Malamud,
Art, and the Artist

1. Quoted in an interview with Joseph Wershba, "Not in Sorrow but Sadness," *New York Post*, 14 September 1958, M2.
2. Wershba, M2.
3. Bernard Malamud, "Suppose a Wedding," *Idiots First* (New York: Farrar, Straus and Cudahy, 1963), p. 177.
4. Bernard Malamud, *The Assistant* (New York: Farrar, Straus and Cudahy, 1957), p. 131. All citations are from this edition, and further page references will appear in brackets in the text.
5. "Suppose a Wedding," p. 182.
6. Irving Howe and Eliezer Greenberg, "Introduction," *A Treasury of Yiddish Stories* (New York: Viking Press, 1954), pp. 30-31. This essay provides an excellent introduction to the historical, social, and cultural forces that shaped the Eastern European heritage of such major Yiddish writers as I. L. Peretz, Sholem Aleichem, the brothers Singer, and Joseph Opatoshu. Howe's *World of Our Fathers*, Chapters Thirteen to Sixteen, offers important insights into the problems faced by the Yiddish artist in the puzzling and demanding world of America, where assimilation into the mainstream of society

was the watchword, rather than the retention of the traditions and cultural heritage of the Old World.

7. "Master of Dreams," *Partisan Review*, 34(Summer, 1967), 346. The major contention of this provocative article, that the characteristic cultural role of the Jew is that of vendor of dreams or interpreter of dreams—either poet or therapist—has been severely criticized, although not entirely to my satisfaction, by Robert Alter, "Jewish Dreams and Nightmares," in *After the Tradition*, pp. 17-34.

8. Wershba, M2.

9. For this brief history of romantic and post-romantic attitudes toward the artist, I have relied on M. H. Abrams, *The Mirror and the Lamp: Romantic Theory and the Critical Tradition* (New York: W. W. Norton, 1958), Chapter Nine, pp. 229-244; Chapter Ten, pp. 290-297; Chapter Eleven, pp. 303-312; Harold Bloom, *The Visionary Company*, rev. edn. (Ithaca: Cornell University Press, 1968); and Ihab Hassan, *The Dismemberment of Orpheus* (New York: Oxford University Press, 1971). But a sampling of poets from Wordsworth to Yeats, including Coleridge, Byron, Shelley, Keats, and the "decadent" poets of the nineties, will reveal with equal clarity these same accumulated perceptions about the nature of artistic creativity.

10. Joseph Campbell, *The Hero with a Thousand Faces*, p. 24.

11. According to Henry F. May, *The Enlightenment in America* (New York: Oxford University Press, 1976), pp. 34-36, writers' complaints of neglect and disrespect begin, in some cases, as early as the colonial period.

12. *America's Coming of Age* (New York: Doubleday Anchor Books, 1958), p. 99.

13. "The Chair Recognizes Senator Saul Bellow of Illinois," *The New York Times*, 5 February 1977, 19.

14. Quoted by Merle Curti in *The Growth of American Thought*, p. 13. Curti provides an excellent history of the changing attitudes toward artists and intellectual achievements with the increasing democratization of the country. He also traces the division between patrician and popular conceptions of culture.

15. *Democracy in America*, II, p. 50.

16. Richard Hofstadter in *Anti-Intellectualism in American Life* examines this particular brand of pragmatic hostility toward certain kinds of cultural developments. See especially Part II: "The Religion of the Heart" and Part IV: "The Practical Culture."

17. Tocqueville, *Democracy in America*, II, pp. 52-54.

18. It is one of Arthur Mizener's contentions in *The Far Side of Paradise* (New York: Avon Books, 1974) that for Fitzgerald the relationship between money, success, and creativity was debilitating, and ultimately destructive. A more recent example of how popular the assumption is can be seen in V. S. Pritchett's comments about Mary Hemingway's book, *How It Was*, appearing in *The New Yorker*, 1 November 1976, 163: "It is commonly said that the American ethos puts a destructive pressure on writers. In Hemingway, there is a

desperate attempt to retain his youth without going soft. He had overloaded himself with the he-man's persona and nostalgia." And this belief that success somehow corrupts the creative imagination informs Saul Bellow's most recent novel, *Humboldt's Gift* (New York: Avon Books, 1975).

19. Tocqueville, *Democracy in America*, II, pp. 62-63.

20. Bernard Malamud, "Girl of My Dreams," in *The Magic Barrel* (New York: Farrar, Straus and Cudahy, 1958), p. 27. All citations are from this edition, and further page references will appear in brackets in the text.

21. Bernard Malamud, *Pictures of Fidelman* (New York: Farrar, Straus and Giroux, 1969), p. 102. All citations are from this edition, and further page references will appear in brackets in the text.

22. Tony Tanner in his essay on Malamud in *City of Words*, p. 341, notes that this search for the appropriate mother is a binding theme in *Pictures of Fidelman*.

23. The symbolic hymeneal dance reappears in *The Tenants*, this time as Harry Lesser's ironically elaborate fantasy of color-blind brotherhood, occurring at a point in the novel where that possibility has become unlikely, and all hope for continuity seems lost in apocalyptic fury.

24. This appears to be the major assertion of Barbara Lefcowitz's "The Hybris of Neurosis: Malamud's *Pictures of Fidelman*," *Literature and Psychology*, 20(1970), 115-120. While this article is an excellent analysis of Fidelman's obsessive-compulsive behavior, Lefcowitz seems unable to realize that Fidelman is an artist as well as a neurotic.

25. *City of Words*, p. 339. Tanner's discussion of *Pictures of Fidelman* is one of the best.

26. Wershba, M2.

27. This figure of the beggar exists, according to Theodore Reik, *Jewish Wit* (New York: Gamut Press, 1962), just so that the Jew might have the opportunity to be charitable; without this figure, to whom could a man give? The beggar, in his symbolic context, appears again in *The Fixer*, approaching Bok as he is about to leave the protection and isolation of the *shtetl*. That Yakov does not give illustrates one of his major flaws and is a clear sign that trouble will follow him. As Shmuel, his father-in-law, says of Bok, "Charity you were always short of" [6].

28. Fidelman here seems almost a parodic inversion of Harold Bloom's theory that art, specifically poetry, is rooted in a creative Oedipal hostility, growing out of a given poet's rebellion against the influences of the father, as Shelley's poetry is a reaction against the artistic fatherhood of Milton or Mailer's fiction a response to Hemingway; see *The Anxiety of Influence* (New York: Oxford University Press, 1973).

29. I would, at this point, like to disagree with Anatole Broyard's review of *Pictures of Fidelman* that appeared in *The New York Times Book Review*, 4 May 1969, 5, 45. He wrongly assumes, it seems to me, that

Pictures of Fidelman should be about a *realistic* Italian environment—"This is even less than the tourist sees—a mishmash of
rhetoric, rather than national characters"—instead of its symbolic or
spiritual identity. Even worse, Broyard virtually dismisses the theme
of the artist as merely a gimmick or a trick on which to hang
"suffering, for achieving exile and displacement." Given the
structure of the novel and Fidelman's absolute absorption in the
world of art, his compulsive need to create a masterpiece, Broyard's
rather cavalier dismissal is foolhardy.

30. This inability to complete a work of art because of the potential
    self-knowledge that completion might entail recurs as a motif in *The
    Tenants*, where Lazar Kohn is unable to finish or perfect his image of
    "Woman." Although it becomes a masterpiece in its very fragmenta-
    tion, the artist himself commits suicide. And, of course, there is also
    Harry Lesser's inability to complete his third and best novel.

31. "The Hybris of Neurosis," 119.

32. Bernard Malamud, *The Tenants* (New York: Farrar, Straus and
    Giroux, 1971), pp. 21-22. All citations are from this edition, and
    further page references will appear in brackets in the text.

33. Morris Dickstein, in a review of *The Tenants* in *The New York
    Times Book Review*, 3 October 1971, 1, 14-17, is disappointed in
    Harry's comments about his craft: ". . . what we get are mostly
    reverential mutterings about the lambent flame of art and a 1950s
    cant about craft and technique. . . . More shopworn still is the whole
    motif of art versus experience already conventional when Henry
    James exploited it for his marvelous fables about artists and writers,
    some eighty years ago." It would seem that Dickstein has lost the
    capacity for recognizing irony, and is taking Harry Lesser as a
    straightforward representation of the artist, and, perhaps, of
    Malamud himself, which is always a dangerous proposition. Of
    course, much of what Harry Lesser says *is* cant or covert hypocrisy,
    and is meant to be regarded as such. Harry does have to justify a
    withdrawal from the world of experience, something Malamud
    hardly approves of. Harry is a failed artist, and it is a mistake to
    accept his words as a literal statement of Malamud's artistic creed. As
    to the "shopworn" quality of the motif of art versus experience—
    simply because James used the same theme eighty years ago does not
    necessarily mean it is irrelevant. Perhaps it indicates, instead, that the
    dilemma is still of some concern to the creative imagination.

34. From a review in *The New York Times*, 21 September 1971, 35.

35. The burned manuscript or the destroyed painting occurs with some
    frequency in Malamud's work. It signifies not only the most
    frightening fantasy that can haunt the artist, but also the destruction
    of some portion of civilized existence that man must continue if he is
    to survive with honor, dignity, and humanity.

36. *Idiots First*, pp. 195-212.

37. Bernard Malamud, *Rembrandt's Hat* (New York: Farrar, Straus and
    Giroux, 1973), pp. 127-141. All citations are from this edition, and
    further page references will appear in brackets in the text.

38. Much of what Levitansky has to say about the actual making of fiction (59-60) echoes what Malamud himself has said in an interview with Israel Shenker in *The New York Times Book Review*, 3 October 1971, 17-18.

CHAPTER 6

The Good Man's Dilemma: *The Fixer,* *The Tenants,* and the Historical Perspective

1. *The Trial of Judaism in Contemporary Jewish Writing*; see also Chapter One, pp. 19-20, of this study.
2. Robert Alter, in "Malamud: Jewishness as Metaphor," in *After the Tradition*, pp. 121-122, has examined the images of imprisonment that mark Malamud's work, culminating in the actual Russian prison of *The Fixer*. This is also a concern of Ihab Hassan, *Radical Innocence*, Chapter Six, "The Qualified Encounter," pp. 169-179.
3. It is odd that one of the few factors not usually ascribed to Malamud's Jewishness is this interest in history.
4. Mircea Eliade, *The Myth of the Eternal Return*, pp. 104-107. I have also depended upon several others, besides Eliade, who have attempted to explore the interaction between the historical process and the Jews: Martin Buber, *The Prophetic Faith*; Arthur A. Cohen, *The Natural and the Supernatural Jew: An Historical and Theological Introduction* (London: Valentine, Mitchell, 1967); Isidore Epstein, *Judaism: A Historical Representation* (Baltimore: Penguin Books, 1968); Will Herberg, *Judaism and Modern Man* (New York: Atheneum, 1970); Abraham Joshua Heschel, *God in Search of Man* (New York: Harper Torchbooks, 1966); and Theodore Reik, *Jewish Wit*.
5. Eliade, pp. 102-103.
6. *Judaism and Modern Man*, p. 287.
7. Israel Knox, in "The Traditional Roots of Jewish Humor," *Judaism*, 12 (Summer, 1963), 327-337, has produced much the best analysis of the philosophical significance of Jewish humor, followed closely by Theodore Reik, *Jewish Wit*, who establishes the historical and psychological context of Jewish humor.
8. *American Nationalism: An Interpretive Essay* (New York: Collier Books, 1961); *Redeemer Nation: The Idea of America's Millennial Role* (Chicago: University of Chicago Press, 1968); *The American Image of the Old World* (New York: Harper and Row, 1963).
9. "Getting Religion," *The New York Review of Books*, 23:17(28 October 1976), 20.
10. *The Magic Barrel* (New York: Farrar, Straus and Cudahy, 1958), pp. 105-133.

11. "The Apocalyptic Temper," in *After the Tradition*, p. 50.
12. Bernard Malamud, *The Fixer* (New York: Farrar, Straus and Giroux, 1966), p. 297. All citations are from this edition, and further page references will appear in brackets in the text.
13. Norman Cohn, *The Pursuit of the Millennium* (New York: Harper Torchbooks, 1961), pp. 71-73. One of the issues this seminal work attempts to deal with is the socio-cultural roots of anti-semitism within the changing environments of the Middle Ages, conditions not unlike those of the pre-Revolutionary Russia that is the setting of *The Fixer*.
14. Cohn, pp. 62-63.
15. *City of Words*, pp. 334-336.
16. James Mellard, "Malamud's Novels: Four Versions of the Pastoral," *Critique*, 9(1967), 9-10, traces the Christian design in *The Fixer* as well as the mythic patterns that seem to underlie the novel's structure.
17. It is this notion of God that seems to dominate the theology presented in both Abraham Joshua Heschel, *God in Search of Man* and Will Herberg, *Judaism and Modern Man*.
18. *The Survivor* (New York: Oxford University Press, 1976), p. 13.
19. This particular model of the Jewish experience is observed by Malamud in an interview with Joseph Wershba, "Not in Horror but Sadness," *New York Post*, 14 September 1958, M2.
20. *Judaism and Modern Man*, p. 287.
21. It is important to emphasize here a peculiar fact concerning the quality of Malamud's endings. While it is true that affirmation appears to be the controlling direction taken by his fiction, it is worth noting how often that optimism occurs in the equivocal context of fantasy. It is as if the actuality presented in the novels and short stories cannot quite justify that sense of hopefulness. Only when a work's ending confronts a disillusioning experience directly do we get a conclusion that is anchored in a version of reality. The exception, of course, is *The Tenants* where pessimism dominates the tone and narrative from the outset. It does not simply appear in the concluding apocalyptic visions. Lesser's imprisonment has been deliberately chosen in order to evade the demands of life. Friendship is limited by racial hostility. There are no counterparts in *The Tenants* to Bibikov, or Shmuel, of even Kogin. Irene Bell, who embodies the possibility of redemption through love, abandons both Willie and Harry for a more fruitful environment. And Lesser's island fantasies grow increasingly bleak. It is the hymeneal dream of brotherhood that seems anomalous, while the final images of violence seem a more accurate reflection of the novel's mood.
22. By a fortuitous set of circumstances, Maurice Samuel's account of the Beiliss case, *Blood Accusation* (Philadelphia: Jewish Publication Society of America, 1966), was published at about the same time as Malamud's novel, permitting a comparison between the real and fictive histories. What Malamud has chosen to do is to isolate Yakov Bok far more than Mendel Beiliss ever was, creating a primal conflict

between a solitary man and his religion, his society, and his history. Malamud has stripped Yakov down to his essence as a human being, without the mitigating factors of friends, family, and permission to live in a non-Jewish quarter of Kiev. In the end, however, those mitigating factors did not prevent Beiliss from undergoing the accusation, imprisonment, and trial. A Jew, after all, will always be a Jew, and therefore, vulnerable to history's claims—which is precisely Malamud's point.

23. "The Apocalyptic Temper," in *After the Tradition*, p. 50.

EPILOGUE

Some Notes on *Dubin's Lives*: Biography and the Art of Possibilities

1. The critic referred to here is Robert Towers in his front page review of *Dubin's Lives* in *The New York Times Book Review*, 18 February 1979, 1, 29-31. But Christopher Lehmann-Haupt makes a not unsimilar assertion in his daily review appearing in *The New York Times*, 2 February 1979, C3.

2. Ralph Tyler, "A Talk with the Novelist," *The New York Times Book Review*, 18 February 1979, 31.

3. Bernard Malamud, *Dubin's Lives*, (New York: Farrar Straus Giroux, 1979), p. 326. All citations are from this edition, and further page references will appear in brackets in the text.

4. Ralph Tyler, "A Talk with the Novelist," 34.

5. Frank Pike, "Life of Letters," *TLS*, 7 December 1979, 103.

Bibliography

Abrams, M. H. *The Mirror and the Lamp*: *Romantic Theory and the Critical Tradition*. New York: W. W. Norton, 1958.

Alter, Robert. *After the Tradition*: *Essays on Modern Jewish Writing*. New York: E. P. Dutton, 1969.

Asinof, Eliot. *Eight Men Out*. New York: Holt, Rinehart and Winston, 1963.

Astro, Richard, and Jackson J. Benson. eds. *The Fiction of Bernard Malamud*. Corvallis, Oregon: Oregon State University Press, 1977.

Baldwin, James. *Nobody Knows My Name*. New York: Delta Books, 1962.

Baldwin, James. *Notes of a Native Son*. Boston: Beacon Press, 1957.

Barsness, John A. "*A New Life*: The Frontier Myth in Perspective." *Western American Literature*, 3(Winter, 1969), 297-302.

Baum, Charlotte, *et al. Jewish Women in America*. New York: Dial Press, 1976.

Baumbach, Jonathan. "The Economy of Love: The Novels of Bernard Malamud." *Kenyon Review*, 25(1963), 438-457.

Baumbach, Jonathan. *Landscape of Nightmare*: *Studies in the Contemporary American Novel*. New York: New York University Press, 1965.

Baumbach, Jonathan. "Malamud's Heroes." *Commonweal*, 85(28 October 1966), 97-98.

Bell, Daniel. *An End to Ideology*: *On the Exhaustion of the Political Ideas in the Fifties*. New York: Collier Books, 1961.

Bellman, Samuel Irving. "Women, Children and Idiots First: The Transformational Psychology of Bernard Malamud." *Critique*, 7(1965), 123-138.

Bellow, Saul. "Some Notes on Recent American Fiction." *Encounter*, 21(November, 1963), 22-29.

Bellow, Saul. "The Writer as Moralist." *Atlantic*, 211(March, 1963), 58-62.

Bercovitch, Sacvan. *The Puritan Origins of the American Self.* New Haven: Yale University Press, 1975.

Berson, Lenora E. *The Negroes and the Jews.* New York: Random House, 1971.

Blaufarb, Sam. "Bernard Malamud: The Scope of Caricature." *English Journal*, 23(1964), 319-326, 335.

Bloom, Harold. *The Anxiety of Influence: A Theory of Poetry.* New York: Oxford University Press, 1973.

Bloom, Harold. *The Visionary Company: A Reading of English Romantic Poetry.* Revised Edition. Ithaca: Cornell University Press, 1968.

Brooks, Van Wyck. *America's Coming of Age.* New York: Doubleday Anchor Books, 1958.

Brownmiller, Susan. *Against Our Will.* New York: Bantam Books, 1976.

Broyard, Anatole. Review of *Pictures of Fidelman. The New York Times Book Review*, 4 May 1969, 5, 45.

Broyard, Anatole. "View from the Tenement," review in two parts of *The Tenants. The New York Times*, 20 September 1971, 21, and 21 September 1971, 35.

Buber, Martin. *Good and Evil, Two Interpretations*: I. Right and Wrong. [Translated by Ronald Gregor Smith.] II. Images of Good and Evil. [Translated by Michael Bullock.] New York: Charles Scribner's Sons, 1953.

Buber, Martin. *I and Thou.* Translated by Ronald Gregor Smith. Second Edition. New York: Charles Scribner's Sons, 1958.

Buber, Martin. *Kingship of God.* Translated by Richard Scheimann. New York: Harper & Row, 1967.

Buber, Martin. *The Prophetic Faith.* Translated by Carlyle Witton-Davies. New York: Macmillan Co., 1949.

Buchen, Irving M. "Jewish-American Writers as a Literary Group." *Renascence*, 19(1967), 142-150.

Campbell, Joseph. *The Hero with a Thousand Faces.* Cleveland and New York: Meridian Books, 1970.

Campbell, Joseph. *The Masks of God: Occidental Mythology.* New York: Viking Press, 1964.

Cleaver, Eldridge. *Soul on Ice.* New York: Delta Books, 1968.

Cohen, Arthur A. *The Natural and Supernatural Jew: An Historical and Theological Introduction.* London: Valentine, Mitchell, 1967.

Cohn, Norman. *The Pursuit of the Millennium.* Second Edition. New York: Harper Torchbooks, 1961.

Curti, Merle. *The Growth of American Thought.* Second Edition. New York: Harper and Brothers, 1951.

Delany, Janice, Mary Jane Lupton, and Emily Toth. *The Curse—A Cultural History of Menstruation.* New York: E. P. Dutton, 1976.

DeMott, Benjamin. "Jewish Writers in America." *Commentary*, 31(February, 1961), 135-141; 32(August, 1961), 163-166.

Des Pres, Terrence. *The Survivor*. New York: Oxford University Press, 1976.

Dickstein, Morris. Review of *The Tenants*. *The New York Times Book Review*, 3 October 1971, 1, 14-17.

Dupee, F. W. "The Power of Positive Sex." *Partisan Review*, 31(Summer, 1964), 425-430.

Durso, Joseph. *Casey: The Life and Legend of Charles Dillon Stengel*. Englewood Cliffs: Prentice-Hall, Inc., 1967.

Eigner, Edwin. "Malamud's Use of Quest Romance." *Genre*, I(1968), 55-75.

Eliade, Mircea. *The Myth of the Eternal Return*. trans. Willard Trask. New York: Pantheon Books, 1954.

Eliade, Mircea. *Myths, Dreams, and Mysteries*. trans. Philip Maireit. London: Harvill Press, 1960.

Ellison, Ralph. *Shadow and Act*. New York: Signet Books, 1966.

Elman, Richard. "Malamud on the Campus." *Commonweal*, 75(27 October 1961), 114-115.

Emerson, Gloria. *Winners and Losers: Battles, Retreats, Gains, Losses and Ruins from a Long War*. New York: Random House, 1977.

Empson, William. *Some Versions of Pastoral*. New York: New Directions, 1960.

Epstein, Isidore. *Judaism: A Historical Representation*. Baltimore: Penguin Books, 1968.

Featherstone, A. J. "Bernard Malamud." *Atlantic*, 219(March, 1967), 95-98.

Fiedler, Leslie. "The Breakthrough: The American Jewish Novelist and the Fictional Image of the Jew." *Midstream*, 4(1958), 21-33.

Fiedler, Leslie. "In the Interest of Surprise and Delight." *Folio*, 20(Summer, 1955), 17-20.

Fiedler, Leslie. "The Jew as Mythic American." *Ramparts*, 2(Autumn, 1963), 32-48.

Fiedler, Leslie. *The Jew in the American Novel*. New York: Herzl Institute Pamphlet, n.d.

Fiedler, Leslie. *Love and Death in the American Novel*. New York: Dell Books, 1969.

Fiedler, Leslie. "Master of Dreams." *Partisan Review*, 34(Summer, 1967), 339-356.

Fiedler, Leslie. *No! in Thunder*. Boston: Beacon Press, 1960.

Fiedler, Leslie. *Waiting for the End*. New York: Delta Books, 1965.

Field, Leslie A., and Joyce W. Field, eds. *Bernard Malamud: A Collection of Critical Essays*. "Twentieth Century Views." Englewood Cliffs, New Jersey: Prentice-Hall, Inc., 1975.

Field, Leslie A., and Joyce W. Field, eds. *Bernard Malamud and the Critics*. "The Gotham Library." New York: New York University Press, 1970.

Foster, Stephen. *Their Solitary Way: The Puritan Social Ethic in the*

First Century of Settlement in New England. New Haven: Yale University Press, 1971.

Francis, H. E. "Bernard Malamud's Everyman." *Midstream*, 7(1961), 93-97.

Frazer, Sir James George. *The Golden Bough: A Study in Magic and Religion*. New York: Macmillan and Co., 1969.

Friedman, Alan W. "Bernard Malamud: The Hero as Schnook." *Southern Review*, 4(1968), 927-944.

Frye, Northrop. *The Anatomy of Criticism: Four Essays*. Princeton: Princeton University Press, 1957.

Genovese, Eugene D. *In Red and Black: Marxian Explorations in Southern and Afro-American History*. New York: Pantheon, 1973.

Genovese, Eugene D. *Roll, Jordan, Roll: The World the Slaves Made*. New York: Pantheon, 1974.

Goldman, Eric F. *The Crucial Decade—and After*. New York: Vintage Books, 1960.

Goldman, Mark. "Bernard Malamud's Comic Vision and the Theme of Identity." *Critique*, 7(1965), 92-109.

Gornick, Vivian. "Why Do These Men Hate Women? American Writers and Misogyny." *The Village Voice*, 21:49(6 December 1976), 12-15.

Graves, Robert. *The White Goddess: A Historical Grammar of Poetic Myth*. Revised and enlarged edition. New York: Noonday Press, 1966.

Grieff, Louis K. "Quest and Defeat in *The Natural*." *Thoth*, 8(1967), 23-34.

Harcave, Sidney. *First Blood: The Russian Revolution of 1905*. New York: Macmillan Co., 1964.

Hassan, Ihab. *The Dismemberment of Orpheus: Toward a Postmodern Literature*. New York: Oxford University Press, 1971.

Hassan, Ihab. *Radical Innocence: The Contemporary American Novel*. Princeton: Princeton University Press, 1961.

Herberg, Will. *Judaism and Modern Man: An Interpretation of Jewish Religion*. New York: Atheneum, 1970.

Hernton, Calvin C. *Coming Together: Black Power, White Hatred and Sexual Hang-Ups*. New York: Random House, 1971.

Heschel, Abraham Joshua. *God in Search of Man: A Philosophy of Judaism*. New York: Harper Torchbooks, 1966.

Hicks, Granville. "His Hopes on the Human Heart." *Saturday Review*, 46(14 October 1963), 31-32.

Hofstadter, Richard. *Anti-Intellectualism in American Life*. New York: Alfred A. Knopf, 1963.

Hollander, John. "To Find the Westward Path." *Partisan Review*, 29(Winter, 1962), 137-139.

Honour, Hugh. *The New Golden Land: European Images of America from the Discoveries to the Present Time*. New York: Pantheon Books, 1975.

Howe, Irving. "Mass Society and Post-Modern Fiction." *Partisan Review*, 26(Summer, 1959), 420-436.

Howe, Irving. *World of Our Fathers*. New York: Harcourt Brace Jovanovich, 1976.

Howe, Irving, and Eliezer Greenberg, eds. *A Treasury of Yiddish Stories*. New York: Viking Press, 1954.

Huizinga, Johan. *Homo Ludens*. Boston: Beacon Press, 1966.

Hyman, Stanley Edgar. *Standards*. New York: Horizon Press, 1966.

Jung, Carl G. *Four Archetypes: Mother/Rebirth/Spirit/Trickster*. trans. R. S. C. Hull. *Collected Works of C. G. Jung*. Vol. 9. Bollingen Series XX. Princeton: Princeton University Press, 1971.

Jung, Carl G., ed. *Man and His Symbols*. New York: Doubleday, 1964.

Kahn, Roger. *The Boys of Summer: Ceremonies of Innocence*. New York: Harper and Row, 1972.

Kazin, Alfred. *Bright Book of Life*. New York: Delta Books, 1973.

Kazin, Alfred. *Contemporaries*. Boston: Little, Brown, 1962.

Kazin, Alfred. "Fantasist of the Ordinary." *Commentary*, 24(July, 1957), 89-92.

Kazin, Alfred. "The Jew as Modern Writer." *Commentary*, 41(April, 1966), 37-41.

Kennan, George. "The Breakdown of Tsarist Autocracy." in *Revolutionary Russia*. ed. Richard Pipes. (Cambridge, Mass.: Harvard University Press, 1967), pp. 1-15.

Klein, Marcus. *After Alienation: American Novels in Mid-Century*. Cleveland: World Publishing Co., 1964.

Knopp, Josephine Zadovsky. *The Trial of Judaism in Contemporary Jewish Writing*. Urbana: University of Illinois Press, 1975.

Knox, Israel. "The Traditional Roots of Jewish Humor." *Judaism*, 12(Summer, 1963), 327-337.

Kohn, Hans. *American Nationalism: An Interpretive Essay*. New York: Collier Books, 1961.

Koppett, Leonard. *All About Baseball*. New York: Quadrangle Books, 1974.

Lask, Thomas. "The Creative Itch," review of *Pictures of Fidelman*. *The New York Times*, 3 May 1969, 33.

Lawrence, D. H. *Studies in Classic American Literature*. New York: Doubleday Anchor Books, 1951.

Leer, Norman. "Three American Novels and Contemporary Society: A Search for Commitment." *Wisconsin Studies in Contemporary Literature*, 3(1962), 67-86.

Lefcowitz, Barbara. "The Hybris of Neurosis: Malamud's *Pictures of Fidelman*." *Literature and Psychology*, 20(1970), 115-120.

Lehmann-Haupt, Christopher. Review of *Dubin's Lives*. *The New York Times*. 2 February 1979, C23.

Lewis, R. W. B. *The American Adam: Innocence, Tragedy, and Tradition in the Nineteenth Century*. Chicago: Phoenix Books, 1959.

Locke, John. "An Essay Concerning ... Civil Government." in *The English Philosophers from Bacon to Mill*. ed. E. A. Burtt. New York: Modern Library, 1939.

Lyons, John O. *The College Novel in America.* Carbondale: Southern Illinois University Press, 1962.

Mailer, Norman. *Advertisements of Myself.* New York: Signet Books, 1960.

Malamud, Bernard. *The Assistant.* New York: Farrar, Straus and Cudahy, 1957.

Malamud, Bernard. *Dubin's Lives.* New York: Farrar Straus Giroux, 1979.

Malamud, Bernard. *The Fixer.* New York: Farrar, Straus, and Giroux, 1966.

Malamud, Bernard. *Idiots First.* New York: Farrar, Straus and Giroux, 1963.

Malamud, Bernard. *The Magic Barrel.* New York: Farrar, Straus and Cudahy, 1958.

Malamud, Bernard. *The Natural.* New York: Farrar, Straus and Cudahy, 1952.

Malamud, Bernard. *A New Life.* New York: Farrar, Straus and Cudahy, 1961.

Malamud, Bernard. *Pictures of Fidelman: An Exhibition.* New York: Farrar, Straus, and Giroux, 1969.

Malamud, Bernard. *Rembrandt's Hat.* New York: Farrar, Straus and Giroux, 1973.

Malamud, Bernard. *The Tenants.* New York: Farrar, Straus and Giroux, 1971.

Mandel, Ruth B. "Bernard Malamud's *The Assistant* and *A New Life*: Ironic Affirmation." *Critique,* 7(1965), 110-121.

Marx, Leo. *The American Revolution and the American Landscape.* Washington, D. C.: American Enterprise Institute for Public Policy Research, 1974.

Marx, Leo. *The Machine in the Garden: Technology and the Pastoral Ideal in America.* New York: Oxford University Press, 1969.

May, Henry F. *The Enlightenment in America.* New York: Oxford University Press, 1976.

Meier, August, Elliot Rudwick, and Francis L. Broderick, eds. *Black Protest Thought in the Twentieth Century.* Second Edition. Indianapolis and New York: Bobbs-Merrill Company, Inc., 1971.

Mellard, James M. "Malamud's *The Assistant*: The City Novel as Pastoral." *Studies in Short Fiction,* 5(1967), 1-11.

Mellard, James M. "Malamud's Novels: Four Versions of the Pastoral." *Critique,* 9(1967), 5-19.

Middlekauff, Robert. *The Mathers: Three Generations of Puritan Intellectuals, 1596-1728.* New York: Oxford University Press, 1971.

Moynihan, Daniel P. "Politics as the Art of the Impossible." *The American Scholar,* 38(Autumn, 1969), 573-583.

Mudrick, Marivn. "Who Killed Herzog? or Three American Novelists." *University of Denver Quarterly,* 1(1966), 61-97.

Nisbet, Robert. "Many Tocquevilles." *The American Scholar,* 46(Winter, 1976/77), 59-75.

Pike, Frank. "Life of Letters." *TLS*. 7 December 1979. 103.

Pinsker, Sanford. "The Achievement of Bernard Malamud." *Midwest Quarterly*, 10(1969), 379-389.

Pinsker, Sanford. *The Schlemiel As Metaphor: Studies in the Yiddish and American Jewish Novel*. "Crosscurrents-Modern Critiques Series." Carbondale, Illinois: Southern Illinois University Press, 1971.

Podhoretz, Norman. "Achilles in Left Field." *Commentary*, 15(March, 1953), 321-326.

Podhoretz, Norman. *Doings and Undoings: The Fifties and After in American Writing*. New York: Farrar, Straus and Company, 1964.

Podhoretz, Norman. "Jewish Culture and the Intellectuals." *Commentary*, 19(May, 1955), 451-457.

Podhoretz, Norman. "The New Nihilism in the American Novel." *Partisan Review*, 25(Fall, 1958), 589-590.

Ratner, Marc L. "Style and Humanity in Malamud's Fiction." *Massachusetts Review*, 5(1963), 663-683.

Reik, Theodore. *Jewish Wit*. New York: Gamut Books, 1962.

Richman, Sidney. *Bernard Malamud*. New Haven: Twayne Publishers, Inc.—College and University Press, 1966.

Rosenthal, M. L. "The Chair Recognizes Senator Saul Bellow of Illinois." *The New York Times*, 5 February 1977, 19.

Roth, Philip. "Writing American Fiction." *Commentary*, 31(March, 1961), 228-229.

Rovit, Earl. "Bernard Malamud and the Jewish Literary Tradition." *Critique*, 3(1961), 3-10.

Sale, Roger. "Love and War." *The New York Review of Books*. 26:2 (22 February 1979), 19-20.

Samuel, Maurice. *Blood Accusation: The Strange History of the Beiliss Case*. Philadelphia: The Jewish Publication Society of America, 1966.

Schaar, John. "Getting Religion." *The New York Review of Books*, 23:17(28 October 1976), 16-21.

Scholes, Robert. "Portrait of the Artist as an Escape-Goat." *Saturday Review*, 52(May, 1969), 32-34.

Schulz, Max. *Radical Sophistication: Studies in Contemporary Jewish-American Novelists*. Athens, Ohio: Ohio University Press, 1969.

Schwartz, Delmore. *Summer Knowledge: New and Selected Poems, 1938-1958*. Garden City, New York: Doubleday & Co., Inc., 1959.

Seymour, Harold. *Baseball: The Golden Age*. New York: Oxford University Press, 1971.

Shear, Walter. "Culture Conflict in *The Assistant*." *Midwest Quarterly*, 7(1966), 367-380.

Shechner, Mark. "Jewish Writers." in *Harvard Guide to Contemporary American Writing*, ed. Daniel Hoffman. (Cambridge, Mass., and London, England: The Belknap Press of Harvard University Press, 1979), pp. 191-239.

Shenker, Israel. "For Malamud It's Story." Interview in *The New York*

Times Book Review, 3 October 1971, 17-18.

Sherman, Bernard. "The Jewish-American Initiation Novel." *Chicago Jewish Forum*, 24(1966), 10-14.

Shticker, Mayer. "The Blossoming Epoch of Jewish-American Creativity." trans. Sylvia Protter and Iska Alter. *The Forward*, 16 January 1977, 6.

Siegel, Ben. "Victims in Motion: Bernard Malamud's Sad and Bitter Clowns." *Northwest Review*, 5(Spring, 1962), 77-90.

Smith, Henry Nash. *The Virgin Land: The American West as Symbol and Myth*. New York: Vintage Books, 1961.

Smith, Robert. *Illustrated History of Baseball*. New York: Grosset and Dunlap, 1973.

Solotaroff, Theodore. "Bernard Malamud's Fiction: Old Life and the New." *Commentary*, 33(March, 1962), 197-204.

Starr, Kevin. *Americans and the California Dream, 1850-1915*. New York: Oxford University Press, 1973.

Stavrou, Theofanis George, ed. *Russia Under the Last Tsar*. Minneapolis: University of Minnesota Press, 1969.

Strout, Cushing. *The American Image of the Old World*. New York: Harper and Row, 1963.

Strout, Cushing. *The New Heavens and New Earth: Political Religion in America*. New York: Harper and Row, 1974.

Tanner, Tony. *City of Words: American Fiction, 1950-1970*. New York: Harper and Row, 1971.

Thorpe, Earl E. *Eros and Freedom in Southern Life and Thought*. Durham, N. C.: Seeman Printery, 1967.

Tocqueville, Alexis de. *Democracy in America*. 2 vols. trans. Henry Reeve, rev. Francis Bowen. New York: Vintage Books, 1959.

Towers, Robert. "A Biographical Novel." *The New York Times Book Review*. 18 February 1979, 1, 29-31.

Treadgold, Donald W. *Twentieth Century Russia*. Chicago: Rand McNally and Company, 1959.

Tuveson, Ernest Lee. *Redeemer Nation: The Idea of America's Millennial Role*. Chicago: University of Chicago Press, 1968.

Tyler, Ralph. "A Talk with the Novelist." *The New York Times Book Review*. 18 February 1979, 1, 31-34.

Veeck, Bill. *Veeck as in Wreck*. New York: G. P. Putnam's Sons, 1962.

Vernadsky, George. *A History of Russia*. Third Edition. New Haven: Yale University Press, 1951.

Wasserman, Earl R. "*The Natural*: Malamud's World Ceres." *The Centennial Review of Arts and Science*, 9(1965), 438-460.

Weinberg, Helen. *The New Novel in America: The Kafkan Mode in Contemporary Fiction*. Ithaca: Cornell University Press, 1970.

Weiss, Samuel A. "Notes on Bernard Malamud." *Chicago Jewish Forum*, 21(1963), 155-158.

Weiss, Samuel A. "Passion and Purgation in Bernard Malamud." *University of Windsor Review*, 2(1966), 93-99.

Wershba, Joseph. "Not Horror But Sadness." Interview in *New York Post*, 14 September 1958, M2.

Wertenbaker, Thomas Jefferson. *The Puritan Oligarchy: The Founding of American Civilization.* New York: Grosset and Dunlap, 1947.

Weston, Jessie L. *From Ritual to Romance.* Garden City: Doubleday Anchor Books, 1957.

Wiesel, Elie. *Souls on Fire.* New York: Random House, 1972.

Wills, Garry. *Nixon Agonistes: The Crisis of the Self-Made Man.* New York: New American Library, Signet Classic, 1971.

Woodward, C. Vann. "The Graying of America." *The New York Times.* 29 December 1976, 25.

Ziff, Larzer. *Puritanism in America: New Culture in a New World.* New York: Viking Press, 1973.

Index